**Making Moral Decisions
in a Morally Complex World**

HARSH
REALITIES

AGONIZING
CHOICES

Making Moral Decisions
in a Morally Complex World

HARSH
REALITIES
AGONIZING
CHOICES

PERRY C. COTHAM

 COLLEGE PRESS
PUBLISHING COMPANY
Joplin, Missouri

Library of Congress Cataloging-in-Publication Data

Cotham, Perry C.
    Harsh realities/agonizing choices: making moral decisions in a
morally complex world/Perry C. Cotham.
        p.   cm.
    Includes bibliographical references.
    ISBN 0-89900-748-1 (pbk.)
    1. Christian ethics.   2. Social ethics.   3. Decision making
(Ethics)   I. Title.
BJ1251.C73 1996
241—dc20   95-50996
                                                            CIP

Table of Contents

Preface

WARNING! PLEASE STOP READING IMMEDIATELY AND PUT DOWN THIS BOOK if you are easily offended by ideas and arguments with which you do not agree.

Actually, this opening statement is designed only to dramatically get your attention and is certainly not intended to insult you as a thoughtful, intelligent reader.

Truth is, however, you will read some statements and arguments in this book to which you are in vehement disagreement. There are statements and arguments included with which even I, as author, disagree. Still other statements I wonder about and may still ponder as long as I live.

When dealing with abortion, sex morality, criminal justice, homosexuality, just to cite a few topics discussed in this book, we are dealing with high-voltage issues. Because some of us espouse intense convictions on these issues, sometimes it is difficult to maintain open, responsible dialogue.

This book is not intended to be the final word on controversial ethical issues. I envision the book being used in adult Sunday School classrooms and in introductory level ethics courses in Christian colleges, perhaps as a supplement to more traditional texts. Along the way, I hope, many individual readers will select it to challenge their thinking in private reading and reflection.

This guide *is* intended for what I call the "thinking Christian," which is not intended to be derogatory. A friend recently challenged me, "Isn't the expression 'thinking Christians' a redundancy? After all, shouldn't all true Christians be thinkers as well?" The question gave me pause. True, Christians should be critical thinkers, but many of us find it more difficult to be open, objective, and fair when controversial issues pull us away from our comfort zone.

In my own mind I have deliberated over the appropriateness of ending each chapter on the controversial issues with a brief personal statement of my own conviction. Thus, for example, in concluding the chapter on abortion I might declare: "I am basically pro-life because everything in human nature, common sense, and God's Word calls us to honor the sanctity and dignity of human life; but, on the other hand, I am always reluctant to establish my position as a moral absolute to be made binding on all society or even as a test of Christian fellowship." Or in concluding chapters on sex morality and homosexuality, I could honestly tell readers: "I believe that God's ideal for intimate human relations is faithful, life-time commitment and fidelity to monogamous marriage between a loving male and a loving female." I could go on, but my guess is that I've selected some of the "hottest" red button issues to make my point.

In the final analysis I decided to present this material along the same style that I would present it in a college classroom or adult Sunday School class. An open, fair discussion accords respect to mature thinkers. There is nothing distinctively "heretical" or "liberal" about being academically serious and culturally informed. How precious are the gifts of freedom of conscience and freedom of expression! And how refreshing and at times unexpectedly enlightening it can be to enter the open marketplace of free ideas!

Believing that we as Christians can only find lasting security beneath the umbrella of God's mercy and grace, having been led there through the atoning blood of Jesus, then certainly we must not fear free expression of ideas. Surely we are secure enough to allow our convictions and values to be tested and sharpened through a persuasive expression by those who take exception to our most cherished insights and understandings. Long a favorite quote of mine has been these words: "Those who do not know their opponent's arguments do not completely understand their own."

Would that we lived in a perfect world where harsh realities did not confront us and agonizing choices were avoidable! Our world rocks us between the eyes with some painful realities about some of the deepest, most personal dimensions of human existence. Seemingly, those who turn to the entertainment media for reinforcement of wholesome values and positive role models will be frightfully disappointed far more than they will be pleased. Sadly, our young people are being engulfed in a media-music orgy of glorified sex, rape, drug addiction, random killings, verbal obscenity, and personal irresponsibility. The pilot light of our cultural conscience seems to flicker at a very low level indeed.

Years ago I ran across a quotation from Reinhold Niebuhr, the essence of which I have never forgotten. Though my paraphrasing here may miss his precise wording, the thought remains powerful and relevant to this entire volume: "We live in two worlds. There is the world of ideals and sentiments and there is the world of harsh and disturbing realities. And Christians must spend their lives negotiating the difference between these two worlds, neither of which they can escape."

A world of ideals? A world of our best sentiments? Dream on.

If we lived in an ideal world where we never encountered agonizing choices and where our moral decisions never had to hurt us or anyone else that we care deeply about, we would never have to decide about abortion. Or about criminal justice. Or about sex morality. In the real world, good women choose to have abortions. In the real world, good people commit sin—some because they rebelliously choose sin and many others because they are weak and vulnerable in the alluring face of temptation.

So, then, no doctrine within the Christian faith leads us to believe that a perfect world can exist this side of eternity. Hopefully, the church of Jesus Christ can be a special community that approximates some degree of divine love and fellowship. Yet even within the church these moral issues and dilemmas crop up, often evoking embarrassment and shame, despite our indefatigable efforts to suppress them.

As we proceed through the maze of controversial issues, keep in mind that this study of ethics may not tell us *what* act is right, but hopefully it gives us direction in *how* we ought to proceed in making our decisions. We will assume as our premise the all-sufficiency of the Bible as God's word in matters of moral authority. Because, on the other hand, we cannot assume the all-sufficiency of human interpretation and opinion in understanding and applying God's word to our contemporary situation, we freely turn to theologians, ethicists, social scientists, and responsible thinkers for insight. Quotations from a wide variety of sources and persuasions are selected to challenge the reader's thinking.

We will begin with two lengthier chapters which are intended to provide a foundation for discussion of issues to follow. The "issues" chapters contain a brief glossary of key terms to enable us to discuss the topics and our convictions with precision and clarity. The questions which conclude each chapter are intended to be a major part of the book and, hopefully, will challenge each reader's thinking and analytical skills. The "pro and con" presentations on the various controversies are couched in the kind of everyday language one might hear when two people are engaged in spontaneous dialogue.

As the dust settles from the pounding of the keys of my trusty "MacPlus" word processor, I would be remiss not to gratefully acknowledge the overall support and assistance of several dear friends. First, thanks to two capable secretaries and fellow staff members at the Fourth Avenue Church in Franklin, Tennessee — Paula Boling and Denise Ellis — for their assistance in keyboarding. They are a pure, unmitigated joy to work with the vast majority of time and they would keep a straight face while telling anyone else the same thing about me.

Much valuable expertise and assistance were rendered by John Hunter, an editor with College Press, in his demonstration of both professional and brotherly editorial assistance. Given the high quality of publications and durable reputation of College Press over many years of service in the Restoration heritage, it is a distinct honor to enjoy association with this firm.

The doors of opportunity to teach ethics and philosophy were opened years ago for me by Dr. Samuel Gant, Nashville State Technical Institute, and by congenial colleagues Professor Randall Harris and Dr. Mac Lynn, professor and chair, both of the Department of Bible, David Lipscomb University, in Nashville.

And, finally, I gratefully acknowledge the general support and encouragement by so many personal friends at two churches I have been blessed to serve — the Fourth Avenue Church in Franklin, Tennessee, and the Sunset Hills Church in McMinnville, Tennesee — whose long-standing friendship has convinced me that they both love and gladly tolerate me. Thanks also to some special people at the Otter Creek Church in Nashville for their friendship and general encouragement.

Time has come to conclude this preface and move on. Hopefully, you the reader will learn a great deal. Maybe I'm a little idealistic, even "pollyannish," but I hope you will do more than simply learn the meaning of some terms and read arguments.

You see, the issues discussed in this book present awesome challenges. Following Jesus' model, the church must continue to address the great ethical and moral issues of our time.

So have the courage to act! Dare to do right! Risk to be wrong! Have the courage to fail! A stumble may prevent a fall.

It is wise to keep in mind that no success or failure is necessarily final. Never forget that grace means that you get what legalists declare that you do not deserve — another chance.

Whatever you think or do, don't lose heart. Jesus is still Lord of all. God is still good. He is still in control. The victory is still ours if we claim it through his Son.

And yes, life is still tough. This is not Disney World. But take heart. No wrong choice can make God love you less. Being right with moral philosophy is not the most important thing in the world. Being right with God is.

Let's join our hearts and minds, if we cannot literally join hands, and journey together. May God bless every minute and every hour we spend earnestly struggling to know his will and grant us the grace and the grit to accomplish that will in our own little world!

Perry C. Cotham
June 30, 1995

CHAPTER ONE

Moral Decision-Making and the Christian

It was a moment on the verge of public glory. It was also a moment in the depth of private anguish.

The time: summer of 1988. The place: Seoul, South Korea, site of the International Olympic games. U. S. Olympic athlete Greg Louganis had seriously botched a high dive by hitting his head on the board. Moments later, blood oozed out of the wound.

One moment in time — a moment for one of the most critical ethical decisions of any person's life! Only six months earlier Louganis had been diagnosed as HIV-positive. There was genuine concern for the doctor who was stitching his wound. There was concern about any potential though remote danger to other divers — would infected blood in the water endanger others in the water?

The championship diver with a chiseled, Adonis-like body that carried the AIDS virus was also concerned about the chaos that a public confession of his condition would stir. He was understandably concerned about his chances of remaining in competition if he acknowledged his condition. He was concerned about his goals, his dreams.

And yet, time was passing. A wound was bleeding. It was a harsh reality. It was an agonizing choice.

Life is sometimes like this. As ordinary people we find ourselves thrust into less dramatic situations, yet still we must face harsh and painful realities. And the choices seem just as agonizing:

✦ Your supervisor asks you to lie about him to a third party and warns you that if you tell the truth everyone in the office will face negative consequences.

✦ Your fifteen-year-old daughter is pregnant and wants you to help her obtain an abortion.

✦ You are not certain your aging grandfather, who has just been diagnosed with a malignant and inoperable tumor, can handle the truth about his condition even though he is asking blunt questions; you want him to have hope and assurance but you know the truth will be a crushing blow.

✦ One of your best friends persists in telling you racist, bigoted jokes and he speaks of minorities only in derogatory terms.

✦ Your boyfriend is pressuring you to have sex and you do not feel emotionally prepared for such intimacy.

✦ One of your good friends confides to you his homosexual interests and asks for your judgment and advice.

✦ Your boss keeps putting his hands on you or brushes up against your body in ways that make you feel uncomfortable.

✦ A fellow classmate comes to you with a purloined copy of the final exam which will be given in a class in which you feel you simply must make an "A" to keep your gradepoint average high enough to enter professional school in your field.

✦ You have reason to believe (but not absolute evidence) that your next door neighbor, a husband and a father, is being physically abusive toward his wife and their children.

✦ After several sessions of psychotherapy, you sense that your therapist, whom you respect and feel some attraction to, is "coming on" to you sexually.

On and on we could go. Some of us can relate directly to one or more of these hypothetical situations cited. Most of us can think of similar moral dilemmas in which we have found ourselves — situations in which there were harsh and gut-wrenching realities, but also situations with irrepressibly painful and agonizing choices.

It's not enough to say that we can escape moral decision-making. All too often, moral choices cannot be avoided. A poster sign seen in the early 70s conveys truth in a few words: "Not To Decide Is To Decide." Indeed, not to decide is to side with the status quo. To evade decision is to share the same mindset with a man named Pilate, a public official who thought he could evade responsibility for the fate of an innocent, itinerant Judean teacher by excusing himself from the case and publicly washing his hands. Few, if any, moral issues can be resolved by indecision; few, if any, moral dilemmas can be solved by "benign neglect."

This book makes an assumption. The assumption can be clearly stated: readers of this material are Christian men and women who seek to make thoughtful, responsible moral decisions. Readers who do not share a mutual Christian calling and commitment may discover herein some interesting information and some mightily assertions, but little else.

Because we, the author and the readers, share a common calling and allegiance to Jesus Christ, then we also seek meaningful and proper answers to a number of vexing questions:

How do Christian women and men make their way to security in the moral jungle of the real world?

Are we called upon to make moral decisions in controversial, difficult cases throughout most of our lives or, as some contend, are such really nettlesome dilemmas only rare?

Does profession of faith in Jesus Christ make any real difference in terms of moral decision-making?

Does the Bible speak out on all the major moral issues that face this generation?

Has God given us moral absolutes to direct our lives and, if so, how do we discover them amidst all the ancient Palestinian cultural concerns and trappings of Holy Scripture? How can we find "black and white" in a world of "grays"?

Why do Christians have such sharp disagreements over the morality of certain actions or options?

How should the silence of the Scriptures on certain moral concerns be respected?

Has the Bible been abused by advocates of certain moral actions or moral judgment?

How would one describe a morally responsible Christian?

Given the imperfectibility of our world, how many of their personal ideals can Christian men and women compromise without sacrificing their distinct commitment as disciples of Jesus of Nazareth?

Since we have discarded the naive optimism of former generations about the moral maturity of our culture, are there actions Christians can take to infuse moral strength and stability into the nation's families, schools, and governmental organizations?

With this chapter we embark on a journey in search of answers to these and other questions. At times we may discover clear direction and indisputable moral judgments. At other times our reading and reflection may produce more confusion and consternation than clarity. Such is the risk assumed by thinking Christians who know the secular world is ever about us, that spiritual commitment is not always easy, and that there seldom exist simple and easy answers.

Specifically, in this chapter our major purposes include: (1) introducing some basic concepts and definitions which lay the groundwork for discussions on issues; (2) defining and stating the uniqueness of Christian ethics; (3) providing an overview of the sources of Christian ethics; and, finally, (4) introducing other ethical systems and philosophies by their names and major contributors.

ETHICS AND MORAL REASONING

What is the difference between ethics and morality? Do not the terms mean the same thing? In everyday communication many people do not make distinctions between ethics and morality, though a subtle difference exists.

Ethics may be defined as the philosophical study of what constitutes good and bad human conduct, including related actions and values. The *study of ethics* is the study of rules and theories about rules by which people live. Ethics may connote a particular moral outlook, such as the Puritan ethic or the Protestant work ethic. Generally, *ethics* and *ethical* are words with strongly positive connotations.

Morality, on the other hand, usually refers to our actual conduct or behavior, to the moral rules we follow, and/or to the moral values that we acknowledge and serve. Morality is a term with both positive and negative connotations. If you were to hear that Professor Zigglebottom, for example, was attempting to teach *morality* in his philosophy class, would you conclude that he was teaching goodness, responsibility, respect for others, tolerance, a humanitarian attitude and so forth? Or, on the other hand, would you conclude that this professor was delivering sermons which advocated judgmentalism, double standards, repression, restrictions, legalism, and so forth? Unfortunately, morality evokes the latter connotation as well as the former, though the latter connotation is more aligned with *moralizing* than morality.

Moral philosophers, then, are concerned about determining what is "good" and "right" and what is "not good" (call it immoral, sinful, wrong, inappropriate, evil, or whatever) and "wrong." If there were widespread agreement about how to use those labels, a great body of ethical literature and moral philosophy encompassing centuries of time and thousands upon thousands of pages might not have been necessary.

You may encounter in your reading and discussions other terms related to ethics and morality. *General ethics* is a more comprehensive, more abstract, formulation of theories about virtues and right behavior. *Applied ethics* attempts a practical application of general moral philosophy to provide guidance in everyday life. *Social ethics* is concerned with applying moral standards to our decisions in group affiliations and group situations. *Normative ethics* makes judgment about obligation and value; it attempts to establish standards or norms about how we ought to behave and what we should pursue; normative ethics has a strong flavor of "oughts" and "shoulds."

When we act, we act for reasons. We exercise physically because it improves our conditioning or it helps us relieve stress or it helps us burn calories, or we exercise for all of the above reasons. We select a movie or a book for certain reasons — we expect to learn something and/or we hope to be entertained. We have reasons for selecting a certain work of art for the living room and another work of art for the office — these reasons are both personal and aesthetic. We choose a hobby or purchase a certain model of automobile for reasons which relate to our schedule, our pocketbook, our family needs, and, most of all, our personal needs and interests.

When our reasons for selections about art or hobbies or automobiles point us in conflicting directions, then we must decide which direction to take. We may seek the advice of others. We may make a flow chart of the advantages and disadvantages of a course of action. We may seek information from specialized journals or magazines, such as *Consumer Reports*. Finally, then, we make a decision. Not to decide is to decide for the status quo, a point we've already made.

Moral decisions are made much the same way. Information may be adduced. Advice may be sought. All relevant factors may be considered. A decision is then made. Moral reasoning is similar to other kinds of reasoning. The major difference is that it considers certain kinds of reasons — moral reasons. To engage in moral reasoning is to employ our rational skills and best judgment in the service of choosing the morally appropriate course of action. Moral reasoning leads us to the "oughtness" of our attitudes and behavior. Ideally, it gives us both direction and motivation to "do the right thing."

Moral concerns are concerns about human beings. Morality is about how we treat people, including ourselves. If you and/or other people are not significantly involved in an issue, the matter is not a moral issue, whatever else may be at stake. And our moral values are our personal assessment of worth about self and other humans. Our moral values inform others of what we cherish and find of great worth or significance in terms of personal behavior and human interaction. The moral values that we espouse constitute the largest part of both who we are as persons and how we live in community with others.

Morality is serious business. It concerns behavior that has serious consequence on oneself or other human beings. When we say that someone is a *moral* person, we may denote that the person's behavior is consistent with ethical standards. A person who is *immoral*, by contrast, is one whose behavior violates ethical standards. *Amoral* issues or behavior possess no moral content. We might say that a mentally retarded person's behavior should be judged as amoral, for such a person is incapable of moral discretion.

All of this can be stated more concretely: High moral standards and excellent moral conduct will render a positive consequence on human beings. Whatever personal attitude or behavior in which we engage that serves to aid, assist, strengthen, affirm, enable (in a positive sense), encourage, enrich, and ultimately even to bless some other person or persons, may be called *moral behavior.*

On the other hand, whatever human behavior or attitudes toward other people tends to *unjustifiably* hurt, injure, harm, weaken, discourage, demonstrate disrespect, bring grief, and ultimately even to destroy some other person or persons (such as in cases of major abuse or murder), may be called *immoral behavior.*

Again, morality is about people. It's about treating people lovingly and fairly. To be morally serious is to be concerned about people. There may be a variety of reasons a person may employ in choosing one's hobbies, home decorations, books and movies, and nursery stock for landscaping a lawn — but, typically, moral reasons are irrelevant. If, for example, I decide that my fragile ego as a middle age male needs bolstering by the purchase and conspicuous driving about town of a new, clear-coat, metallic red Chevrolet Corvette, then (assuming I have paid the fair, negotiated sale price), no moral issue is involved. (Let's not raise at this point the question of whether my $40,000 could have been better spent on my family or on the poor.) If, however, I choose to "floorboard" the accelerator and check out top speed on the Corvette while traversing busy city streets which pedestrians often cross, then my reckless disregard and endangerment of other people renders my behavior a moral concern.

Thus, it is the seriousness of moral standards and moral issues which sets them apart from standards and issues not so serious. We all know people who tend to turn less serious matters, such as appreciation of artistic standards or acknowledgment of grammatical correctness, into moral issues. Likewise, regrettably, we know people who tend to trivialize moral standards and moral rules.

TEN ASSERTIONS ABOUT CHRISTIAN ETHICS

As thinking Christians we give a preferred position to Christian moral philosophy, the essence of which may be captured and summarized in ten assertions. Some assertions will be readily apparent and make good sense to people of a Christian calling. Other assertions may be accepted on the basis of a faith commitment. And even though the assertions are no more than simple declarations, some have been subjected historically to intense and continuing scrutiny and debate. Consider:

1. *The chief sources for Christian ethics are first and foremost the ancient biblical texts, including both the Old Testament and New Testament.* Additionally, historic interpretations, insights, and understandings of these sacred Scriptures by the Christian community through the ages may be included as part and parcel of that chief source of Christian ethics.

Conservative theology holds Scripture to be divinely inspired and binding on all people in all generations. It also contends that biblical truth is absolute truth and that biblical morality contains moral absolutes. Liberal theology holds a respect and appreciation for biblical texts, but will insist that moral directives of Scripture must be understood in light of the historical and cultural contexts in which they emerged. Liberal theology is much less likely to contend for existence of moral absolutes or to regard Scripture alone to be the final, normative revelation from God on moral behavior.

Conservatives have run the risks of inconsistently applying Scripture to various moral issues and of artificially adducing biblical prooftexts to substantiate divine support for some position. On the other hand, liberals have run the twin risks of completely negating the religious and moral authority of the Holy Bible and of subjecting the relevance of every moral commandment in Scripture to each party's evaluation of the time and circumstances. In reality, each camp has much to learn from the other.

In sum, then, Christian ethics owes debts to revelation and faith. Philosophical ethics, by contrast, is rooted in human reason and human consciousness and owes no special debts to supernatural revelation or religion. Christian ethicists need not disparage the contributions and discussions of philosophers outside the community of faith, however, as truth and insights into the human condition may emerge strikingly from various sources.

2. *God is the source of the moral law of the universe and that moral law is the heart of Christian ethics.* If an omniscient, eternal God who could create both humanity and the physical universe did not actually exist, then neither would a real moral law exist. In the absence of a moral law, anything could be permissible.

Even though millions do not know the Divine Lawgiver, every sound-minded adult can know God's moral law clearly or at least adequately. Consequently, everyone is morally responsible before God's moral law. Such is the contention of the Apostle Paul as he builds the case for humanity's need for God's grace in his grand treatise named Romans (see especially 1:18-32). One of the tasks of the Christian missionary, the evangelist, and the apologist is to lead people from a knowledge of morality to a knowledge of God.

3. *Humans have freedom of will and action.* All talk about moral choices would be futile if humans are mere machines, mere robots totally programmed by a superior force, mere beasts of the field or birds of the air, or helpless victims whose alternatives and destinies are completely predetermined by heredity and environment.

Humans possess moral choice. Genesis is a profound book in the Bible because it narrates the entrance of sin into the world. In the experience of the prototypical family, Adam and Eve, we learn of the presence of a divine will and of the human opportunity for moral choice. Thus, human history has always been a struggle of individual effort to know and choose wisely moral right and wrong. Not everyone has made a noble effort to choose and act wisely, of course, but everyone at least possesses the power and opportunity to act wisely. Words such as "should," "ought," "good," "right," "wrong," "evil," "innocence," and "guilt," and admonitions such as "Do the right thing" and "Don't do anything I wouldn't do" would be meaningless if humans were not free to choose.

4. *God's moral rules are not arbitrary and capricious.* They are rooted deeply in human nature and the physical universe as God designed both, as well as consistent with God's own nature and his divine wisdom.

The whole of God's universe possesses a unity far greater than humans can perceive. God designed the laws of *human* nature as meticulously as he designed the laws of *physical* nature. Laws about gravity, animal reproduction, plant growth, harvest, and so forth, are inherent within the laws of the physical universe. Rules about integrity, fidelity, respect, and love are likewise inherent within the nature of humanity as God has created it. Humans may neglect to respect and cooperate with either set of divine laws, but they must encounter consequences of their action. Humans have the freedom to disobey the laws of their nature, but the nonhuman life forms and all matter in the world can only comply with God's laws of nature.

5. *Human beings are the essence of God's moral law, the nucleus of which is located in the Ten Commandments.* The deepest concerns of humans — their spiritual life, their meaning and purpose in existence on earth, their relationships, their sense of security, their lasting happiness, their health of both body and emotions — are all vitally connected in some way with God's moral rules. Sometimes that connection seems weak and tenuous; at other times it is irresistibly strong and undeniable.

To peruse the books of Exodus, Leviticus, Numbers, and Deuteronomy, one is almost washed away by a cascade of commands which seem to cover every conceivable situation that might arise in an ancient agricultural society. The scores upon scores of laws about diets, clothing, crops, slaves, civil penalties, boundaries, and settling civil disputes tend to obscure the fact that a simply stated, yet profound, moral code had been revealed as a foundation for a godly people.

6. *God's moral rules are intended for the entire human family.* God's moral law will work for everyone; therefore, it applies to everyone. The human family is essentially unified by human nature and the need for a consistent moral code for all people regardless of their geographic location, national boundaries, race, political allegiance, social affiliation, or any other interesting description.

Just as Old Testament ethical direction extended beyond the basic moral law and gave real-life application of moral responsibility to ancient Hebrew culture, thus did New Testament epistles give ethical direction to believers who fleshed out their discipleship in the midst of hostile environment and religious persecution. Some of the New Testament commands seem as archaic to modern audiences as do some commands and regulations of the Pentateuch.

Consider, however, that some Christian ethics are intended just for Christians — Christians who know that committed discipleship and moral excellence entail "loving your enemy," "going the second mile" and "turning the other cheek" in the most challenging daily situations. By contrast, God's moral law — the nucleus of which is stated in the Decalogue — is intended for the entire human race.

7. *Christian ethics are not sectarian.* Respect and compliance with God's moral rules do not make one a member of any single religious institution or faith community. And, in fact, a comprehensive study of Christian ethics will lead us to the antecedents of the teaching of Jesus and the establishment of the New Testament church. The ethical doctrine of Jesus cannot be understood apart from its Hebrew background. Apart from his fervent and persistent emphasis on the kingdom of God, precious little that Jesus taught contained anything new. Jesus' emphasis on right motive, genuine and heart-felt worship, the Father's original intention about marriage, and social justice were all rooted in Old Testament doctrine, especially in the writings of Deuteronomy and the prophets.

Every organization and institution devises rules. Rules make life safer and easier for everyone. They take much of the hassle out of knowing the right thing to say or do. Rules tell us how to act in ordinary situations.

There are religious rules. There are moral rules. Rules of morality should be distinguished from the rules of religion. Morality is about behavior; religion is about interpretation and judgment of that behavior. Rules of morality inform us of how to live in a healthy relationship with other men and women. Rules of religion inform us of how to live in a healthy relationship with God. God's basic moral law is about doing right "by" others and "for" others; religion is about being forgiven and reconciled with God for the wrong things we have done.

All of this is oversimplified, of course, because morality and authentic religion are tightly interwoven. Not only does God care about how we relate to other people, but the essence of Christian discipleship is living a life of unselfish love and self-denial in all our relationships. However, in ordinary language most people include rules about prayer, worship, salvation, Bible interpretation, piety, and the like when they mention "religion."

8. *Moral perfection is not possible by mere humans nor, thankfully, is it demanded.* Biblical theology informs us that human beings do not

need to be granted spiritual salvation on the basis of their moral performance, nor do they need to be morally good to be welcomed into the family of God. Right relationship with God is predicated upon relationship with his Son, and not upon religious ritual or moral rectitude (consider, for example, the implications of the conversion of a Roman official named Cornelius, a gentleman whose moral qualities were impeccable; the story is narrated in Acts 10).

Salvation, then, is a gift — a gift of divine grace and limitless love. The response of human gratitude is translated into a lifestyle of everyday moral goodness, but this goodness is the fruit of salvation and not the basis of salvation.

Put another way, Christian theology instructs us that we cannot be saved *by* mere morality, but that God's grace saves us *for* morality. Through the atoning blood of his Son Jesus on the cross, God saves us and places us as his children and heirs into the divine family so that "the righteous requirements of the law might be fully met in us" (Rom. 8:4).

9. *The unregenerate and unredeemed world – that is, a world without Jesus Christ – has not and will not experience major moral improvement apart from Jesus Christ.* Admittedly, this assertion begs major definition and clarification.

Various civilizations have experienced major social reforms. The American political society, for example, has abolished chattel slavery; humans can no longer be purchased, enslaved, and put to work as the property of another in the same way one might purchase and utilize a John Deere tractor. The worst excesses of child labor have been legally abolished; therefore, the scenes of ten year-old girls working as seamstresses in clothing factories or of thirteen year-old boys entering the coal mines, both of which were common in the late nineteenth and early twentieth centuries, will not be repeated. Workers enjoy rights of collective bargaining for better wages and protection against the greatest threats to job-related health and safety.

Despite these and numerous other examples of political and social reform which could be cited, the carnal human nature remains the same. When President Bill Clinton appropriately condemned those who killed innocent men, women, and children in the April 1995 bombing of the Oklahoma City federal building, he invoked the term "evil cowards." Great writers and other artists have grappled with the concept of evil. Shakespeare's "the evil that men do lives after them; the good is often interred with the bones" or "Who knows what evil lurks in the hearts and minds of men?" are statements which come to mind as easily as movie symbols such as Darth Vader.

Men and women are smart in so many ways: Nuclear technology. Computer technology. Sending sounds and images around the world in mini-seconds. Blasting people to the moon. Inventing the Internet, a mind-boggling communications link whose possibilities might have dazzled Einstein or Edison. Certain diseases can be cured. Some forms of cancer can be successfully treated. But unregenerate humans cannot cure war. Cannot end violence. Cannot end the formation of new hate groups. Cannot end racism and persecution. Cannot end dispute over boundaries and resources.

To speak of evil and wickedness is to presume a standard of morality and conduct by which evil and wickedness can be identified and measured. Biblical theology informs us that evil begins in one's heart and moves outward and is not created by one's environment or circumstances. It also informs us that by moral regeneration, and not by advanced technology or all our accumulated knowledge, can the carnal (fleshly or evil) nature be stifled to death and a new life in the Spirit be created which will give new meaning to moral excellence.

10. *Christians cannot solve the world's social and political problems, nor are they called to do so, but they can address them both directly by declaration and action and/or indirectly by living as salt and light in a hostile environment.*

Nowhere in New Testament Scripture are Jesus' disciples mandated to reform the Roman totalitarian government or to end a caste system which included slave labor and relegating all females to a status of mere property. The message and mission of the church were primarily one of God's grace and liberation from sin, but the implications of that mission and message make it impossible for Christians to divorce themselves from the world's problems. Disciples are summoned not simply to proclaim the message of Jesus but also to embody that message. To confront the decaying and darkened elements of society at large, Christian disciples are not called away in cloister but are summoned to live and speak in a worldly environment as "salt" and "light" (Matt. 5:13-16). Salt can quietly preserve valuable perishable items; light can quietly and softly illuminate darkened pathways.

The role of salt and light in an unregenerate society has never been an easy, non-controversial one. Christians ethicists have never found moral consensus easy when faced with historic, deeply-rooted social and political evils. The Christian community has been divided over issues such as direct action or civil disobedience. The imperative of words and action, however, is irrefutable. Particularly at the grass-roots level, Christians can responsibly engage in moral discourse and moral action which challenge and confront the larger community regarding major moral concerns as well as raise sensitivity and demonstrate compassion for the victims of moral failure and systemic evil.

OTHER ETHICAL SYSTEMS

Before providing an overview of Old Testament and New Testament ideas which form the basis for Christian ethics, our discussion here can be balanced by citing names and descriptions of other ethical systems and their major contributions.

The history of moral philosophy is long and varied. Since the Creator gave human beings a conscience we may safely assume that men and women have always reflected at some level or another on the rightness or wrongness of their actions. Some especially gifted and brilliant people have done more than simply reflect on ethics — they have pondered deeply, written extensively, and even systematized their theories and insights. Fortunately, many excellent treatises on ethics have been preserved.

Philosophical ethics may be systematized according to the kinds of questions each system deems to possess the highest significance. Let's consider three sets of questions:

1. *What is the essence of high moral character and the good life?* Ethicists who emphasize character and the highest level of fulfillment are called "virtue" ethicists.

Several centuries before the birth of Jesus, the ancient Greeks raised some of the toughest questions about ethics: What is the essence of good character? What is just, or right, or fair? How does one attain total well-being, a state the Greek philosophers called *eudaimonia*.

Plato and Aristotle, the two best known virtue ethicists inspired by Socrates, grounded their theories of human nature, virtues, and vices in a key assumption: *reasoning is the primary function or purpose that sets humans apart from other creatures.* Humans, therefore, could employ their reason to find inner happiness and fulfillment. The inner person, the Greek ethicists contended, determines true virtue. A virtuous person's soul, perfectly ordered, was a source of inner strength which enabled the "good man" to handle himself well in all circumstances, enjoy tranquility and peace of mind, protect himself and his own, be generous and compassionate with his friends, and exact justice on his enemies.

Plato distinguished three main parts of the soul (or mind) — Reason, the Spirited Element, and the Appetites — each of which possessed a characteristic function to perform. Not only did this analysis pre-date Sigmund Freud's distinctions between id, ego, and superego by many centuries, but Plato proved both spiritually and psychologically sound on another point — mental and emotional health depended on keeping the three elements in balance and harmony.

Ancient Greece bequeathed us the concept of moderation or "the Golden Mean," a notion at the heart of Aristotle's idea of virtue. This great classical philosopher reasoned that virtue was an action or feeling that was highly appropriate to a particular situation at the right time, in the right way, to the right amount, and for the right reason. Furthermore, the "good for man" — what a person is intended to do, where a person can excel, where a person will find genuine meaning and true happiness — is in the "golden mean" between extremes of excessive action and deficient action. True courage, for example, is moderate behavior which avoids the extremes of excess (foolhardiness) and deficiency (cowardice).

2. *What are the major duties of human beings?* Ethicists who emphasize individual duty or "right action" are sometimes called **deontological** (based on the Greek word *deon*, doing what you are supposed to do), and deontologists generally contend that certain actions are good or evil in themselves.

While the Greeks emphasized character, several distinguished ethicists have argued that character is primarily displayed through patterns of conduct, and conduct modifies and shapes character. All of us are required, either by God or by our human nature, to fulfill certain fundamental duties. For Immanuel Kant (1724-1804) and other "duty ethicists," morality consisted of always trying to do our duty because we see it as our duty.

Kant contended that three abstract duties form the foundation for all others: (a) respect others; (b) act on universal principles; and (c) act autonomously. Kant believed so strongly in the "categorical imperative" of always respecting others by telling the truth that, in his ethical system, lying would never be morally permissible.

Some duty ethicists point to the correlation between duties and rights. Duties arise because all people have human rights. To philosophers such as John Locke (1632-1704) and Thomas Jefferson, these rights are inalienable. Thus, people have fundamental rights to life, liberty, and pursuit of happiness (or property in Locke's treatises) simply because they are people. These human rights are given by the Creator and thus cannot be given or taken away. Political rights are simply those rights recognized by a government; human rights exist even when governments do not recognize them.

3. *What action is in everybody's best interest?* Ethicists who raised such a question are called **utilitarians**, thereby asserting that we should always act so as to produce the great possible ratio of good to evil for all concerned.

As formulated by Jeremy Bentham (1748-1832) and John Stuart Mill (1806-1873), utilitarianism maintains that pleasure and happiness are intrinsically good and valuable. The pleasure and pain experienced by an individual, however, must be expanded to consider the pleasure and pain of the group. The basic moral principle of utilitarianism, therefore, is that actions are right to the extent that they promote happiness and pleasure for all, and wrong to the extent that they tend to produce pain and misery for others.

Utilitarianism is forward-looking. It considers only future consequences. What about telling lies? A virtue ethicist would assert that integrity builds inner character and moral virtue. A duty ethicist would assert that lying is morally wrong because we have a moral duty to tell the truth. A utilitarian would agree with Mill, who asserted that lies are usually wrong because they lead to more bad than good effects. (In the next chapter we will consider what a Christian ethicist would say about lying.)

4. *What is the end or goal of an action?* Ethicists who judge morality in terms of what they hope to promote through a certain action are called **teleological** (from the Greek word *telos*) thinkers. Questions such as "What is the meaning of life?" or "Why was I born?" emerge from a teleological perspective.

A teleological viewpoint assumes that something has a purpose, or that the end result of some action is the all-important consideration. Plato believed in the purpose of things, but it was Aristotle who developed his teleology into a complete metaphysical theory of forces. For Aristotle everything had a purpose, woven into the fabric of reality from the beginning. When you bake a cake, you do it for a purpose, whether it turns out that way or not. Everything in nature has a purpose, according to this theory, and life itself has a purpose. In order to determine the purpose of anything, we investigate what the thing in question does best.

Action which enables the worthwhile purpose and valuable outcome to be served is moral action. Some ethicists believe that in deciding the morality of an action, we should consider only the consequences for ourselves. **Egoism** contends that we should always act in ways that promote our own best long-term interests. Defining "self-interests" is always open to debate. If pleasure is the highest goal of life and worth having for its own sake, which is the ethical philosophy of **hedonism,** then a person acts in his/her best interests when doing what is calculated to bring the most pleasure.

Which of these systems is superior? Well, each has many defenders and philosophical debates are centuries-old. Our conviction about the superiority of Christian ethics over any philosophical system based on human reason alone renders this question unnecessary. Regardless, most people who act and speak reflectively will borrow and adapt from several systems in order to justify or reconcile their behavior with their moral values.

"CHOOSE LIFE" (THE OLD TESTAMENT BACKGROUND)

Christian ethics and the doctrine on which it depends can only be understood against the backdrop of Old Testament doctrine and ethics. Christian ethics emerged from Jewish ethics. Jesus was a Jew and so were most of his earliest disciples. When these first century Jews considered and discussed their moral responsibilities, their ultimate source of authority was Moses' law and the prophets. Further sources of Hebrew ethics is the extensive Talmudic literature and the Midrash incorporated in the Mishnah. The Midrash contained commentaries on Moses' law and the prophetic writings. The extra-canonical writings partook of the nature of a modern code book by interpreting, elaborating, and expanding the law.

The Hebrews were radical monotheists. That is, they maintained a strong conviction about the existence of one God, a Supreme Being who was superior to the unworthy gods worshipped by their non-Jewish neighbors. This one great Being, Yahweh, had chosen Israel alone to be his special people. Election

28

was not for political power or material advantage, however, but for the noble moral purpose of being "a light to the Gentiles."

The concept of covenant is vital to understanding Hebrew ethics. A covenant is a contract and a bond, but it is no ordinary contract or bond where money is paid for services rendered. The bond is a special relationship; the contract is enhanced by a high degree of emotional commitment among the covenanting parties. From the Sinai experience onward, the Hebrews, only recently having experienced liberation from Egyptian slave bondage, rendered allegiance to a God who promised his protection and favor to them. In return, the Hebrews pledged to be faithful to Yahweh.

Faithfulness to Yahweh was manifested by the code of laws which had been revealed at Sinai. The core of the Mosaic law was the Decalogue, or Ten Commandments, divided into two tables of responsibility: responsibilities toward God (commandments one through four) and responsibilities within the Jewish community of men, women, parents, and children (commandments five through ten). These "ten words" became the best known summary of the Torah, and even today these commands function in public contexts as a foundational sketch of Western morality.

For the ancient Hebrews, the Ten Commandments were the essence in abbreviated form of what the people had to do to keep faith with Yahweh. Additional instructions, such as commandments regarding diet and circumcision, were given for practical reasons which may be unknown to contemporary readers; however, these supplemental directives granted Israel a sense of identity as a special theocratic community in the ancient world of nations.

The Hebrews could keep their part of the contract by living a consecrated way of life. They did not, however, view God's law as arbitrary restrictions upon their freedom. Instead, it was their good pleasure and honor to obey his commandments, not out of fear of punishment, but because of their gratitude for his liberation and lovingkindness. Without this holiness they could not be intimate with their God. Yahweh had revealed himself to be a jealous God who would not view favorably their wandering spiritual affections and their laxity in following his moral law.

To state it succinctly: the primary ethical principle of the Old Testament is the imperative of obedience to the will of God. Jewish ethics were not concerned with human reason, honor, happiness, power, or reaching human potential, but only about divine will and purpose. Because God had acted decisively in history and had done mighty acts for the Jews, he had the right to speak and command.

The law given through Moses required the Hebrews to demand strict justice but also to demonstrate kindness among their fellow citizens. As centuries passed, the Hebrews became lax about their covenant relationship with their God. At times there was much pride, immorality, idolatry, and exploitation of the weak and poor which corrupted the basis of the Jewish community.

Through the eighth century prophets there developed the greatest ethical ideal among the Jews of the Old Testament era. These courageous and inspired men preserved, through their sermons and their writings, all that was best in the ethics of the early Hebrews and even raised it to a higher level. Amidst the many evidences of social injustice and exploitation of the poor and weak in their own community, the Hebrew prophets protested passionately against the corruption of religious practice.

The chief contribution of the Old Testament prophets is simple yet profound: there is a vital connection between genuine religion and ethics. A corollary to this rule was evident to prophets such as Amos and Hosea: the most magnificent worship assemblies to God and the most elaborate religious ritual will never take the place of justice and compassionate service to others.

What does God really want from the men and women who claim an intimate, spiritual relationship with him? The prophets leave no doubt about the answer.

> I hate, I despise your religious feasts; I cannot stand your assemblies. . . . Away with the noise of your songs! I will not listen to the music of your harps. But let justice roll on like a river, righteousness like a never failing stream! (Amos 5:21, 23-24).
>
> He has showed you, O man, what is good. And what does the LORD require of you? To act justly and to love mercy and to walk humbly with your God (Mic. 6:8).

Clearly, deeds of righteousness and justice are prerequisite to right standing before the God of Israel. When we step back to view the entire Old Testament panorama (the old analogy of "not being able to see the forest for the trees" comes to mind), it is all too easy to focus on the seemingly innumerable "do's" and "don'ts." But the Old Testament is also filled with general exhortation: feel this way, think that way, be a third way. God was truly concerned with forming character more than he was concerned with ritual purity. Deeds were important. Among the greatest saints, such as King David, the Torah and its constant study and meditation delighted the soul. But the heart, the disposition, was of utmost importance.

"But the word is very near you; it is in your mouth and in your heart, so that you can do it," Moses instructed the Hebrew nation in a discourse summarizing their responsibility before God.

> See, I set before you today life and prosperity, death and destruction. For I command you today to love the LORD your God, to walk in his ways, and to keep his commands, decrees and laws; then you will live and increase, and the LORD your God will bless you. . . . Now choose life, so that you and your children may live and that you may love the LORD your God, listen to his voice, and hold fast to him. For the LORD is your life (Deut. 30:15-16; 19b-20a).

"THEREFORE ETHICS"
(THE NEW TESTAMENT BACKGROUND)

Turning to the New Testament we soon learn that it is no easy task to derive a system of ethics from Jesus and the early church. Although Jesus and the inspired writers of New Testament epistles answered questions about day-to-day morality, none was interested in producing a complete code of moral behavior. Jesus and his early apostles were, however, very much concerned with ethics in everyday life; Paul admonished his readers to a life that is "worthy of the gospel" (Phil. 1:27).

From Jesus' ethical teaching, especially his Sermon on the Mount and several of his parables, his followers have received answers to many of their questions; subsequently, this teaching, and the authority to which believers grant it, have wielded far greater influence on the western world than the moral philosophy of Socrates, Plato, Aristotle, or any other philosopher of any age. Rare indeed would be the average "man on the street" who could relate any basic tenets of any of the great Greek philosophers; millions of ordinary folks know at least some moral rule that Jesus taught or exemplified in his ministry.

The Jesus that one encounters in the synoptic Gospels (Matthew, Mark, and Luke) organizes much of his teaching around the concept of the kingdom of God. Many scholars, as well as some noted and thoughtful citizens such as Thomas Jefferson, have attempted to praise Jesus' ethical doctrine while discarding his theology, as if his ethics were the pearl of great price to be extracted from an outer shell of Jesus' doctrine about God and his reign. No such separation is possible, however. The reign of God was a mighty concept that impacted the whole of human existence — what a person valued, how a person thought, how a person felt, how a person treated all others, and even how a person communicated. The lasting result for the faithful disciple was an abundantly rich and joyfully fulfilling existence.

The Sermon on the Mount is the greatest single discourse in Christian ethics. Though relatively brief by modern standards, Jesus candidly laid out the implications in thought and action for those who earnestly sought the kingdom of heaven. This sermon, sometimes called the Magna Carta of the Christian Faith, poignantly describes the character revolution necessary for kingdom preparation and kingdom discipleship. Authentic discipleship transforms ordinary people into extraordinary ones — men and women of purity, mercy, justice, forgiveness, compassion, piety, humility, endurance, and spiritual devotion who courageously go against the cultural grain. These are the people who are equipped in heart and soul to be sources of enlightenment and preservation in the larger environment in which they live.

The Sermon on the Mount presents an impossible ethic, at least in human terms. It presents an ideal for life in the kingdom of God. It presumes a sacrificial commitment to Christian discipleship. Even still, is it possible to measure up to such a radical ethic? To divorce religious devotion from any self-serving motive? To endure persistent and unrelenting persecution? To love your enemies, even to pray for their welfare? To remain totally pure in heart? To shun the temptation to preserve your material blessings? To give no thought about your next plate of food or drink of water? To practice unconditional love? To be perfect as God is perfect?

These questions may lead us to think of the Christian ethic as an "impossible possibility." This phrase is vague enough, to be sure. Let's think of the "impossible" in terms of attaining complete perfection by human effort alone. And let's think of "possibility" in terms of attaining perfection through a process of maturity ("sanctification" in the language of theologians) by the direction and the strength of the Spirit of God. Clearly, Christian ethics are meant for Christians.

The ethic of Jesus is manifestly an "ethic of inwardness." Morality is an inner experience; not an overt act *as much as* a state of the heart. Not coincidentally the Sermon on the Mount opens with the beatitudes, declarations which pronounced God's blessing on those who have espoused an inwardly-driven, counter-culture lifestyle. The beatitudes list the traits of our Lord's ideal moral character and personality.

As Jesus continued his portrayal of the ideal disciple, he took the best of prophetic and rabbinic instruction on the law and further radicalized the existing demand. In each declaration of "You have heard . . . but I say unto you . . . ," the Master Teacher challenged existing Jewish tradition. Thus, the ethic of Jesus makes no allowance for ugly and exploitative dispositions of the heart such as hatred, anger, and lust (see also Mark 7:21).

The basis of the Christian ethic is loving concern. This agape is the "bottom line" in the interpersonal ethics of Jesus. Witness the dominant theme of loving concern in several of the Master's best known stories: the parable of the Good Samaritan (Luke 10:29-37); the parable of rich man and Lazarus (Luke 16:19-30); and the parable of the great judgment scene (Matt. 25:31-46). The Savior's concept of the Fatherhood of God expanded the brotherhood of all people, thus making us all neighbors to one another.

In many ways the early Christian communities gave life and meaning to the basic ethic of Jesus Christ. Christianity's best known disciple and missionary, the apostle Paul, contended that the Spirit-filled "newness of life" impacted every dimension of one's life. Non-conformity to the world and the renewal of the mind are most apparent in the Christian convert's distance from mainstream culture's sexual ethics. Sex for the Greeks had been a trivial fleshly matter, much like eating food to satisfy the appetite, but for Paul it is the body which is to be consecrated to the Lord (Rom. 12:1). On several occasions Paul contrasted what he called works of the "flesh" with works of the "spirit," and with frank language he described behavior that was not, and was, appropriate for members of the body of Christ.

The best known Pauline passage which specifically prescribes both inappropriate and appropriate behavior for Christian converts is the apostle's discussion of vices and virtues in Galatians 5:19-24. Like his Lord, Paul focuses more on the dispositions and heart-felt motives than on external performance. The "fruit of the Spirit," combined with the ethic of the Sermon on the Mount, describes the essence of everyday Christian morality. (We will save a brief discussion of these dispositions until our next chapter.)

Christian ethics may be called "therefore ethics." When one reads some great ethical passages — great texts such as Matthew 5, 6, and 7, or Romans 12, or 1 Corinthians 13, or Colossians 3, to cite a few — one does not reach the sense that inspired directives are absolute commands. Instead, they describe how a loving, caring child of God will act and react in a truly exemplary manner. They describe how moral excellence at the highest level can be fully developed. They are "therefore ethics."

God has filled us with abundant grace at even our lowest moral ebb. God loves us unconditionally. THEREFORE, we live a certain way. We do not consider New Testament commands to be onerous restrictions that curb our liberty and destroy our zest for life. No, instead we find these biblical directives to be excellent counsel about the kind of moral behavior which will demonstrate to a gracious Father our sense of deep gratitude. These are guidelines which shape an enthusiastically willing response in answer to our questions "What shall we do?" and "How shall we then live"? In response to God's grace the question is not so much "What MUST I do?" but, instead, "What WILL I do?"

And it is within the community of faith, the church of Jesus Christ, composed of all who respond in faith to God's grace, that the fellowship encourages and nurtures that common commitment to an uncommon ethic.

HOW CHRISTIANS MAKE MORAL DECISIONS

At the risk of overgeneralizing the entire process by which Christians have made moral decisions over the centuries, we will cite three systems which have major inadequacies: legalism, libertinism, and contextualism.

1. **Legalism** is a lifestyle of careful, disciplined allegiance to a systematic code of law which precisely prescribes laws and rules for all (or nearly all) situations. While "legalism" carries a highly negative connotation — words such as loveless, narrow, rigid, restrictive, and "no way" come to mind — it is instructive to consider that the roots of religious legalism are authority and intense spiritual devotion.

The Pharisees of first century Judaism compose the first major group to come to mind upon mention of legalists or legalism. Indeed, this major Jewish sect received the most scathing rebuke by Jesus for their rank hypocrisy and their rejection of the Messiah (see especially Matt. 23). Saul of Tarsus excelled in unrelenting allegiance and obedience to the Mosaic Law, an achievement in which he took great pride prior to his encounter with the living Lord on the Damascus highway. Contemporary Christians may forget that while Pharisaism was the seedbed for legalism, it was also a network of highly committed and zealous Hebrews, such as Saul of Tarsus, who loved God and wanted to know and obey to the "nth degree" his will as embodied in the complete law of Moses.

Despite the emphasis on the authority of God and obedience to his will, the Pharisees' system of religious devotion degenerated into legalistic Judaism. Throughout the centuries of church history, various religious groups and individual Christians have followed the Pharisees down the same legalistic path. Perhaps no American group epitomizes the degeneracy from rigid commitment to divine authority into rigid legalism any more dramatically than the Puritans of colonial times. (Of course, the Puritans have numerous competitors for any "All-Time Greatest Legalists" award.) Under a legalistic system of pre-packaged morality a person either consciously or unconsciously holds the notion that there is a clear rule or commandment for each moral dilemma that he/she can know and obey.

Legalism and Christian morality are incompatible for several reasons. We'll cite four here:

a. *The New Testament is not essentially a book of laws and rules.* When Christians attempted to substitute a "law of Christ" for a "law of Moses" they have missed the point about grace and have created more division than unity in the Body of Christ.

Though the old law of Moses made an ambitious attempt to codify all aspects of social and cultural life of the ancient Jews, providing literally hundreds of "do's" and "don'ts" to guide their conduct, God's divine love and abundant grace are not expressed toward his children in a "Robert's Rules of God." In their zeal for clear-cut laws to guide and measure all religious matters with precision, some fellowships have transformed descriptive reports about the early church into legalistic formulations for which conformity is demanded. All this in the face of clear statements in Scripture, such as Paul's simple declaration: "A man is not justified by works of law, but through faith in Christ Jesus" (Gal. 2:16).

b. *Legalistic morality is largely negative and restrictive.* Christian ethics is identified largely with a long series of prohibitions, restrictions which tend to multiply with each generation. God's "no" is yelled with thunderous volume; God's "yes" is whispered with almost inaudible tones. Freedom, then, is not freedom at all, or so it seems.

How easily Christian ethics degenerates into a negative, restrictive system! Did not the Lord Jesus call us to self-denial? Did not his great apostle command us to "be not conformed to the world" and to "come out and be separate"? Such commands must be given "teeth" by additional commands that make the Lord's calling clear. Therefore, at least in previous generations, a host of specific acts must be proscribed: "Thou shalt not attend movies." "Thou shalt not play cards." "Thou shalt not dance." And on and on.

Negative Christianity becomes so disillusioning to sincere seekers. Where is the joy overflowing? Where is the fullness of life? Why the repression and why the gloom? Unfortunately, of course, loveless legalism rather than joyous liberty has done more to shape the American media stereotype of Christianity and churches than any other moral style.

c. *Legalism externalizes morality at the expense of heart-felt commitment to principle.* Please consider that there is nothing inherent within moral rules or laws that destroys genuine and wholesome motives; nor is there any incompatibility between one's genuine love for God and his/her meticulous obedience to God's moral law. There is the omnipresent danger, however, when a Christian's roles and duties are defined in a code of laws and ethics that it will not matter in what spirit the laws and rules are obeyed — the only important matter is obedience. Moreover, since outward behavior can be prohibited more easily than unloving and unwholesome attitudes and thoughts, sins of the flesh are made to appear more deadly than sins of the mind and heart.

Legalism fosters a false sense of spiritual security. The man who refrains from defrauding his neighbor because he fears he may be punished in a civil suit has no reason to feel righteous. The woman who decides not to tell a flagrant, blatantly false piece of gossip about a co-worker because she feels the rumor might be traced to her also has no reason to feel righteous. The businessman who pays substandard wages, discriminates on the basis of gender and race in employment practices, and allows dangerous conditions to go uncorrected in his factory may, as a legalistic Christian, feel secure about his faith and spiritual standing before God. Why? Because he attends worship services and mutters grace before every meal at home when guests come to dinner. The hormone-driven, dating teenagers who engage creatively in every stimulating sexual activity they can devise except for actual intercourse may be convinced, in their own mind, they have retained their virtue.

d. *Legalism stifles creativity and individuality in conduct.* It considers only stereotyped moral situations without allowing for the vast variety and complexity of life situations that active Christians encounter in the marketplace, in the family, and at play. As such, legalism repudiates the dynamic, ever-changing dimension of human life in the contemporary age. It also denies there is such a quality as moral excellence wherein Christians of uncommon commitment and courage venture far beyond what is legalistically demanded in the face of moral dilemma. The complexity of life and human relationships is oversimplified.

This system of Christian ethics gives us no grand vision of what life can be. It inspires no lofty vision. It offers no real challenge apart from the call to steadfastness to negative Christianity — always saying "no" and always refraining from doing something.

2. **Libertinism** is a heresy of the Christian doctrine which advocates free-thinking in lifestyle and religious thought. A libertine is unrestrained by conventional morality. Fortunately, full-fledged libertinism is no longer advocated openly among Christians, but it was a serious threat to the purity of apostolic doctrine in the first century Gentile world. Vestiges of libertinism survive in antinomianism or existentialism (for example, act utilitarianism), which contends that no moral guidelines exist, that each situation is unique and so requires a new decision.

The doctrinal argument of the libertine is that the abundance of God's grace and freedom of a new life in Christ mean that any moral law or rules no longer apply. One is free to live without restraint and obligation to anyone. In fact, the greater the amount and frequency of sin, the greater the measure of God's grace; if grace is good, then sin brings more of a good thing.

The Apostle Paul emphatically denounced libertinism in his magnificent epistle to the Romans. The "old man" of sin is so defeated, so repudiated, Paul contended, that new life in Christ leaves no passion or interest for the old life. The idea of persisting in immorality to stimulate a response of God's grace was abhorrent to the apostle. This "death and new life" metaphor is symbolized by the rite of immersion in water (see Rom. 6:1-7).

3. **Contextualism** or **Situation Ethics** is another primary system of making moral decisions. The best known advocate of situation ethics is Joseph Fletcher, whose book by this same title created a firestorm of response from Christian leadership when it appeared in 1966. The author contends that the system he defends is biblical and that it maintains a middle ground between the extremes of legalism, where moral laws become absolutes, and antinomianism (no law).

The essence of Fletcher's *Situation Ethics* may be captured in the following points:

a. *There is no act which is universally right or universally wrong.* Right and wrong or good and bad are not inherent within acts; there should be no pre-definitions of right and wrong.

b. *Moral principles and rules are valuable, but only as guidelines for situations.* A person should know rules and standards to use them as tools in handling a moral dilemma.

c. *Agape is the one unexceptionable principle:* "Only one thing is good, namely love; the ultimate norm of Christian decisions is love." Something is valid only if it serves love in any situation.

d. *At times it may be our duty to break any one of the Ten Commandments.* In this respect, Fletcher agrees with Martin Luther's statement that "when the law impels one against love, it ceases and should no longer be a law. But where no obstacle is in the way, the keeping of the law is a proof of love." Traditional Christian moral laws are fine and even obligatory, but only if they serve love.

e. *Only the end can justify the means.* Justice, which is giving to each person his/her due, is the ultimate end. ("Agape is what is due to all others," Fletcher writes, and "justice is nothing other than love working out its problems.")

f. *Even Jesus broke rules and traditions.* He taught that "Sabbath was made for man, not man for the Sabbath" (Mark 2:27).

Several features of Fletcher's contextualism are appealing. Though he has been scathingly criticized by many who have not read his book, Fletcher does not emphasize a spineless standard that can be used to justify anything; contrariwise, the hallmarks of *agape* are careful evaluation and prudence, characterized by a genuine concern for a neighbor's good. Fletcher is correct in contending that *agape* is the central ethic in the ethical teaching and action of Jesus. And by rejecting legalism, Fletcher repudiates a system under which individuals avoid moral responsibility and creative thinking by meeting only minimal requirements of the moral law.

Despite these strengths, situation ethics is not without serious flaws. First, the system does not offer any systematic decision-making procedure. The same motive (love) might result in different actions depending on how a person views the moral conflict and circumstances. All ethical decisions are thus left to the personal, subjective, spontaneous, and individual responses of someone who loves another person or group.

Second, there is a much closer relationship between love and moral law than the situationist may be willing to admit. Certainly, loving God is the great commandment and loving neighbors as oneself is the second greatest command (Matt. 22:36-49). In the vast majority of situations, however, love and moral law are not antithetical. The meaning and purpose of love are fulfilled when it is given the direction of law. Thus, in the teaching of Jesus there is no sharp distinction between the two. "You are my friends," he instructed his disciples, "if you do what I command" (John 15:14).

Third, even genuine love cannot make an act right. An authentic, deep love may make an act forgivable, but it does not alone make any act justifiable. A father, for example, may love the children that he disciplines with such severity that he is guilty of child abuse. A married woman may love another man so deeply that she justifies infidelity to a wedding vow; she may rationalize that "unmarried love is better than married unlove." Is it possible that, in order to avoid falling into the trap of legalism which he condemns, Fletcher espouses the antinomianism which he rejects?

Fourth, situation ethics may draw the parameters of context too narrowly by failing to take into account the total life situation. Its tendency may be to view each act of life and each decision in moral conflict in grand isolation from other dimensions of life. Major moral decisions carry major consequences. The tentacles of one major decision may grow in all directions to impact other decisions over an indefinite period of time.

Finally, consider that any legal system with exceptions is not good. The kind of law — moral, canon, common, secular — does not matter. Law cannot officially provide for its own violation. Imagine, for a moment, that a constitutional amendment is passed that declares "All serious theft shall be prosecuted in a court of law and the guilty punished except for theft by poor people." Or, suppose the Seventh Command declared: "Thou shalt not commit adultery unless you honestly feel that your mate does not love you or treat you right." What kind of chaos would such legal provisions stir?

Is contextualism the true middle ground between the extremes of legalism and libertinism? Situation ethics presents us with a more appealing and persuasive alternative to the two extremes, to be sure. Admittedly, the abuse of contextualism and the vagueness of its functioning lead thoughtful Christians to reject it as a biblical system. Is there not a more biblically sound system? We turn finally to a declaration about Christian liberty.

4. **Liberty in Christ** is the grand basis for moral decision-making and represents the most biblical, the most authentically Christian, system of ethics. Christian liberty, properly understood and enjoyed, represents the true middle ground between legalism and libertinism.

The ethical life of the Christian is a response of faith to God's abundant grace. The ethical lifestyle is a responsible use of the freedom which Christ's death made possible (Gal. 5:1; 2 Cor. 3:17). As we noted earlier, authentic Christian morality is centered on people and their total welfare. The moral rules of the New Testament are given for several purposes:

a. *Moral rules are guidelines for ordinary behavior.* A Christian husband does not awaken each morning on a business trip and decide if he will be faithful that day to his wife. A Christian employee does not leave for work each day and start deciding if she will steal cash from her employer. Those issues are decided already. Most of our lives are lived in ordinary situations.

b. *New Testament rules provide norms or standards for what we hope and expect to be.* They are guidelines to what the significant people in our lives can expect in our behavior; to them, our behavior will not be unpredictable and capricious. With this commitment we can contribute to the building of community. All others in this community know what to expect from us. If our colleagues and friends know that we are committed to a moral system that commands "Thou shalt not bear false witness," they have an invitation to full confidence in our testimony. If they know our system commands "Thou shalt not steal," they are invited to trust us around their most prized possessions.

c. *A moral rule may be so overwhelmingly valid and relevant that it tells us ahead of time what we should do.* Unlike the situationist, we do not have to wait until we find ourselves in a predicament before we start considering the right thing to do. We know ahead of time that it's wrong to take our friend's car without his permission, that it's wrong to mislead or humiliate a child, that it's wrong to sleep with our best friend's mate, and wrong to betray a major confidence.

d. *A moral rule so informs the conscience and gives a standard for judgment of rightness or wrongness after we have already spoken or acted.* In the process of moral development we must constantly reevaluate our behavior. Without present objective moral standards we have neither a directive for the future nor a measure for the past.

True, Christian liberty is a dangerous concept. It summons us to depth reflection and meditation. It also summons us to wide dimensions of responsibility. How do we proceed across a treacherous moral battlefield that is dotted with loaded mines?

MORAL DECISION-MAKING: TEN TESTS

Would you change the Bible if you had been writing or collecting its contents? Would you prefer the Bible to be similiar to a collection of law books and case studies that a lawyer can consult for case law and precedent? Or like a *Physician's Desk Reference* and *Diagnostic Statistical Manual* with the latest updates on all kinds of human ailments and conditions? Is there not a sense of security about having all the answers and directions in front of us? Wouldn't it be great if there were Bible verses which declared: "Thou shalt not smoke marijuana except for medicinal purposes" or "Thou may dance socially except when there is intense bodily contact with someone not your spouse for more than an hour"?

Sometimes life is that simple. Many times it is not. Even lawyers and attorneys occasionally learn that pat answers and clear precedents are not available in their technical manuals and their only recourse is to their best analysis, reasoning, and judgment.

Moral decision-making in the gray areas will summon the best within us. It calls us to serious knowledge of God's word. It demands that we keep studying Scripture. It means that we continue to keep an open mind. Most of all, it requires that through prayer and meditation we seek the will of God and the guidance of his Holy Spirit.

Ten tests or questions may be raised by thoughtful, serious-minded Christians in making moral decisions in areas in which there seems to be no clear "Thus saith the Lord." Some of the following questions will have more relevance to one moral dilemma and not to others:

1. Test of Specific Scriptures. Are there specific biblical texts that address this issue? Are there direct and specific commands in Scripture that relate to the moral issue?

2. Test of General Biblical/Spiritual Principles. Are there general principles or biblically-based values which can be applied to the moral issue under consideration? For example, Jesus' emphasis on the priority of love, justice, and mercy (Matt. 23:37) provides a powerful sense of moral direction in interpersonal relations. Is what I am about to do a loving act toward the other party? Is it treating another person justly or fairly? Am I really showing mercy?

3. Test of Prima Facie Duties and Values. The term *prima facie* means "at first sight" or "on the surface." By *prima facie* duties philosophers generally mean duties that dictate what we should do when other moral factors are not considered; *prima facie* duties generally obligate us because they are so obviously primary duties.

A twentieth century British ethicist named William David Ross wrestled with the issue of conflicting moral duties. Sometimes our moral choices are between duties, such as when a person has a duty to protect society but, at the same time, has a duty to uphold justice. Which duty must be honored foremost, even at the expense of other duties?

Ross provides his own categories of *prima facie* duties and values. As thinking Christians we may construct our own list of values and priorities, including: justice, human worth and dignity, mercy, caring and nurture of self and others, gratitude, non-abuse and non-harm of others. These are values that clearly suggest major moral duties.

4. Test of Conscience. What are my "gut feelings" telling me about what I am about to do? How will I feel about myself after I do it? In what direction is that "inner ought" prodding me?

Even though we attempt to make moral decisions by reason (the head), which is the classical tradition, in reality our decisions are influenced by feeling, instinct, or intuition (heart, in ordinary parlance). We instruct people to make ethical decisions by thought and logical processes, but without conscience and moral instinct the human family could never have made moral decisions and restrained at least some of its immorality.

Theologians and Christian evangelists easily point to the inadequacy of the human conscience in moral decision-making. Whether pointing to the Apostle Paul who, as Saul the zealot who gave orders for executing the disciples of Jesus, or of Native Americans who counted the scalp of a white European a badge of honor, that inner voice clearly approves or disapproves of our most dramatic behavior toward others on the basis of our indoctrination and convictions. Incidentally, many white settlers apparently had an equally deficient conscience regarding early treatment of Native Americans.

To discuss this test might easily lead us into philosophical and semantic debates over the meanings of head and heart. Do we draw our definitions and concepts from science? From psychology? From general semantics? Or from Scripture? The debate is not necessary here. Suffice it to say, hear the words of your inner voice. Attend your gut feelings. Listen to your heart.

5. **Test of Most Respected/Admired Personality.** Bring your moral decision into the light of the person you esteem most and test it. Ideally, it is wise to seek the counsel of the person you respect most. You might compose your "short list" of the men and women who have the highest spiritual dedication and godly wisdom that you know personally and ask: "If these people were to do what I am considering, would my estimate of them be altered?"

Ultimately, what would Jesus do? Can you imagine Jesus doing what you are considering? (see Paul's admonition in 1 Cor. 11:1). Obviously, it is appropriate and easy to raise this question. Sometimes it is quite difficult to answer.

6. **Test of Long-Range Consequences on Self.** What will this behavior lead to? The test is pragmatic. It asks you to look down the road into the distant scene. Impossible? Well, it is certainly a challenging test.

The formation of a habit is a powerful experience. Habits and addictions alone are amoral. A pleasure which becomes a major addiction, however, is not high morality. Things and activities can grip us. An old Greek once stated that there were only two questions about any pleasure: "Do I possess it" or "Am I possessed by it?" and "Do I control it?" or "Am I controlled by it?" Surely it is better to steer away from pleasures or commitments that become so addictive that we slight the very highest priorities of personal life and family.

7. **Test of Sportsmanship.** This test, drawn from the world of sports, offers a simple rule for the whole of life: Morally sensitive people do not take for themselves special favors which they deny to other players but, making rules equal to all, abide by them.

In daily life this test means that we must question whether our behavior, if everyone else acted accordingly on the same principle, would undermine community and decency. This is the test of the Golden Rule, a timeless and almost universal moral standard, which demands that we treat others as we desire to be treated. Following such a standard, one does not break in a line to avoid a longer wait for tickets or seating, to cite an obvious example. Nor does a perfectly healthy shopper seeking closer proximity to a store in the mall park an automobile in a space reserved for handicapped motorists.

8. **Test of Publicity.** What if everyone knew what I am proposing to do? Does the success of my moral venture depend on secrecy and furtiveness. This is a searching and healthy test, for behavior that cannot stand sunlight may not be healthy (cf. John 3:19-20).

9. **Test of Immediate or Long-range Consequences on Others.** Christian ethics has always been concerned with relationships and how our everyday decisions impact others. The Apostle Paul applied the principle of potential impact on spiritual brothers and sisters as a standard for decisions about selecting meats, drinking wine, or acknowledging holidays (Rom. 14:1-15:13).

10. **Test of Common Sense.** Is this a sensible thing to do? Or is it silly and stupid? Speeding and reckless driving, apart from endangering others, is just plain stupid. The colonial custom of dueling was ended because it dawned on thinking men that such a dangerous contest was an incredibly senseless way to determine who was right and resolve conflict. How many young men have been spared from senseless endangerment of life and property by a girlfriend who simply admonishes: "Look, don't be stupid!" or "Don't act crazy" or "Hey, get a grip!"

A "MORALLY RESPONSIBLE CHRISTIAN"?

Let's summarize the varied concepts and insights presented in this foundational chapter by attempting an answer to an important question: "How does one describe a "morally responsible Christian"?

The question may be the most important one raised in this volume. At times the application of Christian ethics to everyday life becomes complex and confusing because multiple moral reasons exist, moral duties may conflict, and there is no easy consensus on a simple hierarchy of relative importance of values and duties.

At least five important character traits capture the heart and soul of a morally responsible Christian: (1) *Autonomous* or *independent* in the sense of using one's own reasoning with the Word and grappling with reality rather than passively falling back on the inertia of tradition or influence of another; (2) *Courageous* or *tenacious* in the sense of steadfastly acting out one's convictions against all temptations toward rationalization and self-deceit, against all foes who would forsake or even persecute a moral person, and against all inevitable discouragement about results and disillusionment with others; (3) *Intellectually honest* in the use of the Bible, in the facing of facts, and in moral analysis and reasoning, thus avoiding fallacious reasoning and strategies of deceiving others; (4) *Accountable to God, to self, and to significant others* in the accepting of the full consequences for the moral decision.

Oh yes, there is a fifth requirement: the *morally responsible* Christian *maintains a deep, but humble reliance on the guidance of the Almighty God*, through the Holy Spirit, and by his abundant grace! Such trust in God, or abandonment to God's providence and direction, both emboldens us and enables us to do great things.

> Trust in the LORD with all your heart and lean not on your own understanding; in all your ways acknowledge him, and he will make your paths straight. Do not be wise in your own eyes; fear the LORD and shun evil. This will bring health to your body and nourishment to your bones (Prov. 3:5-8).

> And this is my prayer: that your love may abound more and more in knowledge and depth of insight, so that you may be able to discern what is best and may be pure and blameless until the day of Christ, filled with the fruit of righteousness that comes through Jesus Christ — to the glory and praise of God (Phil. 1:9-11).

QUESTIONS FOR DISCUSSION

1. Doesn't this book begin with a preposterous claim: that a few commandments embedded in an ancient religious manuscript intended for one society and one culture many centuries ago possess all encompassing significance and relevance to all human beings living in this modern age of computers and spacecraft?

Do you personally accept this claim? If so, what fundamental assumptions must you make about:

    (a) Human beings?

    (b) God and his moral law?

    (c) The Bible itself?

2. Who or what is the source of moral values? Spiritually devout people speak of God as the source of all moral values, and yet, nowhere in Holy Scripture do we read of "God creating [or inventing] values" in the same sense that we read of "God created the heavens and the earth." If God created values, how and when did such a creation take place? Do you think it is more appropriate to say that God is the source of genuine morality or that God is the best authority on morality?

3. Could it be claimed that the essence of Christian ethics is for his followers always to ask in any moral situation the searching question: "What would Jesus do right here and now?" Such a claim has been made by numerous writers and preachers. Thomas à Kempis's book *Imitation of Christ*, an influential work written in the late-medieval period, argued that the chief task of Christians is to imitate Christ; the book presented a series of meditations which helped readers identify with Jesus, especially in his sufferings. Charles Sheldon's classic *In His Steps* tells the story of a preacher, Henry Maxwell, who, upon neglecting to demonstrate mercy to a derelict, was moved to preach a sermon from 1 Peter 2:21: "To this you were called, because Christ suffered for you, leaving you an example, that you should follow in his steps." In concluding his sermon, Maxwell challenged the congregation to commit for one year to asking one question before making a moral decision: "What would Jesus do?"

To our question: is the literal imitating of Jesus possible? This standard for moral decision-making seems valid at first thought. We can certainly know that Jesus would show mercy and lovingkindness and speak words of comfort and healing whenever there was human need. But when we turn to specific situations can we always ask, "What would Jesus do?" Jesus was not married, so we cannot know what he might say if marital conflict arose over family spending or raising and disciplining teenagers. Jesus did not live in a democracy where he could choose to vote. He did not have discretionary income. He was not on a board of directors of some major institution. He had no savings account. In fact, he didn't own real estate or personal transportation. On and on we could go. So, is the standard of imitating Jesus possible and is it even adequate?

4. The Bible is replete with commands, demands, instructions, counsel, maxims, requests, and maybe even a few subtle hints (for example, Paul's letter to Philemon about his runaway slave Onesimus). How do thoughtful Christians systematize this bewildering array of moral rules? Would that the Bible categorized its rules with sub-headings such as "Absolute Rules," "Almost Absolute Rules," "Relative Rules" and "Wise Advice for the Current Time!"

We may start with a profoundly important question: Do you believe there are moral commands or moral rules which are absolute? Which commands do you consider to be absolute? And how do you separate an absolute rule from those which have valid exceptions?

5. Did Jesus actually break the moral law of God? Were there not times that Jesus violated a legal interpretation of the Torah, for example, when he exonerated his disciples for picking corn in violation of the Sabbath law or when refused to uphold the death penalty for an adulterous woman in the presence of those who had witnessed her sin? Does this mean that Jesus was a "situation ethicist"? Would it be more appropriate to declare that Jesus was so filled with the love and mercy of God and so convinced of the presence of his Father in his earthly ministry, that if a legalistic interpretation of the Torah seemed an obstacle to lovingkindness, he had to set it aside?

6. Do you think that Jesus "revised" the Ten Commandments in the Sermon on the Mount or did he simply state the original intent of some of the commandments, an intent which had been almost forgotten after centuries of mainstream Judaism's apathy to the will of God?

7. This chapter discusses the connection between religion and morality. How do you see that the two are related? Do moral standards need the endorsement and support of religious doctrine to give them validity, or are moral standards and values self-validating?

8. In communicating with non-Christians, have you as a

Christian been effective in appealing to the authority of Scripture? If appealing to the authority of Scripture is not effective, do you have any other recourse in moral reasoning which is persuasive?

9. Is etiquette a moral issue? By etiquette we mean a special code of behavior or politeness. We may think of "table manners" or socially appropriate and socially inappropriate behaviors. "Miss Manners," and sometimes Abby and Ann Landers, tell us how to behave in a socially acceptable manner in all kinds of situations. Typically, the rules of etiquette are non-moral directives (e.g., "Don't lean on the table," "Say 'please' when making a request," etc.). Does etiquette ever raise moral issues? What about, for example, when a boss calls a female employee "honey," "girl," or "doll"? What about a white male addressing a minority group as "you people"?

10. Why do you think that different religious traditions give conflicting answers to various moral questions? Take just one example. How nations settle conflict among each other is a crucially important moral issue which determines the destinies and fortunes of millions of people. How is it that Christians reading the same Bible can be divided over whether they can morally enter armed conflict and kill enemies of their home nation? Is it unreasonable to insist that the greater the moral issue and the greater the consequences on people, the higher degree of moral consensus should be expected?

11. Is the Golden Rule (Matt. 7:12) the best principle of fairness? Certainly, it is a standard that most of us memorized quite early in our moral education and one that still figures significantly in our moral decision-making. Do you think this standard is the closest thing to an innate moral principle, the wisdom of which people have recognized long before and long after Jesus lived on earth? (In the literature of Hinduism, for example, we read, "Do naught to others which, if done to thee, would cause thee pain: this is the sum of duty." Confucius is quoted as saying, "What you would not want done to yourself, do not do unto others.")

Do you find it easy to obey the Golden Rule? Isn't doing unto others as you would have them do unto you much more than you are ordinarily inclined to do? Wouldn't you be pleasantly pleased if a complete stranger walked up to you and handed you the keys and title to a brand new Lexus, for example? Or would you like for someone to hand you a wad of large denomination bills? Why do we usually not think of such outlandish illustrations when we reflect on the Golden Rule?

Would it be dangerous to attempt an intimate relationship with certain people when they are actually practicing the Golden Rule? Consider that there are masochists who enjoy inflicting pain and punishment on their bodies. What about people who prefer to be lied to rather than to face unpleasant truths?

Would the negative version of the Golden Rule ("do not treat others in ways that you would not want to be treated") give us more assistance in properly applying its meaning?

12. Do you see social ethics as the sum of personal ethics? If every individual measured up to high moral standards, then would we Christians have settled all issues of social ethics? Before you answer yes, consider that many citizens in Nazi Germany of the 30s and 40s measured up to high individual moral standards — they read the Bible, attended worship, loved their families, practiced honesty and loyal friendship with their neighbor, paid their debts and felt deeply patriotic toward their homeland and nation. Actually, what more is there to high morality?

13. Ethical relativism is the doctrine that moral truths are not absolutely true, but are true relative to a particular society or individual. Thus, no absolute moral standard exists by which differing rules, commitments, or actions can be judged. Fletcher's doctrine of situation ethics, discussed earlier, is a variation of ethical relativism.

The cultural relativist believes that the rightness or wrongness of an action or policy depends on society's norms or the advancement of civilization at that point. The individual relativist contends that the morality of an action depends on the individual's own commitments and values.

What is your evaluation of either individual and/or cultural relativism? Is it possible that slavery would have been a greater evil for our generation than it was for eighteenth century America? If so, on what basis? Realistically, different societies do develop different moral standards, and individuals do make different moral commitments. And it is possible for an individual to hold certain rules to be morally absolute, such as a prohibition against murder of innocent life, while holding other moral rules to be relative, such as sexual morality.

On the other hand, the fact that some people hold moral truth to be relative no more proves the validity of ethical relativism than the fact that variation in scientific belief proves that scientific truth is relative. Have relativists relinquished the credibility and authority to criticize the moral action of any other person or any society?

14. What is the connection between constitutional and statutory law and morality? We have frequently heard two sayings that are "pulled out of the hat" suddenly, depending on whose interests are at stake: "there ought to be a law" and "you can't legislate morality." Can one reconcile these two sayings? Should law legalize morality and criminalize immorality? If you answer that only some immorality must be legally punished, where do you draw the line?

15. Distinguish between these terms: mores, morals, and moralism. Which are created and which are discovered?

16. Can a person live a good, moral life without believing in God or practicing Christianity? Bluntly stated, do we need God to be good? What do you think when you see a morally good atheist practicing Christianity better than many Christians do?

17. Clearly, the early disciples of Jesus did not confront systemic evils, that is, the deeply entrenched social and political injustices of their age. They did not demonstrate to overthrow the totalitarianism of Rome, sign petitions of protest to the emperor to institute democracy and legal reforms, petition Pilate or Herod to institute social programs for the redistribution of wealth among the Jews, protest slavery, or seek to elevate the social standing of women. Why do you think the early disciples did not address these major socio-political injustices directly? Select from these possibilities and offer your own explanation:

(a) The kingdom of God concerned priorities, spiritual salvation, attitudes and interpersonal relations; social and political issues are beyond the scope of kingdom concerns.

(b) The disciples believed that if proper attention was given to the inner person and if true agape was practiced by the growing number of disciples, then major reform in society would come through a gradual, but inevitable process.

(c) The early Christians possessed no real political power. They had no voice and no military strength. They possessed no resources or tool to effect reform.

(d) The early Christians believed in the imminent return of Jesus Christ to establish a new age; therefore, there was insufficient time to become involved in major social reform.

18. Should Christians study philosophical ethics? Is there anything we can learn from philosophers such as Socrates, Plato, or Aristotle? Do you believe that moral philosophy and Christian ethics complement and reinforce each other even though the two

fields are distinctive in emphasis? What are some areas of agreement between the two disciplines?

19. (The final four questions are more personal, but are intended to provoke critical thinking.) In facing moral dilemmas, all of us give more or less conscious attention to a process of decision-making. The author stated several tests or questions that may be applied. List the steps that you the student or reader go through, or feel that you *should* go through, in making a major moral decision.

20. Most of us will compromise goals or accommodate others for the sake of peace or good will. Yet, what values or virtues do you esteem to be so vital, so precious, that you will not compromise them *regardless*?

21. What one person, book, or other resource has influenced your moral life and moral philosophy than any other resource?

22. Moral excellence is living life and making decisions at the very highest pinnacle of ethical thought and life. It may mean great sacrifices or "going against the grain" of conventional ethics or typical lifestyles.

Select one man or woman (not including Jesus Christ, the ultimate example) that you believe exemplifies moral excellence. In one or two paragraphs explain and defend your choice. The person should be someone, living or dead, whose life you have studied or heard about. Examples might include Socrates, Mother Teresa, Henry David Thoreau, Albert Schweitzer, Victor Frankl, Maximilian Kolbe, Dietrich Bonhoeffer, Corrie Ten Boom, Mahatma Gandhi, Martin Luther, Arthur Ashe, Terry Anderson, Scott O'Grady, Rosa Parks, Martin Luther King, Jr., Yitzhak Rabin, Abraham Lincoln or some other U. S. president, or someone from the world of sports and athletics such as Dave Dravecki, Jesse Owens, Wilma Rudolph, or Dan Johnson. The list of possibilities could almost be limitless, as you can see.

CHAPTER 2

Foundations of the Everyday Moral Life

One of the most popular movies of 1994, acclaimed as Oscar-winning "Best Picture" at the 1995 Academy Awards, is named after the lead character, Forrest Gump, a young man whose life was one mighty adventure.

Forrest Gump was a common person, not one who would expect to find himself in the midst of historic events. Actually, Forrest was slightly mentally handicapped, with an I.Q. of 75, but that did not squelch his curiosity about life, his genuine interest in others or his refreshing childlike faith and sincerity. He always saw the best in people and trusted his best instincts. If he was ridiculed as "stupid" he would simply quote his mother: "Stupid is as stupid does."

Though Forrest Gump came from a poor Southern state and lived in a poor, obscure town, he developed several endearing qualities. In addition to his faith and sincerity, Forrest lived life free from deep anxieties about power and position. Rather than fret about material advantages he did not possess, Forrest felt free to enjoy whatever experiences came his way and frequently quoted a simple saying imparted to him by his mother: "Life is like a box of chocolates. You never know what you are going to get." Forrest also kept his word. When a black man, apparently as low in intelligence as Forrest, befriends him on a bus loaded with Army recruits, Forrest establishes a bond of faithful friendship that later led to a successful business operation in shrimp boating.

This disarming trust and simplicity, as well as his bold courage and good timing, placed Forrest Gump in the center of some of the most remarkable events of the turbulent 1960s and 1970s — an encounter with a young Elvis Presley; the George Wallace stand against integration on the steps at the University of Alabama; at the White House for visits with Kennedy and later with Johnson, in the Vietnam War where he rescued soldiers in his company from certain death on the battlefield and thereby won a Congressional

Medal of Honor, and at the Watergate complex on the night of the infamous break-in, June, 1972 — just to name a few places.

Through all the turbulence, Forrest Gump remained passionate about only two people in his life — his mother and Jenny, his childhood girlfriend. To these two he was committed to a devoted, loyal, and loving relationship. Forrest's fidelity to Jenny remains steadfast, even when Jenny devotes heart and soul to the counter-culture which debunks the "establishment," rebels against traditional morality, protests government policies, and experiments with free sex and illegal drugs. Forrest never stops thinking about Jenny and always comes to her defense by putting the best possible "spin" on her dissent and rebellion. In time, Jenny realizes she loves Forrest and, despite an earlier rejection of his proposal to marry, this time asks him to marry her. They marry. They find happiness. They raise a son. When Jenny dies at an early age, a wounded Forrest stands at her grave and weeps.

Many film reviewers have interpreted the movie as something more than a delightful story with "golden oldies" played on the sound track. To them, the movie raises an overriding issue: What is the most moral, the most rewarding, life? What is the truly good, the truly gratifying, life to live?

The lifestyle depicted by Jenny is based on rebellion and "doing your own thing;" it draws from doctrines that philosophers would call hedonism and existentialism. The end result of this lifestyle, at least as depicted in the movie, is loneliness, despair, and alienation. The lifestyle depicted by Forrest Gump, again, as depicted in the movie, leads to optimism, meaningfulness, and incredible fame and fortune.

The story in this movie does not actually *prove* anything about what is right and good or wrong and harmful in anyone's lifestyle. The story does, however, in expressing its philosophy, lead us to think about our moral choices, about real freedom, about our relationships, about our values, and about our everyday morality.

What are the foundations of the good and moral life? Volumes could be written in answering this question. Before jumping into the moral debates over several major socio-political issues in our culture, a survey of personal qualities which are linked with everyday morality is essential. For, you see, both individual morality and social morality are intimately linked. When we as responsible individuals must decide what we should do or how we should feel on the major social issues, we must, if we are to decide morally, consider whether we are showing respect or disrepect for self and others, whether we are being honest or dishonest with self or others, whether we are being loyal to our commitments or being unfaithful to them. Therefore, considerations of private, individual morality will necessarily and inevitably play an important role in moral decision-making on larger issues.

From this point, the purpose of this chapter is merely to survey the personal foundations of everyday moral life. What are the major character traits that render you or me a morally responsible person? Of necessity we must cite duties of the individual toward others in his/her social environment, but we begin with discussing duties toward self.

SELF-RESPECT

Some philosophers believe that individuals have moral duties toward themselves. There is no universal consensus on this thesis, as other philosophers have argued that morality is about promoting the good of others. Kant contended that "proper self respect" meant appreciating our own moral worth and demonstrating that appreciation by treating ourselves with respect. Just as we show disrespect for others by perpetrating unjust harm and suffering on them, so do we show disrespect for ourselves when we inflict undeserved harm and suffering on ourselves. We respect ourselves by honoring duties regarding our bodies, our hearts (emotional and mental life), and our souls (our spiritual life).

Duties Not to Harm the Body
1) Drug Abuse ("Just Say Maybe"?). Drug abuse is an obvious example of harming oneself. Of course, there are many forms of drug abuse: addiction, dependence, continual abuse, and occasional misuse.

Addiction is evident by a compulsion to continue using a drug, whether through a deeply rooted habit or a physiological dependence. Sometimes the compulsion to use a drug is so powerful that resistance seems nearly impossible without major assistance from others. Dependence involves a desire which is more easily resisted, as with an affinity for caffeine-filled beverages. Continual abuse involves a pattern of abuse which impacts normal emotional life over an extended span of time. Periodic misuse involves lapsing into occasional abuse of a drug in such a manner that creates problems for oneself or others; for example, binge drinking (involving five consecutive alcoholic drinks for men and four for women) may create conditions conducive to abuse, violence, and drunken driving.

Obviously, there is such a wide range of ways to abuse drugs. The person who occasionally smokes cigarettes or drinks socially would not be placed in the same moral category as the person who uses cocaine regularly to add glamor to his/her life, to flirt with danger, and/or to escape reality. Consciousness-altering drugs are especially dangerous, not simply for their addictive nature, but for the false sense of power and security which they engender.

While there is some evidence that the use of cocaine and marijuana has experienced some decline among college-age young adults, the incidents of binge drinking and public drunkenness in the same age category continues to rise. Students spend $5.5 billion on alcohol annually, more than they spend on nonalcoholic drinks and books combined. Drunkenness is a major factor in fraternity fights and campus violence; studies have shown that two-thirds of student suicides were legally drunk at the time.

2) Masochism ("No Pain No Gain"?). The term masochism is derived from the name of the Austrian novelist Leopold V. Sacher-Masoch (1836-1895), whose fictional characters dwelt sympathetically with the sexual pleasure of pain. As with the term sadism, the meaning of masochism has been broadened beyond sexual connotations, so that it includes the deriving of pleasure from self-denial, expiatory physical suffering, and self-inflicted pain and suffering in general.

The masochist causes and enjoys his/her own severe pain without justification. Many an athlete has inflicted pain on the body in both workouts and field or court competition, but such discipline obviously does not constitute masochism because a healthy, valued goal was kept in mind. Therefore, the key to distinguishing masochism from other kinds of physical pain is the motivation behind the pain and the role it plays in a person's emotional life.

Admittedly, there are borderline cases: The man who "works out" and jogs in order to cope with stress and depression may increase the amount of time, energy and distance invested in exercise so that his muscle and joint system is irreparably damaged. Or the woman who undertakes a healthy diet in order to lose weight and become more attractive to the opposite sex may continue to reduce her nutritional intake and show symptoms of anorexia nervosa. Who knows when a line is crossed between healthy motivation and worthwhile physical discipline and neurotic motivation and self-destructive tendencies?

3) Abuse of Body/Reckless endangerment. There are still other ways to abuse the body in addition to drug abuse and masochism. There are several ways to risk one's health: obesity and other kinds of total disregard for body health, such as lack of meaningful exercise, workaholism, and heavy cigarette smoking (cigarette smokers may be under an incredible addictive power of nicotine, a drug more addicting than heroin or cocaine). Reckless endangerment might include taking up high risk sports, carelessness with firearms, and driving under the influence of drugs, to cite just a few examples.

Duties Not to Harm Heart and Soul

1) *Irrational Guilt and Shame.* Guilt and shame are heavy feelings — highly painful, intensely self-critical, sometimes irrepressible. They are part and parcel of the human condition. If we did not have values, goals, dreams, and moral standards we would not experience guilt and shame. We may live in fear of the psychopath, the person who can inflict cruelty on any living creature and feel no guilt. We do not enjoy the company of one who is shameless, a person who disregards ideals and standards.

Guilt and shame have no intelligence. They do not reason with us. They are feelings. We may think of guilt as focused on the harm done to other people; we may think of shame as focused on personal shortcomings. Guilt is about what people have done; shame is about what people are.

Guilt and shame can be healthy emotions, emerging from a sense of who we really are and what we have actually done in the presence of God. David expressed both guilt and shame in several of his Psalms. The prophet Isaiah, upon catching a vision of the Almighty, exclaimed: "Woe is me! I am lost; for I am a man of unclean lips . . . my eyes have seen the King, the Lord of hosts." The apostle Peter experienced shame and guilt after denying Jesus, but rose from repentance to become a stronger, more mature disciple.

Saddling ourselves with guilt and shame around our neck like a mighty albatross harms both our emotions and our spiritual life. These emotions led Judas to hang himself after the consequences of his betrayal of Jesus fully impacted him. Irrational shame and guilt display both low self-esteem and low self-respect and are usually based on irrational beliefs about our wrongdoing or vices and what can be done about them. The healthy Christian has a mature understanding of God's grace and understands the therapeutic power of both honest confession and supportive fellowship.

2) *Negative Self-concept/Low Self-esteem.* Your self-concept is your perception or understanding of who and what you really are and is one of your most important possessions. Going a step beyond your self-understanding and self-perception is your personal appraisal or evaluation of who and what you really are: your self-esteem. The self-concept and self-esteem of any individual may have little connection with the world of reality or others' opinions.

Certainly, a major duty to ourselves is to maintain a positive self-image and good self-esteem. This is not to contend that either is simple or easy. The self-esteem that we bring into adulthood is largely shaped by what our parental/guardian figures have bequeathed us. We build our self-concept by interpreting selected experiences with ourselves and with others in a positive manner. We build self-esteem by making fair and favorable appraisal of ourselves as unique creatures of value to ourselves and others and as persons created by God in his image and loved and accepted by him and summoned to be his heirs (Gen. 1:23; Rom. 8; 1 John 3:1-2).

True enough, there are many people who have an inflated sense of their personal value to others and of their "indispensable" place on a team or in an organization. There are many others, however, who ignore or discount their worthwhile traits of character and personality, and limp through life with the burden of guilt, shame, self-criticism, moral weakness, and self-doubt. The moral person who is self-respecting is the person who is self-tending and self-nurturing.

3) *Servility/Inferiority* (". . . such a worm as I"). Servility is an attitude that one lacks inherent moral worth or at least lacks moral worth equal to the value of other people. It is an attitude befitting a slave or a servant in a menial position.

Servility can assume a number of forms. A woman or man with an "inferiority complex" may undervalue her/his notable traits, genuine achievements, or noblest aspirations. An obsequious person is one who possesses an excessively submissive or deferential attitude. The flatterer or sycophant may be much akin to the court prophets of the Old Testament who enjoyed their proximity to the throne of power and offered only utterances that the king wanted to hear. The excessive altruist carries doing good and involvement in worthwhile activities to the point of sacrificing health or primary relationships; consider, for example, the church leader who spends such vast amounts of time in church business meetings and church activities that he becomes alienated from his wife and children.

An attitude of servility must be distinguished from that of genuine humility. Humility is both a repudiation of selfish pride, self-importance, and arrogance and then is the honest recognition of one's lesser gifts and talents as well as one's moral imperfections and standing before God as a sinner. Humble people do not "put themselves down" and do not devalue their own genuine achievements and worthwhile activities and interests. Humble people are able to keep themselves, their standing before God and other people, and their role in the world all in proper perpective.

4) *Codependence* ("if you only understood him . . ."). The codependent person may exhibit some of the above traits, especially low self-esteem, while submerging his/her identity and personality into the life of another person.

Far from being a self-tending person, the codependent spends excessive time and energy in the process of rescuing, saving, explaining, and/or helping the other person, as well as fixing blame for the addictions or other problems of the other person (often a mate or lover, sometimes a child, parent, or good friend). Most of all, the codependent hopes to save the other person from the painful consequences of his/her personal problem, for example, alcoholism and uncontrolled drinking. In time, the codependent has so disregarded his/her own emotional needs and personal identity that serious consequences to mental and emotional health and to other relationships may develop.

In sum, morality concerns our relationship with ourselves as well as with others. We may justifiably believe that we have as much moral value as do other people and just as we are called to respect others we must also respect ourselves. Self-respect goes beyond feeling good about ourselves and entails an honest effort to live up to duties to self and to treat oneself in a loving, nurturing way.

INTEGRITY

The story is told of an ancient philosopher named Diogenes who went about the streets of Athens with his lantern and a declaration: "I'm looking for an honest man." Pascal once stated that we should not expect to meet more than three or four honest people in one lifetime. When we reflect on the credibililty problems of contemporary politicians, sales people, and advertisers, only to name a few, we are tempted to conclude that Diogenes and Pascal were not off target.

Self-respect demands a high degree of honesty about oneself and about others. There must be a candid recognition of one's moral commitments and moral relationships. And as for Christians, a simple, basic integrity is a vital part of the foundation of discipleship. A dishonest Christian is a contradiction in terms. Integrity is absolutely basic to our witness in the world. No matter how faithfully we keep the rituals, recite the creed, restore the pattern, or donate to the poor, if we are not honest men and women in the eyes of our peers we have nullified the faith and destroyed our witness.

Definition. A lie is any intentional effort to deceive. To deceive other people is to purposely misstate something, to purposely mislead them with some verbal or nonverbal language, or to conceal some truth from them which they have a right to know.

Kinds of Lies. Not all lies are created equal. There are "little white lies" and there are "big whoppers." Augustine identified eight kinds of lies. The relationship between lying and the truth has always been complex. But can thinking Christians make a distinction between "acceptable" lying and "unacceptable" deception?

At the risk of oversimplifying the phenomenon of deceit, consider three general categories of lies (as cited by *Time*, October 5, 1992):

1) *Lies to protect others,* as in "I love your new hairdo" or "a great party." These are well-intentioned lies intended to grease the gears of society. Few people want searing honesty when they are guests at a dinner party or viewing a newborn baby for the first time. Of course, lying to protect others may be a literal survival issue. Consider the lies told by families hiding Jewish refugees during World War II.

2) *Lies to promote self-interest,* as in "the computer swallowed my term paper" or "my car wouldn't start." All of us fear reprisal, reprimand, disgrace, embarrassment, or penalty. To tell a lie is tempting when seeking to avoid such strongly negative repercussions to what we've done or who we've become. Undiluted greed may motivate much deception, as in the celebrated case of author Clifford Irving who stood to reap large sums of royalty money from a bogus manu-

script which he claimed was an authorized biography of recluse billionaire Howard Hughes.

3) *Lies to cause harm,* as in "trust me on this one" or "my opponent in this campaign has a big skeleton in his closet." Little wonder we do not trust used car salesmen (or sales people in general, for that matter). Surveys show that citizens believe there is less honesty in government than even ten years ago and that government officials cannot be counted on to tell the truth when discussing a volatile issue.

What is the value of commitment to truthfulness? First, to be true to ourselves is a matter of emotional and spiritual self-preservation. To be dishonest is to destroy a portion of our wholeness (*integer* is a Latin word meaning whole, complete, solid) and to lower our self-respect. Second, dishonesty is a betrayal of another person, the abuse of the faith and confidence of another person. Third, wilful deception undermines the trust which is the fabric of a community. The apostle Paul's admonition for everyone to speak the truth with his neighbor was a practical one: "for we are all members one of another" (Eph. 4:25).

Self-deception: Is it possible to "lie to oneself"? If the phrase is taken literally it would not seem possible to tell an outright lie to oneself and then simultaneously be deceived and hurt by it; this would involve one person playing the roles of both perpetrator and victim. On the other hand, if we understand "lying to oneself" as a figure of speech that must not be taken too literally we will observe many strategies by which people show disrespect for themselves and others by evading the whole truth.

1) *Rationalization* is reasoning in a biased, though socially approvable, way. It aids in justifying specific decisions and behaviors and aids in softening the disappointment connected with unattainable goals. Even callous brutality can be rationalized as necessary or even praiseworthy; Adolf Hitler saw the extermination of all European Jews as his patriotic duty.

2) *Compartmentalization* involves keeping certain areas of our lives free from moral scrutiny and moral reflection. Many a combatant during warfare has simply said, "I'm just a soldier doing my duty." A cabinet member in a corrupt administration could say, "I'm just doing what the president ordered me to do."

3) *Non-reflection* is akin to both compartmentalization and wilful ignorance. It means divorcing one's behavior or decision-making from moral consideration.

4) *Selective attention* means ignoring the unpleasant and focusing only on immediate matters. A mother who may fear the possibility of her husband's infidelity may clean the house and do laundry and turn her attention away from physical evidence of intimacy with another woman that she might encounter accidentally in those duties.

5) *Emotional detachment* means numbing our emotions from unpleasant realities.

6) *Repression* is "selective forgetting," or a defense mechanism by which threatening or painful thoughts and desires are excluded from consciousness. One becomes an "amnesic" with regard to piercing truth.

MORAL INTEGRITY

Moral integrity is a vital foundation for the everyday moral life. Knowing the right thing to do is one thing. Doing the right thing is something else. A person with high moral integrity is continually active in determining his/her moral convictions and making an honest, courageous effort to live up to them.

a. *Virtues.* Historically, moral philosophy has paid close attention to character traits and activities that are distinctively human and, taken together, constitute the good life for human beings. Qualities which make for excellence philosophers call virtues. These may include natural qualities such as speed, strength, or intelligence; acquired qualities such as expertise at public speaking or accomplishment in playing the piano; qualities of temperament such as a good disposition or a sense of humor; spiritual qualities such as faith, piety, or fidelity to vows; or qualities of character such as benevolence, kindness, courage, perseverance, or wisdom.

By a "good person," most people usually mean someone who is morally good, whether or not he/she exhibits any other qualities we admire. Albert Speer, the official state architect under Hitler in the Nazi regime and eventually second only to Hitler in power, possessed both great intelligence and remarkable administrative skills; additionally, he was a sensitive and caring man with his family and friends. Nonetheless, his involvement and leadership in the Nazi war agenda preclude our judging Speer as a man of moral integrity and goodness. Christians may be especially reluctant to label a man or woman "good," for their conviction is that God is the ultimate judge and the only one who can attain infallible knowledge of the heart and soul.

b. *Vices.* While "good" traits of character are often called virtues, the "bad" traits are called "vices." A vice is a trait of human character or a habit that is considered to run counter to the welfare of an individual or his/her relationships. Vices, like other habits, may develop unconsciously and deeply entrench themselves in the person's behavioral patterns.

In popular thinking, vices may only be little habits of indulgence — such as occasional drinks of whiskey, smoking, personal wagers, overeating — which seldom present major threats to the social fabric of a community or organization. Perhaps we should remember that Jesus himself was accused of being both a drunkard and a glutton (Matt. 11:19) since he came "eating and drinking." Recall that Jesus declared that "nothing outside a man which by going into him can defile him; but the things which come out of a man are what defile him" (Mark 7:15). This radical statement may lead us to the tenable conclusion that motive and intention have more to do with virtue and vice than individual actions.

When one is kindly, lovingly, and generously disposed, when his/her utmost desire is to be a blessing, then one is virtuous, even if the actions seem to obscure such disposition. A vice is essentially the opposite: a disposition toward selfishness, greed, and harm which then cloaks itself in deceit, including self-deceit.

c. *Sin/sins.* That humans are in serious trouble from which they need deliverance by a Force greater than themselves is a fact assumed everywhere in the Bible. The plight of humans is one of sin, not merely one of fate, finiteness, ignorance, or mere mortality. Biblical writers generally assumed the fact of sin as sufficiently obvious and drew from several words to discuss it: *hamartia* (the most commonly used term in the New Testament for sin) means to transgress, to do wrong; *anomia* denotes lawlessness, defiance; *apistia* indicates unfaithfulness, lack of belief; *asebia* indicates impiety, lack of reverence; *kakia* indicates wickedness or depravity as opposed to virtue (to cite a few of the words for sin).

Moral theologians properly distinguish between "sins," violations of individual commands and expectations that God expects of all morally accountable people, and "Sin" (best noted, perhaps, with a capital "S"), one's rejection and denial of our true relationship with God and the attempt to organize life on some other basis. Consequently, any definition of sin must involve both humans and

God in the wrong relationship to each other. Saints are sinners who have been forgiven by God's grace and, though they still commit and confess "sins," they steadfastly remain faithful to God.

d. *Moral defects and weaknesses* become evident in the thinking of most of us as we struggle to honor our moral values and live up to our moral convictions. Our spiritual experience may become much like that of the apostle Paul: "So I find this law at work: When I want to do good, evil is right there with me. For in my inner being I delight in God's law, but I see another law at work in the members of my body, waging war against the law of my mind and making me a prisoner of the law of sin at work within my members. What a wretched man I am! Who will rescue me from this body of death?" (Rom. 7:21-24).

There are various ways in which one may display moral weakness:

1) *Lack of discipline:* Most people are conscious of times in which they have failed to exercise discipline or self-control. We may commit ourselves to being chaste in our sexual relationships and then fail. We may commit ourselves to a certain weight reduction diet and then fail. A commitment to exercise according a prescribed regimen may not be honored.

2) *Inner conflict:* When we are pulled strongly in two directions, the self can be divided against itself, thus evoking intense inner conflict. Unless these inherently disturbing feelings of inner turmoil are successfully resolved, we face possible suffering from feelings of shame for who we are and guilt for what we've done. There are both healthy and unhealthy ways of avoiding these negative responses to weakness of will.

3) *Excuses:* An excuse is a personal explanation offered as a justification or as grounds for being pardoned from failure to live up to one's standards. To be human is to be prone to excuse-making, for all of us seek to maintain our self-image and self-respect.

Excuse-making can be categorized according to two purposes: lessening blameworthiness and justifying the behavior. Adam and Eve used a *blame-lessening strategy* when the man said, "The woman which you gave to me, she gave me the fruit, and thus I ate it" and the woman declared, "This serpent beguiled me and I ate it."

A *behavior-justifying strategy* is intended to convince others that the act was justified. Imagine, for example, that Adam and Eve had answered the Lord: "Yes, God, you're mighty right, we did eat of that forbidden fruit, but what's so wrong about that? You put it there and said it gave knowledge of good and evil. If you hadn't wanted us to eat it, you shouldn't have stuck it right in front of our faces!"

Again, all of us offer excuses for failures, big or small, to live up to our standards or commitments. Some excuses are weak and totally self-serving; other explanations are valid excuses. Assessment of excuses is complicated. Reality is, of course, that just as *we* can pass private judgment on the excuses we offer to *others*, so do others pass their own private judgment on the validity of excuses we offer them.

4) *Fanaticism.* A fanatic is characterized by excessive enthusiasm and intense uncritical devotion to some cause or point of view. In social conversation, a fanatic is someone who will not change his/her mind and does not change the subject. Fanaticism is a moral weakness because the fanatic has lost balance and proper perspective in the pursuit of even good objectives.

The most extreme fanatics may pursue goals with methods that harm other people. Terrorists undertake goals with an excess of zeal and personal danger to everyone who is in harm's way. Thus did John Brown seek to end slavery, by personally taking up arms against slaveholders. And thus, in recent times, have "pro-life" fanatics such as Paul Hill and John Salvi felt compelled to take up arms against abortion providers near or inside their own clinics in Florida and Massachusetts respectively. And thus did — on April 19, 1995 — right-wing militia members in their own dementedly fanatic way make a strong statement against the federal government by maliciously bombing one of its office buildings in Oklahoma City.

5) *Hypocrisy.* Another defect in moral integrity is to proclaim oneself to the world as being morally committed to a cause but then failing to make an honest effort to live up to that commitment. Words of concern and commitment are usually spoken effortlessly. Action may be costly.

COURAGE

Moral integrity requires honesty about who one is and how earnest and committed one is to moral causes. Additionally, it may require bold action in the face of danger or significant risk to live up to one's commitments and moral convictions. While cowardice leads one to shrink from strong opposition and danger, courage leads one to confront and deal with obstacles when risk, danger, and/or hardship are inherent within the situation. Synonyms for courage include mettle, spirit, resolution, and tenacity.

a. *Physical courage* refers to courage in the face of risks to body and life. One remembers, for example, the courage displayed by a young North Dakota man who almost completely severed both arms from his body while working alone with farming equipment. While bleeding profusely, he made his way to the farm house, kicked in the door, picked up an instrument and clutched it in his teeth and thus dialed his phone for medical assistance. A less courageous man might have been traumatized so that he could not act or in such panic that he bled to death.

In military history, the name Scott O'Grady may come to be synonymous with courage. O'Grady was an Air Force captain who survived six days in June 1995 in war-torn Bosnia countryside after his F-16 jet fighter was shot down. O'Grady survived the ordeal by eating plants and insects and evading enemy troops by camouflage and laying low. Upon rescue he refused to wear the label "hero" and gave credit to God's miracle and his own spiritual faith for the rescue.

b. *Courage of convictions.* There are times when people act courageously because of a strong commitment to abstract principles of justice, fairness, integrity, kindness, or goodness. One might think of the courage of convictions held by Martin Luther when he nailed his protest in the form of 95 theses to the door of the church at Wittenberg. Or, one might think of Martin Luther King, Jr.'s determined commitment to civil rights; whatever one may think about King the person, as a reformer for equal justice and equal rights this young Southern Baptist minister risked his life almost daily before he was eventually assasinated in Memphis, April 1968.

Actually, the most striking examples of courage manifest long-term patterns of *both* physical and intellectual courage. One might think of an Old Testament hero, a young man named Daniel, whose steadfast loyalty to Yahweh on foreign soil landed him in a den of lions. A reading of Revelation in the New Testament offered encouragement to early Christian disciples whose confession "Jesus is Lord" rather than "Caesar is Lord" usually carried the penalty of violent death. Finally, to cite one more example, one might think of Winnie and Nelson Mandela, whose faithful devotion to ending *apartheid* in South Africa entailed perseverance through many years of unjust imprisonment, even months of solitary confinement.

RESPECT FOR OTHERS

Three kinds of respect may be delineated:

1) *Minimal Respect.* All individuals, simply because they are human beings like ourselves, deserve a minimal amount of respect. The human being — with his/her capacity for moral reasoning, memory, moral discretion, autonomous decision-making, making and keeping vows, penitence, and so forth — is different from all other animals in God's creation. Because of such uniqueness, each human merits respect.

2) *Character Respect.* When we admire or value other individuals for their general character or for specific character virtues, we have accorded them character respect. While minimal respect is totally inclusive, character respect is highly subjective and exclusive. One, for example, might accord great respect to Mother Teresa for her compassion and life-time devotion to the poor and dying on the streets of Calcutta, India (character respect), while insisting simply that an apprehended criminal not be beaten by his arresting officers simply because he is a human being (minimal respect).

3) *Divine Respect.* The Bible depicts a God who created human beings in his own image and who loves and cares deeply for every woman and man, girl and boy, simply because he gave them life and spirit. This same God who created us also seeks our salvation from the guilt of our wrongdoings and wants us to have fellowship with him. This God does not show partiality toward his created children, regardless of their race, nationality, or ethnic background (Acts 10:34; Titus 2:11-14).

Moral philosophers have long dealt with the issue of how respect is shown to other people; some take respect for persons to be the fundamental moral principle. This kind of respect is not simply a matter of calling people by their proper titles, such as "Your Highness" or "Mister President," nor is it a matter of proper politeness in social situations. Respect for others is a special kind of respect, often called "Kantian respect," after the German philosopher Immanuel Kant (1724-1804), and is captured in a familiar moral principle: *Never use other people merely as a means to your own ends.*

When we respect others we recognize the reality that all adult humans are autonomous beings and free moral agents. Our behavior is the product of our choices, big and small, and our choices emerge from our values, our convictions, our training, the major influences on our life, and our moral reasoning. That is what makes people free, autonomous individuals. To respect others is to accord the freedom and understanding, perhaps even appreciation, for their choices about convictions, lifestyle, goals, and aspirations.

Respect for others is such a powerful moral concept, a concept we have attempted to state positively. Respect means that we do not erect barriers and throw obstacles in the way of people attempting to exercise their freedom and autonomy. Perhaps the concept of respect for others can also be understood by citing some of the more common *violations* of minimal respect.

Some major violations of minimal respect:

1) *Cruelty/coercion.* As a free moral agent, each of us possesses autonomy and freedom to be the kind of person we are capable of becoming. Cruelty is the infliction of pain, either physical or emotional; it is causing injury, grief, or pain by someone devoid of humane feelings. Coercion entails unjustifiable interference with another person's freedom and autonomy.

Domestic violence may constitute one of the most common forms of cruelty and coercion. Testimony before the U. S. Congress in the early '90s revealed that at least four million incidents of domestic violence are reported by women every year; almost a fifth of these cases are aggravated assaults in the home. And about 16% of American couples experience a violent incident in any one year and about one-third do over the course of a marriage. Though the media seem to exploit certain cases of abuse — O. J. Simpson's abuse of his second wife, Nicole Brown Simpson, and Lorena Bobbitt's impulsive slicing off of her abusive husband's penis, to cite just two notorious examples — at least our national consciousness about domestic violence has been raised during the '90s. On the other hand, with all the media coverage of everyday shootings, slashings, and stabbings, even greater amounts of blood, guts, gore, and sensationalism seem to be required to shock the nation!

2) *Rape/date rape.* In recent years rape has been the fastest growing violent crime in the United States. Some studies project that one out of three women and one out of eleven men will be sexually assaulted during her/his lifetime.

Rape is both cruel and coercive. It directly assaults the dignity of another person. Its immorality is not rooted simply in the physical and emotional pain inflicted on the victim, but also in the fact that the act is a violation of a person's right to self-determination or personal autonomy. The rapist violates another person in a way quite unlike any other violation (except for murder). The rapist's motive is never pleasure in sex per se, but is a desperate expression of malice and cruelty based on his exercise of power as well as on his indifference to the pain and anguish of the victim.

Date rape, or "acquaintance rape," is nonaggravated sexual assault, nonconsensual sex that does not involve physical injury or the explicit threat of physical injury. Since physical injury is not involved, what is actually sexual assault is mistaken for seduction. The celebrated cases of Mike Tyson, who invited a young beauty pageant contestant named Desiree Washington to his hotel room, and of William Kennedy Smith, who invited a young woman named Patricia Bowman to join him in an early morning stroll on a private beach, have served to stir national debate on date rape issues: Does a woman by her dress, her speech, or her behavior precipitate the rape incident? Can a female victim share any responsibility and blame? Can sexual intimacy reach a point of intensity where it is untenable and unreasonable for a woman to say "no" to a man? Is there an unfair double standard concerning sexual activities? Answering these questions will compel us to separate sexual facts from sexual myths.

3) *Sexual harassment.* In the fall of 1991 much of the nation was riveted to a series of televised Senate hearings. Ordinarily, Senate hearings spawn boredom and apathy. This time, however, the principals were Supreme Court nominee (and now Justice) Clarence Thomas and Professor Anita Hill. The subject was neither new nor was the phenomenon uncommon: sexual harassment.

Sexual harassment is any sexually-oriented act or practice involving coercion, intimidation, or unfair sexual conduct. This includes unwanted and inappropriate behavior: comments about someone's body, clothing, or personal sexual activity; jokes, remarks or teasing of a sexual nature; requests or demands for any sexual favor that also comes with hints or stated threats about a job, grade, or reputation; obscene gestures, insulting sounds and leering at someone's body; touching, pinching and brushing against someone's body; unwanted, coerced sexual acts including intercourse. Any unwanted attention that causes the recipient to feel annoyance, unnecessary discomfort, or a sense of threat, and is not discontinued upon request of the victim, is sexual harassment.

Although sexual harassment takes many forms, the message is always the same: "I have power over you and you have a lot to lose if you complain." Sexual harassment generally occurs in an environment where authority relationships are unequal; for example: the workplace, where an employer or supervisor can threaten to fire or demote an employee unless sexual favors are granted and inappropriate touching and comments are freely made; in academia, where close relationships between professors and students are encouraged by some schools and where students seek to influence the process of final grades; in church, where honest attraction can develop between a preacher and a church member, especially in a counseling situation which leads to transference and counter-transference of emotions that are appropriate only in each party's primary relationship.

4) *Prejudice* is an unfair and unreasonable attitude towards other people based on a categorical judgment about their physical characteristics, such as race, gender, or ethnic origin, or based on their group affiliations such as social class or religion. A prejudiced attitude may be expressed in oral communication and in behavior or in practices, laws, and institutional policy.

Prejudice can be either overt or covert. Overt prejudice is easily discernible to others and even to the prejudiced person. The sexist boss may claim that female employees are inferior. The white racist may claim that all blacks are inferior in intelligence. The anti-Semite may denounce all Jews as shrewd, conniving opportunists. The most dangerous, insidious form of prejudice, however, is covert (hidden, concealed). Covert prejudice is also called "visceral" because it is so deeply rooted in the psyche that it is not recognized or acknowledged; a person with covert prejudice uncritically and unconsciously adopts and acts on prejudiced attitudes toward other people or groups of people.

5) *Stereotyping* is holding a standardized mental picture of all members of a certain group based superficial characteristics, incomplete information, unmerited value judgments or preconceived beliefs and attitudes. Stereotyping literally means "to repeat without variation." Negative stereotypes violate basic respect of others by denying them acceptance and standing as a unique man or woman whose emotions, needs, goals, aspirations, and life situation are different from all other men and women.

6) *Racism* is prejudice and unfair discrimination based on race or, as one person expressed it, "racial prejudice plus power." Racism is expressed in the intentional or unconscious use of power to separate, isolate, or discriminate against others. The racist

believes that his/her own racial origin and racial traits are superior to those of other races and that, consequently, discrimination is legally and morally justified.

7) *Sexism* is prejudice and unfair discrimination based on gender; the term is typically applied to males who entertain prejudiced views against females. Sexism is a term which emerged in the 1960s with the women's movement, which also popularized terms such as *male chauvinist* (to which "pig" is often suffixed), *misogyny* (hatred of women), and *patriarchy* (socially sanctioned male dominance). For Bible-believing Christians, the view toward women's role in the workplace and society may be colored by one's view of biblical teaching on woman's role in the church and in the home.

8) *Passive-aggressiveness,* a seemingly contradictory term, refers to behavior that is widespread in important relationships. It is a method of game-playing and manipulation through silence or neglect or failure to attend/respond to another's needs. Passive-aggressiveness has been called "sugar-coated hostility." Passive-aggressive people use silence as a weapon, refusing to deliver the greatly needed words of assurance, love, and encouragement; they are an hour late, a dollar short, a block away, and armed with excuses to deflect responsibility. Passive-aggressiveness is an attempt by a weak person to demonstrate disrespect for another or to thwart authority rather than to confront interpersonal issues in a healthy and direct manner.

Some "lesser" violations of minimal respect:

1) *Ridicule.* To ridicule someone is to treat someone as an object of scorn or mockery. Ridicule implies a deliberate, often malicious, belittling of some person or cause. Mockery implies scorn often ironically expressed as by mimicry or sham deference, as in youngsters mocking a helpless "wino." One may ridicule through malicious humor which camouflages one's spite and mockery of an individual or group.

2) *"Put-downs."* When Archie Bunker called Edith a "dingbat" and admonished her, "Stifle yourself," audiences laughed. In real life, verbal abuse and put-downs, admittedly among the most familiar indignities of everyday life, are anything but funny. Although some put-downs may seem appropriate responses to someone's arrogance and pomposity, most put-downs reflect malice and contempt toward someone else.

Both ridicule and put-downs can warn of physical violence to come, and verbal abuse alone can destroy a relationship. While everyone can lose his/her temper now and then, and even throw mean, acid-laced statements at a loved one, the verbal abuser has a different style and motivation. The abuser uses words and emotions (such as anger and aloofness) to punish, belittle, and control his/her partner; the abuse and ridicule continue compulsively and constantly with little empathy and rare apologies. Just as with physical abuse, practitioners of ridicule and put-downs express a need for domination and control. And, not surprisingly, most practitioners are men — men who find it easier to give up physical abuse than verbal abuse.

3) *Bigoted humor.* Telling and enjoying jokes is an almost universal experience which seems to make daily burdens lighter and bonds jokester and listener together. Joke-telling is also a popular avenue for conveying covert prejudice. A bigot is someone who is obstinately and intolerantly devoted to his/her own opinions and prejudices about other individuals or groups.

Bigoted humor violates a basic respect for other people. Almost every group of people in the American society, with the sole exception of the white American male — women, Indians, the Polish, blacks, Jews, blond-haired women, overweight people, short people, homosexuals, Southern white mountaineers, just to name a few — has been the subject of bigoted humor and bigoted stereotyping. Whether we tell or laugh at a bigoted joke, we are usually sharing the prejudiced attitudes expressed in the joke or story.

4) *"Off-color" jokes and stories* often contain an element of scorn and ridicule for certain individuals and groups. Since sexuality is such a vital part of life, few would contend that a joke or story containing a sexual theme is automatically "dirty" or "off-color." Consider, however, two points: first, to tell someone a joke or story that the hearer will consider to be "crude" or "off-color" is to show disrespect for the listener; second, sexual or scatological humor may convey derogatory and scornful views toward certain individuals or groups. Humor about the sexual activities or bodies of very old people in health care facilities, for example, may berate all older people.

5) *Rudeness* is a major violation of accepted standards of proper behavior, dress, and speech in a given society; it is being in a rough, non-refined state (uncouth). As such, rudeness may seem simply a matter of etiquette and not everyday morality. After all, rudeness may be defined more by the context and culture than by absolute

rules; a frank sexual comment that is flattering to one woman may be a devastating offense to another woman. However, rudeness may be much more than a violation of etiquette and entail demonstrating disrespect for others.

The following are some traits of the functionally inconsiderate and as you read them consider which behaviors are excusable lapses in ideal etiquette and which of them demonstrates an insensitive disrespect for other people: ignore phone messages; never ask how you are or how your family and work are doing; talk loudly to their friends while you try to watch a movie or play; spend more than fifteen minutes rehearsing a vacation they've taken or an operation they've had; are always late and never offer an excuse; never use their car signal for changing lanes; break dates at the last minute; say "I'll get right back to you" and never do; bring a week's worth of groceries to the "10 Items or Less" express lane; park in the handicapped space when they are able-bodied; turn in front of you but give no signal; offer no apology when they interrupt or inconvenience you; do not know the meaning of phrases "It's on me" or "What's your opinion?" or "What's happening in your life?" or "What can I do to help you?"

6) *Snobbery* is an attitude that one is superior to all other people except for the group in which one belongs. A snob tends to rebuff, avoid, or ignore those he/she regards as inferior and may seek to associate only with those he/she considers equal or superior in importance and worth. The snob may project an offensive air of superiority in matters of morality, wisdom, intelligence, and taste. The snob may impair the self-esteem of others in his/her immediate social environment.

Snobbery becomes a moral issue when one's intention is to cause others to suffer — to feel inferior — because of one's alleged superiority. Snobbery is frequently accompanied by hypocrisy, as when one pretends to be better or more important than one actually is, and by arrogance, in which one makes unwarranted claims of superiority or flaunts authentic superiority in offensive ways.

CARING FOR OTHERS

Caring for others means desiring their well-being and, when appropriate, seeking to promote their good for their sake alone. Caring goes beyond respecting people's rights and according them minimal respect. We want the people that we care for to prosper, to enjoy health and overall well-being, and to reach their full potential as a unique human being.

Caring for others is a distinctly Christian virtue, though the theme is such an important one in other world religions and in general moral philosophy. As we consider some controversial issues in chapters following, it is clear that there are many ways that we can relate to other people and the world about us. We can dominate and exploit other people and animals to serve our own selfish agenda; we can try to appreciate the interesting and worthwhile in all environments and systems as do multiculturalists; we can take an appreciative interest in aesthetic matters, such as students in art and music do, and so on.

From our Christian perspective, however, we can first and foremost engage the world and others by caring. A caring relationship involves two or more conscious beings, at least one of whom cares about the other. When we care for others (as well as care for the projects, ideas, and agenda in which we and others are engaged), we view them as having inherent worth and value. We can commit ourselves to treating others as genuine persons, interested in them as whole people, helping them to mature, flourish, and find meaning in life without trying to mold them into what we want them to become. All the while we are aware that the only way in which we can know our loved ones and neighbors is by identification with their lives in all their interests, hopes, fears, joys, and sorrows.

(Note: The purpose of the remainder of this chapter is to simply cite and define or illustrate several of the traits of the everyday moral life. Non-professing citizens or Christians at low commitment levels may possess these traits to a lesser degree; highly committed Christians will measure personal moral excellence by these standards. Several major scriptural texts in the New Testament may be consulted for further study: Jesus' listing of the Beatitudes, character traits which are counter-culture in nature and reflect his "ethic of inwardness" [Matt. 5:3-12]; the great love chapter of Paul in which love is described not simply as a sentiment but as attitude and action [1 Cor. 13]; the fruit of the Spirit passage, the best known of Paul's passages on Christian virtues [Gal. 5:22-23], and two other passages dealing with Christian virtues [Phil. 4:8; Col. 3:12-17]. Love is brought to its peak of meaning in the writings of the apostle John.)

1) *Agape (Christian love)*. The heart of the ethic espoused by

Jesus is the primary virtue of *agape* (Christian love). Agape is the supreme virtue of the disciple of Christ. Such a love resembles and approximates the love God has for all human beings. Accordingly, the commandment which Jesus regarded as of ultimate importance was to love God with every fiber of one's being (heart, soul, strength, mind), and to love one's neighbor as oneself (Matt. 22:37-40). Such love will enable one to perform incredibly noble deeds, for, in fact, there is no greater love that a person can demonstrate than to lay down one's life for one's friends (John 15:13).

Christian love, which is first concerned with the inner heart or intention, has two radical implications: First, this ideal, God-motivated neighbor-love is indiscriminate and inclusive in its scope of care. Agape differs from *philia*, the Greek term for friendship; *philia*-love is selective and exclusive. Christian love respects and nourishes the individuality of each woman and man since we encounter in that person someone who is unlike any other person. "Unconditional positive regard" (to use language of psychologist Carl Rogers) ought never to be based on color, class, nationality, or group affiliation.

Second, genuine Christian love is extended even to enemies and hurtful people as well as to powerless and unattractive people who have nothing to offer us in return. Christian love is disinterested. Not uninterested but disinterested, in the sense that "love seeks not its own." Agapic love is not linked with "game playing" where a payoff awaits the lover (as in *eros*). This love is unselfish and uncalculating. Jesus instructed his disciples to love and do good in ways that surpass the love and goodness shown by ordinary citizens, else disciples merit no special credit (Luke 6:32-35).

2) *Compassion/Mercy* (The virtues of kindness and goodness, two traits cited in Gal. 5:22, are virtually synonymous with compassion and mercy). A caring perspective leads one to demonstrate compassion to one's less fortunate neighbor, else one does not possess the love of God (1 John 3:17). Compassion is a deeply empathetic consciousness of another's pain and distress coupled with merciful action to minister in healing and helpful ways to the hurting person. It is tender mercy.

The ultimate model for tender mercy and compassion is God himself. There are times that God meted punishment to his wayward people. On many other occasions God's grief over a wayward people turned into compassion that was "warm and tender." Jesus taught his disciples that his Father's compassion and tender mercy were overflowing. When we have left our family, mocked our religious heritage, squandered our precious resources, and, having no place else to seek refuge, come home a beggar, the Father's compassion will not only grant us a place but will throw a big party. Through the everyday moral character of his disciples, the Lord's compassion reaches into hospital and hearse, into unemployment lines and welfare offices, and it surely grows warm and tender when we seem overwhelmed by disease or death or misfortune or hard times.

While many seem to isolate themselves from their brothers and sisters because of indifference to their life situation or a sense of their own moral superiority, neighbor-love treats each person as a unique person and seeks community with him/her. Such neighbor-love demonstrates itself most fundamentally by refusing to be separated from one's neighbor by artificial barriers of race, gender, nationality, or social status.

The best biblical illustration of neighbor-love is narrated in Jesus' story of the Good Samaritan (Luke 10:29-37). The story is primarily about compassion; it illustrates a merciful outpouring of love that went far beyond what is understood as the Golden Rule and touched one of the most "untouchable" people of society. The parable of the Great Judgment Scene instructs disciples that even their smallest acts of kindness toward the lowliest of fellow citizens are not overlooked by the Great Judge but, instead, are rewarded as valuable service in the Lord's name (Matt. 25:31-46).

3) *Patience.* We live in an era of speed. Products, machinery, and services are often touted for their speed of operation or delivery. Our generation emphasizes instant gratification. Little wonder that patience is seldom considered a virtue.

The word translated "patience" in Galatians 5:22-23 (*makrothymia*) is a compound word which joins "large, big, grand" with "large emotions" — hence, the capacity for holding in check large quantities of emotion, such as anger or frustration. Christian patience is not a matter of suppressing emotions but of "longsuffering" through all kinds of emotion.

Both Old and New Testaments praise God for his patience. This trait of God is for the sinner's hope — God is slow to anger and longsuffering in love that awaits our coming to him. For us, patience is the discipline of the mind and spirit that allows one to bear with difficult people and difficult circumstances until God brings his solution and purpose to light.

4) *Gentleness.* Another virtue in the fruit of the Spirit is gentleness, as translated from the Greek, *prautes.* Some translations render *prautes* as meekness, though sometimes meekness connotes weakness and spinelessness. A gentle person has a certain soothing and kind manner; he/she is polite, courteous, and humble. Meekness and humility are characteristics of the Christian walk (Eph. 4:2).

Gentleness and meekness can be understood by contrasting them with their opposite traits — sternness, pride, contentiousness, belligerence, rudeness, and harshness. Gentleness is most certainly rooted in a proper respect for self and others.

Gentleness and meekness are associated with Jesus. Moses was considered the great example of meekness in the Old Testament, and yet he was no spineless, "low key" leader of the Hebrew nation.

5) *Gratitude.* One of the most important yet complex emotions is gratitude. Like love, gratitude is more than a series of inner twitches and tingling, but instead is a structure involving beliefs, attitudes, desires, and actions.

Gratitude as a virtue implies that it is something that is owed to someone. Actually, it may not be that simple. Gratitude involves progressive elements: (1) believing that someone or others voluntarily performed a deed that was good and helpful, or intended as such; (2) having a positive attitude toward the gracious party; (3) having a desire to express appreciation to this one; (4) appreciating and properly using the gift. Gratitude, like love, is a feeling that we may be encouraged to demonstrate.

The primary motive for Christian service is gratitude for the grace of God in Jesus Christ; all other motives are secondary to Christian love. The words "grace" and "gratitude" are at root one (*charis*). Because God pours out his *charis* (grace), regenerate men and women respond in thankful *charis* (gratitude). Ingratitude is indicted by the apostle Paul as one of the major sins of the pagan world of his time (Rom. 1:21). From a Christian perspective, one owes gratitude for acts on our behalf that were required by duty. Thus, one would surely thank a lifeguard or policeman for saving his/her life or graciously thank and respect parents who raised children lovingly in the "nurture and admonition of the Lord."

6) *Self-Control.* Another character trait in the Spirit-filled life is self-control, drawn from the Greek word *enkrateia* which is sometimes translated "temperance." Originally, self-control referred to the practice of chastity in a pagan world filled with sexual impuri-

ties and debauchery. When the apostle Paul preached to a Roman political official named Felix and his wife, Drusilla, political leaders who seemed obsessed with power and sensuality, he discussed the issues of righteousness, self-control, and final judgment (Acts 24:25). Peter urged his readers to add self-control to their list of virtues (2 Pet. 1:6). Shepherds of the flock are required to be self-controlled (Titus 1:8).

Biblical writers did not simply apply the principle of temperance or self-control to power or sexuality. In various passages one reads warnings and directions about controlling our desires, our interests, our eating and drinking, and our emotional expression. Nor is discussion of this virtue unique to the New Testament. Socrates and Plato saw it as one of the principal virtues; Aristotle provided the classical discussion of this virtue, defining it as "the ability to restrain desire by reason." Several of the early church fathers — respected church leaders such as Clement, Hermas, and Polycarp — wrote eloquently about the virtue of self-control.

7) *Forgiveness.* One January morning in 1984, Pope John Paul walked into a cell of Rebibbia prison in Rome to meet Mehmet Ali Agca, a man who had tried to kill him. The pope extended his hand and forgave the one who had aimed a gun at his heart. While it might have been easy for a religious professional to forgive when he knows the entire world will be informed of his magnanimous mercy, it is a far greater moral challenge for an ordinary person to forgive a major offense when there are no media present to offer praise.

All of us have felt the stabs of hurt and betrayal. We have been wronged, even when the offending person was stirred by noble intentions. Quite ordinary people can do extraordinary evil, a lesson so easily chronicled in the history of Hitler's Third Reich. All people are sinful and, bound to one another by the invisible and visible ties of their common life, we are all guilty of inflicting hurt and pain on one another.

Despite it all, an essential element in everyday morality is the capacity and willingness to forgive. And for Christian disciples, the many injunctions to forgive, especially in the teachings of Jesus (see Matt. 5:23-24; 6:12-15; 18:21,22 and 23-35), are closely connected with the commandment to love one's neighbor. Forgiveness is the natural response of one who knows personal forgiveness from God by grace and mercy and knows that he/she should be moved by the same grace and mercy in dealing with others.

Thus the *ground* of human forgiveness is divine grace and mercy; the *aim* of human forgiveness is the restoration of fellowship and community which has been broken by moral offense.

The general principle not only of forgiveness but of other character traits of everyday moral excellence is set forth in a text by the apostle Paul: "Get rid of all bitterness, rage and anger, brawling and slander, along with every form of malice. Be kind and compassionate to one another, forgiving each other, just as in Christ God forgave you" (Eph. 4:31-32).

QUESTIONS FOR DISCUSSION

(The preceding chapter has been intended only as an overview and as such we have only touched on a wide range of topics. Likewise, any listing of questions raised by these topics could be lengthy. Only a few questions emerging from these topics will be cited here.)

1. Do you feel that the fictional character Forrest Gump depicts an ideal moral character and role model for today's youth? Do you feel that the movie equates low I.Q. with inner goodness? Is virtue linked in any way with lack of intelligence? Is there a kind of anti-intellectualism in light and breezy films such as *Forrest Gump, I. Q., Nell*, and *Dumb and Dumber*?

2. What is the connection, if any, between everyday morality and moral decision-making on major socio-political issues such as abortion or euthanasia?

3. Do you agree that all individuals have duties toward self?

4. All of us seek to enjoy life and to experience happiness. When we are cheerful, the world and all that we encounter appear brighter to us. Is there any moral wrong in the regular use of drugs for the purpose of elevating one's mood so that life continues to be more enjoyable than it would be otherwise?

5. Does the personal use of food, alcohol, and tobacco constitute a major moral issue? Is excess with these substances a sin or is it a vice?

6. Is it masochistic to use drugs to enhance performance during a stressful challenge? How about the athlete who takes steroids to build muscle for weight-lifting? How about the student who takes stimulants to stay awake for long hours of study? How about the young woman who takes diet pills each day to curb her appetite and lose weight?

7. How does one distinguish between healthy guilt and neurotic guilt? What are some morally appropriate responses to guilt and shame?

8. Is self-esteem a moral issue? That is, are people morally responsible for the level of their self-esteem?

9. What are some healthy ways to build self-esteem and to develop a more positive self-concept?

10. How are servility and an inferiority complex contrasted with genuine humility? Is it possible for a person who has reached a truly high or important position (for example, a president or sena-

tor, a CEO of a large corporation, an administrator of a big hospital, a pulpit minister of a big church) to retain genuine humility?

11. Is there anything morally wrong with being "codependent?" After all, are not Christians encouraged to be mutually dependent on one another, to enable one another to do great things, and to share one another's burdens? Rather than to feel that the codependent is a candidate for psychotherapy, should we not praise that man or woman who enables a loved one to fight a personal battle?

12. Is it ever morally right to tell a lie? If so, under what circumstances?

13. Should a morally responsible person make distinctions in deception? Are some lies worse than others? Is it appropriate to lie when protecting the feelings people hold about themselves or their families? How about information you have been told in confidence? How about bad news that you think someone is not ready to handle? What about a little exaggeration on a job resume? What about a small amount of unreported income on a tax return?

14. Case study (contributed by Prof. Randall Harris and used by permission):

A member of the Lipscomb University faculty is notorious for his difficult essay questions on finals. A member of the class steals these questions prior to the test. In the interest of fairness this class member offers to share these questions with all the other class members, some who accept and others who refuse the offer. So everyone in the class knows who the thief is, except the instructor. When the exams are passed out on test day, the questions are indeed the ones expected. But at the bottom of the page is a note from the professor:

"I have heard rumors that someone in this class has stolen the questions to this test, though I can't be sure. If you know this to be true and who is responsible please indicate this on your test. No one will know you informed me, but me. Just leave this space blank if you know nothing about this."

If you were a member of this class, what would be the ethical thing for you to do? Use the eight step method to answer this question.

15. Is it possible to lie to oneself? If so, what are some of the most effective strategies people use in self-deception? What would motivate people to lie to themselves?

16. Could self-deception ever be beneficial and supportive of self-respect and self-esteem? Consider how an athlete gets "pumped

up" to play a championship ballgame. Consider a person who has an intense case of stage fright and is required to make a speech to a large audience. Might that person get "psyched up" to make the speech by engaging in innocent self-deception about his/her public speaking skills or the desire to the audience to hear the speech?

17. Do you agree that virtues and vices have as much or more to do with motives and intentions than with actions or neglect?

18. What are some moral and highly creative ways to handle inner conflict and weakness of will in order to build self-respect?

19. Are persistence, perseverance, self-discipline, and strength of will always virtues? Manifestly, highly immoral and misguided people sometimes demonstrate great strength of will and self-control. Consider, for example, Adolf Hitler and Joseph Stalin; consider the Ayatollah Khomeni and Islamic fundamentalists. Consider also the courage displayed by terrorists who risk their lives in radical action for the causes they believe in.

Courage and strength of will empowered these people to accomplish their horrors and wreak havoc on others. If we condemn the conduct of these extremists, should we not also condemn the character traits that enabled them to succeed in their pernicious causes? Could the villains of history be admired in some sense for the virtues they displayed in pursuing their ends? Is not an irony involved when one considers that true virtue can promote real vice?

20. Is procrastination a moral weakness? Consider that some people seem to need to procrastinate until the pressure point of schedule forces them to prepare for a task or performance.

21. Is excuse-making an act of deliberate deception? Are all excuses lies?

22. How can a zealous activist for a cause know when he/she has become a fanatic?

23. Can one distinguish between courage and foolhardiness? Why is it that one person's courageous hero is another person's foolish zealot?

24. Is there any significant difference between physical courage and intellectual courage? Which is greater?

25. How many ways are there to demonstrate courage? For example, is it more courageous to live for a cause or to die for a cause?

26. Remember the 1955 hit movie *Rebel Without a Cause*? The film is best known for being one of only three films James Dean

starred in before his untimely death at age twenty-four. Though somewhat dated, it depicted eerily the seductive nature of gang violence to teenagers of Los Angeles in the '50s.

An incident which stands out in the film is the deadly game of "chicken." The James Dean character competes with another teenager, racing at top speed in separate automobiles toward the edge of a cliff with the first driver to bail out as "chicken." In the story, the other teen perishes when he hangs an item of clothing on the door handle.

Could we say that the person who wins at playing "chicken" is demonstrating courage? Must courage always contribute to the good of others? How about athletes who practice a dangerous sport such as hang-gliding or sky diving? Is the frightened, first-time bungee jumper displaying courage once he/she jumps? How about the one who commits a painful suicide, such as jumping from a tall building or high bridge, as opposed the one who swallows an overdose of drugs?

27. Who do you know that has displayed a high degree of courage of one's convictions?

28. Is every individual human being worthy of being accorded minimal respect because each is a human? What about psychopaths, for example, who lack any conscience about what is morally right and wrong and may be capable of committing a gruesome murder and then sleep soundly for eight hours the following night? How about the sadistic torturers among the Nazis who performed grisly experiments on Jewish subjects? Is it possible that we might respect some animals more than we would respect certain humans?

29. When a man rapes a woman, is it ever possible that the woman shares some portion of blame and responsibility for the crime?

30. Does current interest in sexual harassment represent an emerging sensitivity to issues that have been too long suppressed or does it represent an extreme fastidiousness by which women can exercise power over men? Is the concern valid or is it "much ado about nothing"? Is it possible for a woman to sexually harass a man and, if so, would such harassment be taken seriously by others?

31. Should there be absolute prohibitions on romantic relationships between professors and their students, at least during the time that the two parties are in a classroom situation together? Should there be an absolute prohibition by a company policy which

would forbid a romantic relationship between a supervisor and one of his/her supervisees? If you answer in the affirmative, would not such policies violate the sexual freedom of consenting adults?

32. Is there a moral difference between a man who rapes a woman he does not know and a husband who forces his wife to have sex when she insists that she does not feel like it?

33. Is it possible to eradicate all racial or ethnic prejudice from our minds?

34. How "politically correct" should our language choices be in order to respect sensitivities about race, ethnicity, handicaps, and gender?

35. Do you agree that "whether we tell or laugh at a bigoted joke we are usually sharing the prejudiced attitudes expressed in the joke"?

36. Is it appropriate for Christians to tell jokes which have sex as the main story-line or punch-line?

37. Is rudeness really a moral issue? Can you think of examples where rude behavior indicates a low moral view of others?

38. Is it humanly possible to have pure agape-love for our neighbors, to love someone unconditionally?

39. Do we owe gratitude to people such as police officers, school counselors, rescue workers, physicians and nurses, etc., who are simply acting in the line of their duties as assigned and as compensated by a fair salary?

40. Does moral excellence actually require that we literally "forget" an offense against us as part of the forgiveness we grant to the offender?

41. Consider, for a moment, the radio talk shows which discuss politics and government. Some of these shows, such as ones hosted by Rush Limbaugh and G. Gordon Liddy, have come under attack, especially since the Oklahoma City bombing of the Murrah federal office building, for alleged abusive and contemptuous criticism of government officials. Do you think that these shows tend to justify vicious personal attacks against people with whom we disagree? Do opinion-makers show disrespect for government officials when they subject them or their families to ridicule or derisive humor? Was it right, for example, for Howard Stern to use the airwaves to ridicule Spanish music just after the murder of a popular Mexican singer? What about Senator Jesse Helms' declaration that the president had better bring a bodyguard if he visited North Carolina? How about Jerry Falwell marketing anti-Clinton videotapes featuring alle-

gations about the president's complicity in murder and drug trafficking? Is there a loss of respect for public officials and others in authority in our society? Is there a loss of civility in terms of how we treat and talk to one another?

42. What do you think about the "trash talk" that is transmitted by airwaves and cable on radio and TV talk shows? Are we losing our ability to community with each other civilly? Have we become a society obsessed with the bizarre, with sexuality, and with hostile confrontation?

43. Case study: In January 1995, Jewish survivors of the Holocaust commemorated the fiftieth anniversary of the liberation of the Auschwitz-Birkenau death camps by Russian troops. Over one million Jews had been killed by Nazis at these camps. To most historians and moral philosophers, what happened at Auschwitz and other Nazi concentration camps in the '40s represented the darkest and most terrible chapter in German history and demonstrated the depths of evil of which people are capable.

In an observance on the site of Birkenau's crematoria, Elie Wiesel, a survivor of eleven months at Auschwitz and Nobel Peace Prize winner, intoned in a public prayer: "Merciful Father, do not have mercy on those who had no mercy on Jewish children."

Did this prayer express in any way a Christian attitude? Are there ordinary people who have committed such extraordinary evil that no humans should be expected to forgive them? Are some evil acts simply unforgivable? What does it mean to deny the possibility of forgiveness to certain people? Does today's generation of Americans have any business passing judgment on any Holocaust survivor's refusal to forgive Nazi war criminals?

CHAPTER THREE

Abortion/Reproductive
Technologies

One of the most pressing social and moral issues of our day is abortion. Second only to circumcision, abortion is the next most common surgical procedure in the United States. Since the famous *Roe v. Wade* (1973) decision, wherein the Supreme Court ruled that the constitutional right to privacy applies to a woman's decision on whether to terminate her pregnancy, abortions have risen from 775,000 in 1973 to about 1.6 million annually. Statistics indicate that about one in four pregnancies in the U. S. end in an abortion. The largest percentage of abortions (about 65%) is among unmarried women and twice as many white women were responsible for abortions as nonwhite women.

Abortion is prevalent in other nations and is usually viewed as an appropriate means of birth control. Forty percent of the world's population live in countries where abortion is legally available on request (largely in the U.S., China, the former Soviet Union, and Europe). Nations comprising another 37% of the population allow abortion when a woman's life is endangered or her general health is threatened or in the case of rape or incest. Abortion rates are highest in nations such as Romania where contraceptives are still difficult to obtain; the nation with the lowest rate is the Netherlands, a nation with a liberal abortion law but with high contraceptive use.

The debate over abortion has been fervent and heated in the United States. Finding a middle ground has been difficult. For one reason, the issue is more of an ethical and moral issue than a political one. Also, people are willing to compromise only when they can see the validity or possible merit in the position of the opposing party. "Pro-life" advocates tend to absolutize the rights of the fetus, contending that the fetus must be protected at all costs against the so-called rights of the woman. At the other extreme in this debate are those who maintain that the fetus is essentially tissue belonging to the woman, possessing no independent identity and humanity of its own. Each of these positions denies the moral validity of the opposing position and contends that there is a clear-cut answer to this vexing issue without any need to consider the circumstances in each separate case.

Some who seek a moderate position on the issue contend that liberal abortion policies tend to dehumanize and degrade a nation of people, but that no absolute prohibition against abortion need be enacted. Moderates would say an abortion is right if: (1) it is therapeutic, that is, if it is necessary to preserve the mental and physical health of the female; (2) it prevents the birth of a severely mentally and/or physically handicapped child; or (3) it ends a pregnancy resulting from rape or incest; (4) it is performed early in the pregnancy, usually before the end of the second trimester. "Right to life" absolutists will argue that the above situations do not morally justify an abortion decision and that the providence of God to bring good out of difficult and even evil circumstances must be honored. "Right to choose" absolutists believe that at any point in time a pregnant woman in consulting with her physician may choose an abortion for any reason.

What is the key issue in this moral debate? The term *ontology* in philosophy refers to the theory and nature of being and existence. When we ask about the ontological status of the fetus we are asking what kind of entity the fetus is. Determining the ontological status of the fetus bears directly on the issue of fetal rights and, subsequently, on the morality of aborting fetuses.

Is the fetus a human being? Is the fetus a person? Does the fetus have a soul? What standards or criteria must be met for a fetus to have personhood? To affirm that a fetus is a person would be to assign significant legal and moral status to the fetus. The meaning of "human life" further complicates this issue. Conservatives might contend that the fertilized human egg is "human life" because it possesses all forty-six chromosomes present in an independent human being and has certain biological characteristics which distinguish it from nonhuman species. Liberals might contend that biological characteristics and potentialities are not sufficient requisites for the presence of human life. To liberals, human life must refer to psychological human life which is characterized by traits which are strictly human: ability to use symbols, to think, to reason, and to imagine.

The concept of personhood is also at the root of the debate over abortion as well as over euthanasia. Some contend that to be a person is simply to have the biological and/or psychological properties that make an organism human. Others propose that true personhood involves additional faculties such as consciousness, self-consciousness, awareness, rationality, ability to communicate, and ability to make moral judgment; accordingly, for an entity to be a full person, he/she must possess some or all of these capacities.

A final consideration related to the key issue: When does a fetus gain full ontological and moral status? Clearly the conditions that one believes are necessary for "human life" and "person" status directly affect both the ontological status of the fetus and one's moral judgment of the permissibility of abortion. If an organism becomes a human being with minimal biological characteristics then abortion at any point of fetal development becomes morally indefensible. On the other hand, those who would agree that abortion involves the taking of human life in the biological sense would deny that it involves taking human life in the psychological sense; such liberals would find nothing objectional about taking life in an exclusively biological sense, but would render taking life in the psychological sense morally reprehensible.

In the final analysis, the ontological status of the fetus will remain an open issue because it will never be settled by scientific evidence or laboratory experiments. But some viewpoint ultimately underpins any stand on the morality of abortion. Whether you consider yourself to be a conservative, a liberal, or a moderate, be prepared eventually to defend your view of the ontological status of the unborn organism.

Most of all, we do well to remember that behind the avalanche of words that comprise the heated debate there are real people, real feelings, real hopes, triumphs, fears, and tragedies.

REPRODUCTIVE TECHNOLOGY

A Tennessee couple continued to make national headlines in the early '90s. Junior and Mary Sue Davis had stayed together through nine years of marriage and five unsuccessful pregnancies. Exasperated, they turned for help to in vitro fertilization. Several eggs were taken and fertilized. Two eggs were implanted, but neither produced a pregnancy. The other embryos were frozen. When the couple filed for divorce it was natural to inquire about the custody of the seven frozen embryos. Both Junior and Mary Sue wanted them and neither wanted the other to own them. Legal remedy was sought. Pundits quipped that each could keep the embryos in his or her personal freezers on a rotating basis for six months at a time. On June 1, 1992, the state's Supreme Court ruled that Mary Sue could not use the embryos to induce pregnancy, for such action would force her former husband into unwanted fatherhood. Under the rights of both privacy and "procreational autonomy," the Court ruled that each person has rights to avoid as well as to enjoy procreation.

What a brave new world we live in! The impact of research and technology on the medical and biological sciences during the past two generations has been staggering. And who knows what the future holds as technology dramatically impacts both terminal points of human existence — birth and death. Some of our discoveries in biomedicine bring unquestionable, manifold blessing to millions of families. Other discoveries about biomedical techniques — involving methods of enhancing fertility, fertilization, gene splicing or genetic "engineering," diagnosing and treating genetic defects *in utero*, organ transplanting, behavior modification, and the prolongation of life — pose unprecedented ethical problems.

In this chapter we simply mention several dimensions of reproductive technology, an area in which rapid development has spawned a number of nettlesome moral dilemmas. When a married couple earnestly desire to have children but, for reasons of infertility or impotence are unable to conceive, artificial means can induce pregnancy. One procedure, called AIH (artificial-insemination-husband) involves using instruments to inject the husband's sperm into the wife's vagina. In another procedure, called AID (artificial-insemination-donor), the semen injected is from a man other than the woman's husband. In still another method, in vitro fertilization (IVF, "in vitro" meaning "in glass"), the male sperm is joined with the female egg in a test tube; if the egg is fertilized, it is inserted into the hopeful mother's uterus and if implantation is successful the pregnancy has begun.

One notorious variation of the in vitro fertilization process, the fertilized egg is placed into the body of a third person. Surrogate mothers may either receive a woman's fertilized ovum or be artificially inseminated with the partner's sperm. The model of Abraham, Sarah, and Hagar (Gen. 16) suggests a natural model of surrogacy. Sarah was barren, but God had promised an heir for

Abraham. Sarah took the lead in arranging for Hagar's availability for her husband. Abraham had sexual relations with Hagar. A son was born. This was not God's way of introducing an heir into the world, but the surrogacy as such does not seem to be condemned in Scripture.

Does surrogate mothering present a moral issue or should we conclude that the experience is not radically different from other recognized practices in which the child is removed from its biological mother? How does surrogacy differ from artificial insemination, adoption, and blended families? Do not all involve the intentional separation of biological and social parenting functions?

Since what is technically possible is not for that very reason morally admissible, many other questions emerge for Christian ethicists: Is all this advancing of reproductive technology one grand assault on God's natural law? Does it matter if a woman enters the experience of surrogate motherhood solely for the purpose of making a large sum of money? What about males who seek to earn money through sperm donation? Should the gestational mother (and her spouse, if any) possess any rearing rights and obligations? What if the surrogate mother decides she does not want to relinquish the child she carries, an issue which came to the fore in 1987 with the famous "Baby M" case in Michigan? Should there be a connection from a moral point of view between procreation and sexual intercourse in marriage? Are we as a society moving toward one grand loss of the sanctity of life? Is it morally wrong to attempt to control and manipulate human reproduction? Have we lost the biblical concept of parenthood and family?

Christian thinkers will answer these vexing questions in different ways, perhaps depending on whether they consider themselves to be liberal or conservative. Try as we might to imagine a simpler world, the triangulating challenges of law, theology, and medicine simply will not disappear.

KEY TERMS

Abortion — The termination of a pregnancy. From the Latin, *abortare*, to disappear. It means the premature expulsion of the fetus from the womb. The abortion can happen for a number of reasons. A "spontaneous" abortion may occur because of internal biochemical factors or because of an injury to the woman. Such spontaneous abortions are ordinarily called "miscarriages" and they generally involve no moral issues. Abortions also can result directly from human intervention, which can occur in a variety of ways (most methods are included in this listing).

Amniocentesis — Procedure in which a needle is inserted through the mother's abdomen into the fetal sac, and fluid is removed and examined to determine any abnormalities.

Artificial insemination — A simple technique of injecting sperm obtained through masturbation into the vagina. Its most common application today is in the alleviation of male infertility with the use of donor sperm. Artificial insemination is a mirror image of the surrogate mother. As a surrogate mother helps an infertile woman, artificial insemination helps an infertile man. By the use of donor sperm, his wife can become pregnant. Many couples find this more desirable than adoption because the child will at least have characteristics of one parent.

Aspiration — (Uterine or vacuum aspiration) — The cervix is dilated, and a suction tube is inserted into the womb. The suction removes both the fetus and the placenta from the uterus, sucking them into a jar.

Birth — The baby's expulsion or removal from the mother's uterus, either naturally or by Caesarean section.

Blastocyst — The life form which develops when the multicell zygote reaches the uterus and floats free in the intrauterine fluid (from second day through second week).

Cryopreservation — Freezing of sperm or eggs (fertilized or not fertilized) in liquid nitrogen for future use.

Dilation and curettage ("D & C") — A system of abortion wherein the cervix is dilated, and the contents of the uterus are scraped out by means of a spoon-shaped surgical instrument called a curette.

Ectopic or tubal pregnancy — A rare pregnancy in which the fertilized egg does not implant in the uterus but in the fallopian tube.

Embryo — The name for the growing life form from the end of the second week, when the blastocyst implants itself in the uterine wall, until the eighth week, at which point the unborn entity is called a "fetus."

Ensoulment — An issue of special concern for medieval theologians, the act of God in endowing a separate human life with an eternal soul; after ensoulment the fetus was considered a fully

92

human being and abortion was considered a homicide. Some medievals followed Aristotle in placing ensoulment at forty days after conception for a male fetus and eighty days after conception for a female fetus.

Fetus — Unborn young entity from the ninth week until birth. Fetus is from Latin, meaning *offspring*. In common parlance, fetus designates the unborn entity at whatever stage.

In Vitro Fertilization (IVF) — Eggs are removed from the ovaries and mixed with sperm in the laboratory where fertilization occurs. The fertilized eggs are then placed in the uterus.

Ovum — Female germ cell.

Quickening — Stage at which the fetus makes moves which can be felt by the mother.

RU-486 — A drug, first discovered in 1980 by a French biochemist, capable of terminating an early pregnancy. Popularly known as the "morning after" pill, RU-486, a laboratory name and molecule number, functions by blocking the action of the hormone progesterone, thus preventing the fertilized egg from implanting in the uterus.

Roe v. Wade; Doe v. Bolton (1973) — In this decision the Supreme Court struck down both the older, more restrictive legislation operative in thirty states and the more lenient legislation of sixteen other states. By a 7:2 vote the Court affirmed the right of a woman to have an abortion in the first trimester of her pregnancy; it also declared that the state's interest in the health of the mother and in the potentiality of human life may lead it to regulate abortion procedures in the second trimester and to regulate and possibly proscribe abortion after viability of the fetus. Even after viability, however, abortion must be permitted if there would be danger to the life or health of the mother. Judge Harry Blackmun, author of the majority opinion, attempted to skirt the complicated moral questions concerning abortion ("We need not resolve the difficult question of when life begins"); he retired from the bench in 1994.

Saline injection — A method of abortion in which the needle is inserted through the mother's abdomen into the sac. Some of the amniotic fluid is removed and replaced with a solution of concentrated salt. The fetus dies which leads to a miscarriage.

Spermatozoon — male germ cell.

Surrogate — One appointed to act in place of another or one that serves as a substitute. A surrogate mother acts in the place of the potential "mother" by carrying and delivering a baby. A surrogate is one who is impregnated with the sperm from a man whose wife is unable to become pregnant. The surrogate mother agrees to carry and deliver the child and then relinquish it to the man and his wife.

Viability — The point at which the fetus is capable of surviving outside the womb; the fetus generally reaches viability around the twenty-fourth week.

Zygote — The result of conception, when a single cell, containing a full genetic code of forty-six chromosomes, develops (first through third day) and then makes its journey down a fallopian tube to the uterus.

KEY SCRIPTURES

There is no single Scripture which specifically addresses the issue of abortion. When considering this tough moral issue, the thinking Christian will consider certain core principles that are drawn from biblical doctrine.

The most frequently cited text on this issue is Exodus 21:22-25, a "special case" passage which has been used by both sides in this debate. The text states a penalty for compensation in a situation wherein two men are fighting near a pregnant woman and accidentally strike her so that she miscarries her baby. If the woman is not injured, then the penalty is only what the woman's husband demands and the court allows. If the woman is injured, the law of *lex talionis* (the law of retaliation) is required. A common sense interpretation of this passage concludes that the personhood of the woman is more valued than the non- or limited-personhood of the fetus.

Consider the following, however: Even if the above interpretation is correct, this passage does not authorize abortion, because (1) the death that is referred to in verse 22 is accidental, not intentional; (2) the fact that a penalty is required for the death of a fetus indicates that it is an injury or wrong of some kind; (3) a mere fine does not mean less value to the fetus because the law of Moses made exceptions to the death penalty in the case of accidental death. Conclude, then, say conservatives, that this passage *does* place a high value on the fetus.

KEY ISSUES/ARGUMENTS
Arguments against Acceptance and Condoning of Abortion (Pro-Life)

1. Abortion is murder, pure and simple.

"You don't have to be a Philadelphia lawyer to know what murder means — the intentional termination of an innocent human life. This is a life that the mother and abortionist cannot return. How can anything be more outrageous than killing the helpless and innocent? If you attempt to kill an adult, at least an adult might have an opportunity for self-defense."

2. Every human life is sacred to God and to self.

"Every human life has special, irrevocable value. God created that life. Life is precious to him. Every human life is sacred. Its value is absolute — not relevant to the circumstances of its conception, to the wealth of the parents, to the convenience of the timing, to other people's desires, or to society's opinions. The value of your life does not depend on whether you are convenient or inconvenient to me or whether my friends and family like you. You and I both have a right to live and enjoy liberty. A black southerner before the Civil War had as much right to live and be free as a white southerner. A German Jew possessed the same right to life and liberty as a German Gentile, even if the German Gentiles did not acknowledge that right.

"Let's state this is the form of a proposition: Every person is an end and not a means to someone else's end. This proposition is not subject to public opinion polls or to scientific research. It is true whether we believe it to be true, want it to be true, practice it to be true. Whatever is sacred has absolute value and must be guarded and cherished."

3. Reasonable alternatives to abortion are easily available.

"A woman has no alternative to abortion? Ridiculous! There are countless individuals and couples who are longing to have children but cannot. Adoption is always an available alternative. If a woman does not want to carry a child to term, that's no reason to abort it. Just put it up for adoption at birth. The demand for children is so great that many couples are willing to wait many months and encounter complex legal barriers and extravagant costs to be granted a child.

"What a bizarre morality that says, 'Oh, I just couldn't possibly give up my baby for adoption. It's just too precious to send to another home' — and then chooses to kill that 'too precious' baby instead!"

4. Biblical Scripture (by example and inference) clearly condemns abortion.

"How could anyone read the Bible and not see that God finds abortion abhorrent. There's too much evidence to believe otherwise. The Bible infers that one's personal history begins at conception [see Gen. 4:1; Psa. 51:5; note that the Psalmist declared in 139:13 '. . . thou didst weave me in my mother's womb.']

"The Bible also presents the idea that conception is the gift of God. Godly women considered it an honor to conceive a child while the barren womb was considered a curse. God has a personal relationship with the unborn. While in his mother's womb, Jacob was chosen over Esau for special blessing [Gen. 25:22]; the Lord told Jeremiah that "before you were born I consecrated you' [1:5]; John the Baptist was filled with the Holy Spirit 'even from his mother's womb' [Luke 1:15; 41-44]; a pregnant Mary was declared to be 'blessed' already even before Jesus was born [Luke 1:42]. God has a plan for every single child who is conceived. How can a woman thwart that plan without considering that she is fighting the will of God?

It may be true that the Bible does not issue a single command, such as 'Thou shalt not abort thy child.' The absence of such a command does not make abortion a moral act. People in biblical times surely knew about abortion procedures, but they believed that all life, including fetal life, was protected by the sixth commandment. Just because the Bible does not say 'Thou shalt not shoot and kill your neighbor's pet,' does that make it moral and legal to shoot your neighbor's dog when it does you no harm? Some things are too complex to be decided by a single, specific phrase.

5. Abortion takes a heavy psychological toll on the female.

"As anyone knows, a mother and her child she's bearing are as close as any two humans can become. This closeness comes out of an organic unity, but it creates an emotional and psychological bond as well. For a woman to allow anyone to harm and destroy her unborn child will violate the deepest level of her unconscious needs, desires, and impulses. Thousands of women have sought psychological help and support for the pain and guilt they have experienced after an abortion they thought would be easy. Hence, a woman who chooses an abortion does not simply harm an unborn child — she harms herself."

6. A liberal abortion policy establishes a dangerous and degenerative precedent, weakening the moral fabric of a society.

"Any public policy which creates a casual or indifferent attitude toward human life provides a dangerous precedent. And that just what abortion does. Once we become so callous and indifferent to the nearly two million abortions each year in our country, the next step will be indifference to the severely deformed, the dysfunctional, the senile, the victims of Alzheimer's disease, and the incurably ill in our society. Shall we pass some laws that will 'put them away,' too?"

7. Females must be responsible for their sexual activity.

"Nobody has to get pregnant. If a woman is mature enough to have sex with a man, she's also mature enough to take responsibility for her actions. You don't have to be a high-priced call girl to know that all kinds of contraceptives are available. The problem with our society now is that too many people are trying to avoid the consequences for the decisions that they alone made of their own free will. For a female to sacrifice an innocent human life just because she's been ignorant, careless, undisciplined, or indiscreet during a time of passion is the height of moral irresponsibility."

Arguments for Acceptance and Condoning of Abortion (Pro-Choice)

1. Abortion terminates a growing life form, but it need not be labeled "murder."

"To talk about the 'slaughter of innocent babies' is to use language in the most judgmental manner. Murder is the illegal termination of human life. Pro-life advocates may have a valid point when they object to the destruction of a fertilized ovum. But what they are objecting to is the prevention of the development of a human being and not the malicious killing of a person. A potential human being is not the same entity as an actual human being.

"For any woman who believes that abortion is murder, then her response to an unwanted pregnancy is clear: 'don't get an abortion.' To those men who believe abortion is murder, I say, 'Tell the woman you have impregnated that you will be financially responsible for the child.'"

2. The Bible is silent on the issue of abortion specifically, and generally cannot be used to make abortion sinful or immoral.

"Why can't we respect the silence of the Scripture on this issue? Abortion is a complex issue and moralists tend to inject some simple statement, such as 'the Bible condemns abortion,' into the debate and that tends to turn the issue into a crusade rather than a reasonable discussion.

"Not only is the Bible totally silent on abortion, but there are a number of Scriptures which indicate that a person receives a soul when he/she breathes at birth and not prior to birth. In Genesis 2:7 we read an account of human creation: 'God breathed into the nostrils of man the breath of life and man became a living soul.' Another text which makes clear the relationship between the soul *[nephesh]* and breathing is the story of the son of the widow from Zarephath in 1 Kings 17:17-24 ['. . . let this child's soul come into him again'].

"As for the womb passages [Psalm 139; Isa. 49; Jer. 1], these writers were simply saying that God was their Creator and therefore knew them before they were born; these are not passages about abortion. As for John the Baptist being filled with the Holy Spirit in his mother's womb, can we not see this as hyperbole about a truly Spirit-filled man! If this was not a figure of speech, then what practical purpose was served by a fetus having the Holy Spirit — to speak in tongues or perform miracles and signs in the womb?"

3. Women have rights over their own bodies.

"Only women have the burden and responsibility of carrying a fetus from conception to delivery. A baby is a special guest in the body of the woman. In one sense, the fetus is a 'biological parasite' taking resources from the woman's body; for nine months a woman devotes a major portion of her life and energies to this process.

"The woman must bear the pain, the discomfort, the disruption of routine life and career, and the toll on her entire body. Since the unborn is an integral part of the woman's body, only she should have absolute say over whether or not the baby should be allowed to remain in her body. To deny her that right is a violation of her constitutional freedom."

4. Some pregnancies are highly dangerous for the female.

"Sure, there's been much advancement in terms of prenatal care and maternal health during pregnancy, and yet pregnancy can be hazardous to the life and health of some women. Some women are called on to endure heroic suffering. Others must spend months in bed to maintain the pregnancy. Some are in constant pain. Others may expect lifelong health problems if they carry a baby to term. Given all these possibilities, a woman should have the right to decide if she wants to continue a pregnancy."

5. Many females are unfit for motherhood and there are already too many unwanted and unhealthy children.

"Just because one is a female does not mean that she is fit for motherhood. Lots of women are not emotionally or physically fit to be mothers and for them to bring children into the world is to bring them into an environment of dysfunction and possible abuse. Our society already has enough serious poverty and population problems and these serious problems are the seedbed for other serious problems — hunger, crime, drug addiction, and violence. All children who are brought into the world deserve to be wanted and loved. Children who will be born deformed or mentally retarded can tax the emotional and financial resources of the parents. Abortion is not a pretty alternative, but let's face reality here. Sure, there are children who were unwanted when they were conceived and were born and are now considered loved and special, but these are exceptional situations."

6. Some pregnancies result from rape and incest.

"What greater indignity can be foisted upon a woman than by having society demand that she bear a child which is conceived after a criminal act? This is adding insult to injury. All reminders of a rape must be removed as quickly as possible. With incest, there is a high risk of birth defects. Nothing less than a woman's free choice can justify her coping with an incest or rape pregnancy."

7. A legal ban on abortions would not cease the operation, but would lead females to seek costly and/or dangerous abortion procedures.

"We know what it was like before 1973. A lot of abortions were performed, many of them illegal and highly dangerous for the women. A legal ban on abortions would see the emergence of 'back alley' and 'coat hanger' abortions for poor women and high-priced abortions for women with means. It would be a mockery of the law in general to have a statute that was so widely disregarded and disobeyed.

"If a woman feels that an abortion is immoral, no law requires her to have that abortion. Since abortion will occur whether it is legal or not, is it reasonable to make such a simple, safe procedure painful, degrading, dangerous, and possibly even fatal by making it illegal? The law should be left simply as it is — giving women the freedom to make a choice, ideally after consulting with the father and a physician and, perhaps, either parents or counselor."

8. Abortion is not the chief problem in this debate. Unwanted pregnancies are the chief problem and there are steps which can be taken to reduce their number.

"If we as a society could reduce the number of unwanted pregnancies then we could reduce the number of abortions. Half of all American women who become pregnant do so by accident and for too many American women unplanned means 'unwanted.' Women need more and better choices to help them avoid unwanted pregnancy in the first place. Several effective steps can be taken: sex education [abstinence is a valid answer, but it's not the only answer]; more public clinics to dispense contraceptives; giving condoms to sexually active teenagers; and improvement in women's health services."

SELECTED QUOTATIONS

Love your neighbor as yourself. . . . You shall not murder a child by abortion nor shall you kill a newborn.

—Didache

You shall love your neighbor more than your own life. You shall not murder a child by abortion nor shall you kill a newborn.

—Epistle of Barnabas

The greatest destroyer of peace today is abortion, because Jesus said, 'If you receive a little child, you receive me.' So every abortion is the denial of receiving Jesus, the neglect of receiving Jesus. It is a war against the child, a direct killing of the innocent child, murder by the mother herself. And if we accept that a mother can kill even her own child, how can we tell other people not to kill one

100

another? . . . Any country that accepts abortion is not teaching its people to love one another but to use any violence to get what they want.

—Mother Teresa

The irony of our public debate is that the people labeled "conservative" are often those arguing for a more liberal and inclusive understanding of the meaning of human personhood. This language may once have served to include within our common humanity those whose skin color was not white. Now it increasingly serves as a language by which we mark off those human subjects who cannot lay claim to equal protection.

—Gilbert Meilaender

We forthwith acknowledge our awareness of the sensitive and emotional nature of the abortion controversy of the vigorous opposing views. . . of the deep and seemingly absolute convictions that the subject inspires. One's philosophy, one's experiences, one's exposure to the raw edges of human existence, one's religious training. . . are all likely to influence and to color one's thinking.

—Harry Blackmun

The Court in *Roe v. Wade* blithely overturned centuries of precedent in which abortion had been considered both morally and legally unacceptable. Never before nor since has there been such sweeping disregard for fundamental morality in the halls of American justice.

—F. LaGard Smith

I believe that each human life has a definite beginning and that that beginning is conception.

—C. Everett Koop

It is interesting to note that the same Supreme Court that dehumanized unborn babies and withdrew protection from them stopped the construction of a $116 million dam in Tennessee because the life of a three-inch snail darter was endangered, and a $340 million dam in California because the life of a $5/8$" long-legged spider was threatened. What a tragic course we are traveling upon when snails and spiders have more value than unborn babies.

—Knofel Staton

As much as I wish that laws against abortion would solve all our problems, I do not believe they would. We need above all to change the hearts and minds of people. This is really the root of the whole problem. To some extent we have put so much effort into getting laws on the books that we have failed to persuade people of the basis for our moral stance.

Changing hearts and minds is always the most difficult task; it is also the essential. I would like us to spend a lot more time and effort on it. If we did, we might come to more agreement on the profound moral questions involved. Then the development of the legal structure would follow quite quickly.

—Thomas J. Gumbleton

The law will always fail if it is unsustained by the common conscience. But that is no reason for repealing the unsuccessful law, because the law has a further purpose: not to transform people, but to declare and disavow publicly what we commonly believe to be unfair or damaging. Laws are part of our public profession of justice. They are what we, as a people, are willing to promise out loud to one another.

—James T. Burtchaell

I have learned from my earliest medical education that human life begins at the time of conception. . . I submit that human life is present throughout this entire sequence from conception to adulthood and that any interruption at any point throughout this time constitutes a termination of human life.

—Alfred M. Bongioanni

Conception sets in motion a series of events within the womb more complex and wondrous than anything that will ever happen to the body outside the womb. So astonishing are the happenings that transpire in the first moments, days, weeks, and months of life-before-birth that when we come to understand them fully we will very likely possess the answer to such puzzles as cancer and the aging process. By fully understanding life we will almost certainly be able to better understand death.

—Landrum B. Shettles and David Rorvik

Even if I believe the fetus is human — and I do — it exists inside a woman's body. . .Here, one human being is wholly contained within another. Rights are in conflict: The right of the unborn child to life against the right of the woman to decide what to do with a part of her body.

If a woman aborts her unborn child, some may define the act as murder. But if a woman is prevented from having an abortion by allowing society to take control of her body, she may feel imprisoned and invaded. . .

Pro-choice women have accepted the moral responsibility for what they do with their own bodies — and the creature inside. One may not like their choice, but they have claimed the moral responsibility for themselves and said they are comfortable with it. Let them have it.

It is not healthy to mind someone else's business.

—Kenneth Guentert

The society we seek must have as its primary agenda the rights of the born, the improved quality of life for those who come into this marvelous world — adequate care and protection from the first stirrings to the final groans. My grievance is severe with so many anti-abortion advocates who demand justice for the unborn but who also advocate dismantling social programs that provide a decent life for children once they enter the world. If we are to reduce abortions, we must reaffirm by work and action the rights of the born.

—George F. Regas

The horror of abortion is not just that a woman destroys a child, but that a woman destroys *her* own child. We have a duty not to kill any human being, but we owe our children much more: care, protection, the effort of daily love. Abortion is the refusal to acknowledge the unconditional claim children have on our lives. In an aborted society, parental love is hedged in with conditions. I will care for you only if: it seems like it would be gratifying; if it doesn't interrupt my education; if it doesn't interrupt my marriage; if I have the time, and it doesn't interfere with my career; if you love me enough to make it worth my while.

—Maggie Gallagher

Persons of good will and earnest belief standing before the threshold of moral decision take different courses informed by their belief and individual conscience before God. This is not to say that conscience never errs, but even when it is in error it does not lose its dignity. We ask that the dignity of a woman's conscience as she faces the difficult decision involved in an unwanted pregnancy be respected.

—Patricia Wilson-Kastner

An embryo is not a person but the possibility or probability of there being a person many months or even years in the future. Obviously possibilities are important, but to blur the distinction between them and actualities is to darken counsel.

—Charles Hartshorne

DISCUSSION QUESTIONS AND BRIEF CASE STUDIES

1. What constitutes human life? While this question may seem to be easily answered when considered philosophically or in the abstract, defining life in terms of concrete, real-world situations may be more difficult.

As noted earlier in this chapter, when we speak of the ontological status of that which is conceived — whether embryo, fetus, etc. — we are speaking of the nature and kind of that specific life form. Determining the ontological status of a life form has direct bearing on the issue of fetal rights and how the fetus may be treated. Do you consider the fetus to be a human being? At what point in development did it become a human being?

2. Do you consider yourself to be "pro-life" or "pro-choice"? Do you hold an absolutist position? Consider that a "pro-life" advocate would contend that once a sperm fertilizes an egg, that life form must be considered an "absolute value" to be protected at all costs. A "pro-choice" advocate would contend that the potential mother has full and absolute rights over her own body, rights which include terminating a pregnancy at any time.

3. The subject of abortion has been particularly divisive within the American society. At times the debate between pro-life advocates and pro-choice advocates has become greatly heated. What are the specific values which "drive" or motivate each camp? What specific contributions to moral thought could each camp make to the other side?

4. Moderates on this issue attempt to find middle ground between those who absolutize the rights of the woman and those who absolutize the rights of the fetus. A moderate will reject the notion of a clear-cut, simple solution to unwanted pregnancy and will attempt to find resolution based on the circumstances in each particular case.

If you believe that a woman possesses the moral right, at least at some point in time, to prevent conceived life from developing, then where would you draw a line between what is "morally permissible" and what is immoral and sinful? In which of the following cases would you, if you consider yourself a moderate, condone an abortion:

(a) The health and physical survival of the woman is severely threatened by a continuation of the pregnancy.

(b) The pregnant woman is unmarried, does not want the

baby, and is a heavy drug and alcohol abuser.

(c) The pregnant woman is HIV-positive.

(d) The expected baby is likely to be born with severe physical deformities and/or severe mental retardation.

(e) The pregnant female is a fifteen-year-old who does not know the father of the child, lives in an inner city housing development with her single mother and brothers and sisters, all of whom are supported by AFDC payments; this teenaged female does not want this baby.

(f) The expectant mother is an upper middle-class married woman who already has three children. The pregnancy was unplanned and is several years separated from the couple's last child, whom they presumed would "round out" their family. The woman's husband is adamant about not carrying this child full-term and the woman herself has mixed feelings.

(g) A conception occurs because of the liaison of two highly respected, middle-aged, active church members, each married to another person. To carry and deliver this baby would likely mean exposure of this affair and tremendous hurt and pain to the other mates and to the children and other relatives in these two families.

(h) The pregnancy results from an incest between first cousins.

5. Is it possible that language is manipulated in this debate about abortion so that argumentation becomes more propaganda than fair argument? What about words like "fetal products," "murder," "tissue," "mass of cells"? For that matter, what about "pro-life" and "pro-choice"? What about the phrase "unborn baby"? By definition, isn't a baby an individual who has already been born and prior to birth the unborn is merely an embryo or a fetus? How much does how we talk about an issue determine how we think about an issue?

6. Do you agree that the Bible does not deal with the issue of abortion in any specific way? If not, what Scriptures do you employ to prove that biblical writers knew and cared about abortion? If so, in what way should the silence of Scripture be respected? Is it possible that the biblical writers considered abortion to be so offensive to themselves and universally reprehensible to others in their culture that they did not give any thought to its mention? Would you feel better if the Bible declared: "Thou shalt not abort a fetus"?

Do you think the Bible has been used fairly in this whole debate? If not, please cite examples.

7. Seemingly, some of the strongest moral pleas and arguments against abortion have come from Christian males, both in writing and in the pulpit. Is this fair? Do males have the potential for experience and the credibility to address what many consider to be a "feminist" issue? Would men look at the issue differently if they could experience the surprise of an unplanned and unwanted pregnancy?

8. Let us assume, for the point of this question, that a majority of abortions are immoral because the pregnancies which they terminate do not involve cases of rape or incest, nor would continuation to full term be a threat to the emotional or physical health of the mother. Nonetheless, could Christians still support liberal abortion policies as a part of public law because: (1) not all other citizens will view the morality of abortion the same way and people should be given a choice; and (2) women will still seek abortions who are desperate to obtain them by whatever means, safe or not, whether they are legal or illegal?

9. For pro-life advocates: Is the issue of abortion so important that you would:

(a) Refuse to vote for a political candidate in your own party whom you otherwise liked and respected except for his/her stand on abortion?

(b) Disfellowship, or discount the spirituality of, a Christian brother or sister who claimed to be "pro-choice"?

(c) Publicly demonstrate outside an abortion clinic?

(d) Engage in acts of disorderliness or civil disobedience which threaten physicians (or impede their practice) who perform abortions?

10. For pro-life advocates: Should anyone who is prepared to rest the abortion issue on the commandment "Thou shalt not kill" also feel compelled to examine his/her position on capital punishment (a willingness to condemn to death a citizen of one's own country) and carnal warfare (a willingness to kill, or send men and bombs to kill, the citizens of another country)? True, a criminal is likely to be guilty and a baby is surely precious and innocent. However, if this command is absolute, can Christians allow any exceptions?

Also, what about being "pro-quality-of-life"? Do pro-life advocates work as earnestly for policies which enrich life (health, education, and welfare) for the already born? Do abortion opponents contend for the public housing and public welfare needed to provide a minimally decent standard of living for unwanted children who would be born if abortion becomes illegal?

11. It is interesting to note that the same moral arguments used against abortion are the same ones used previously against birth control, an issue thought to have been fought and decided years ago. The two are analogous; both are methods of controlling births. If birth control is right morally, at what point does it become immoral? If it is permissible to keep the sperm cell from fertilizing the ovum and to so restrict the ovum that it cannot be reached by a living sperm cell so as to be fertilized, then what is immoral about frustrating the growth of the ovum and sperm together? What has happened in a few hours or days to make the issue significantly different?

12. The video *The Silent Scream* received notoriety through its use by pro-life activists. The video clearly and dramatically illustrated that the fetus can feel pain. The strong emotional appeal of the video rendered its use controversial. Critics called the video propaganda. Two questions emerge: (1) Do you feel that the use of graphic color photographs and videotaped depictions of actual fetuses should be deployed as means of persuading the general public on this issue? (2) What does the capacity to feel pain prove about the fetus — that it is a full person who deserves equal protection under the law or that it has a nervous system which can react to sharp stimulus? If consciousness and feeling pain determine the morality of terminating life, do we sanction killing the innocent if it can be done painlessly and without the victim's awareness?

13. The noted German theologian Dietrich Bonhoeffer addressed the issue of abortion. He knew of classical theologians who attempted to affix a date for ensoulment to the fetus but felt that such attempts were futile. According to Bonhoeffer, the important matter is potential (not human form, beauty, rationality, contribution to society, etc.). From conception on, what Bonhoeffer called the "nascent human being" passes the only two tests for human status that make any sense: it is of human parentage and it has the potential for rational thought and acts. Given this wonderful potentiality, is not the mother (and anyone else participating in abortion decision-making and action) "playing God" when human life is terminated? Could not God have a plan for this unborn infant, just as he did for Jeremiah, John the Baptist, and other great biblical characters?

14. Drawing from this same logic (Bonhoeffer's argument

above), pro-life advocates contend that the fetus has 46 chromosomes and is thus a potential person who, if not allowed to develop, would be unable to make a valuable contribution to society, such as the discovery of a cure for cancer or for AIDS. Often this contention is stated in highly dramatic ways. One particular version is found in much of the anti-abortion literature:

Two physicians are talking shop. "Doctor," says one, "I'd like your professional opinion. The question is, should the pregnancy have been terminated or not? The father was syphilitic. The mother was tuberculous. They had already had four children: the first was blind, the second died, the third was deaf and dumb and the fourth was tuberculous. The woman was pregnant for the fifth time. As the attending physician, what would you have done?"

"I would have terminated the pregnancy."

"Then you would have murdered Beethoven."

Do you consider this to be a persuasive story? Consider that the genetic blueprints are not the same as the finished product — once a child is born there are many environmental factors (such as whether family and friends encourage one to pursue training and fulfillment in music) that determine what that child will pursue and become. Second, could the story be twisted to say that we should encourage syphilitic and tuberculosis couples to have as many children as they could in hopes of giving birth to another Beethoven? Could it mean that as many eggs as possible should be fertilized so that all kinds of creative and wonderful people could be born into our world? Such questions are absurd, but do they not bring out the emptiness of arguing about the potential person being lost? (If someone like Beethoven or Einstein had been aborted, we would never know what society had lost, for we can't be aware of losing something we never had.)

15. Do you consider the donation of sperm for artificial insemination in order to create life to be the moral equivalent of donating blood in order to save a life?

16. "Playing God" is a vague phrase which is thrown around a great deal by opponents of abortion rights and euthanasia. Would an infertile couple seeking to increase the chances of having children by taking fertility drugs also be "playing God"?

17. Case study: George and Paula wanted desperately to have a baby, but due to a severe case of endometriosis early in life, Paula's ovaries were damaged and she was unable to produce healthy eggs. Paula's sister Suzanne donated some healthy eggs and after being

fertilized by Tom's sperm, one was implanted in Paula. Months later, a healthy baby boy was born. When Suzanne was asked how she felt about her relationship to the baby, she said she sees the child as her nephew and nothing more.

Now, not only is the woman who donates her eggs considered a biological mother, it is also correct to say that the woman who contributes her womb during gestation is a biological mother. Studies have shown that there are many ways that the intrauterine environment and maternal behavior during pregnancy influences the fetus and child development, though difficult to establish just how much. Likewise, it would not be fair to totally diminish the role of the donor since without her contribution the child would not exist.

(a) How would we determine who would be the rightful mother should there be a battle over custody?

(b) How does one explain to the child his/her lineage? (if necessary)

(c) Wouldn't there be cases where the egg donor feels more than a passing responsibility for the child that results from her gift and if so, how would she deal with that?

18. The abortion culture seems to devalue born children as well as the unborn lifeforms by turning them into objects of choice. Does an easy acceptance of liberal abortion laws lead to a devaluation of life in general? Consider that retarded babies with birth defects may be legally allowed to die by neglect and starvation. Does this mean that if abortion remains legal for much longer we will see our laws permit active euthanasia of unwanted citizens or of old people who have lost their productive value to society?

19. Some states now prohibit the unlawful killing of a fetus. The intent of such a law is to prevent the unlawful killing of a viable fetus by anyone except the mother. Some have argued that the Fourteenth Amendment's "equal protection" clause should protect a viable fetus from being killed not only by some third party but also by death from its own mother. Does it make sense that a mother can terminate the life of a viable fetus and the act is not homicide, but that the same act by another person can be prosecuted as homicide? Would our answer to this question depend on whether we are answering it from the point of view of the fetus or of the pregnant female? Why should not the unborn baby be given constitutional protection from any or all other parties, including the mother?

20. Could a Christian make a contention that even pregnancies resulting from rape and incest might be allowed to continue? If a woman is willing to carry the child of a rapist, could she not trust in God to overrule for good the terrible harm done to her? As for a participant in incest, do "two wrongs make a right"? Can one wrong undo another? Have we put too many limits on the providence of God?

21. In the summer of 1995 a Republican-dominated Senate used the threat of filibuster to prevent an open floor vote on President Clinton's nominee for Surgeon General. The nominee, Dr. Henry Foster, a black obstetrician-gynecologist, had delivered up to 10,000 babies in a career that spanned several decades, but he had also performed 39 abortions. Is a person's stand on abortion the one litmus test that determines the credibility and viability of one's career in politics, religion, and medicine?

22. Do you consider artificial insemination from a donor (AID) to be adultery? Obviously, a third party is involved with the marriage bond between two others. Before you answer this question, consider what action constitutes adultery. Is not the essence of faithful marriage a commitment to live together and love another exclusively for a lifetime? How is the donation of another man's sperm a violation of that commitment? Furthermore, is there anything sexually stimulating for a woman being artificially inseminated, especially as she would not ordinarily know the donor and would have no physical or emotional contact with him? On the other hand, one's offspring is considered one's own "flesh and blood." Isn't donated sperm morally different from sperm from the natural father?

23. Does the fact that masturbation is required to produce donor sperm for artificial insemination create a moral consideration?

24. In the mid-90s a California fertility clinic was enabling women in their 50s — women who have already experienced menopause — to bear children. One program for such women uses fertilized eggs from the male partner's sperm in a test tube. Implantation follows. The women, who are rendered naturally infertile after menopause, take hormones to promote the pregnancy. True, there was a higher rate of pregnancy problems, but most were manageable. While some praise these clinical researchers as pioneers, others have contended that natural law is violated.

Do you think a woman has the right to choose artificial fertilization no matter what her age? Is not any limit on pregnancy on the basis of age or marital status unfair to the female, but suggestive of both an age and gender bias since no such limitation is placed on males? We all know of men in their 60s who have fathered children and boast of that achievement. Should it be determined by society when a woman can no longer have a child?

25. In recent years the pro-life movement has assumed new militancy. Abortion opponents have taken to the streets and the clinics to "rescue" mothers and babies. Some "Advocates for Life" are resorting to terms such as "justifiable homicide" and "honorable" to describe the killing and wounding of several abortion doctors. In 1993 Dr. David Gunn, a Florida abortion doctor, was murdered; soon thereafter, a Kansas abortion doctor was wounded by gunfire. There have been clinic shootings in Massachusetts and Virginia. Some abortion opponents called these actions "honorable" because they would save babies' lives.

How do you feel about such extremism? One Oregon pro-life advocate proclaimed: "What we are saying is that there is a legitimate place for a use of force in protecting life in the womb. All we're saying is abortion is murder, it is taking the life of an innocent person, and the obvious response is that if you're forced to use force, it may be lethal force. The bigger question is: Is force ever appropriate, and I've concluded that it is. To say anything else is to diminish the value of the life of the babies." Do you agree with this statement?

Consider also this letter to the editor of the *Tennessean:*

> I shed no tears for the death of an abortion doctor. The hypocrisy of President Clinton to say he is 'outraged' over the 'atrocity' of the killing of an abortion doctor but feels no remorse over the snuffing out of life of 20,000,000 unborn babies. God will make plain on the Judgment Day that life begins at conception.
>
> A March 12 editorial in *The Tennessean* said the abortion doctor's murder 'happened only because respect for the law — and respect for life — were violently ignored.'
>
> Abortion approvers talking about respect for life?
>
> A majority of the Supreme Court justices in 1973 had no respect for the sanctity of life. A majority of Americans have no respect for the sanctity of life.
>
> It took 20 years for someone to make the ultimate statement. It is

the Biblical precept that if you take a life, yours is to be forfeited. This speaks of the sanctity of life. People just can't abide the killing of babies, and indeed, they are babies.

We can't stop an act that is sanctioned by 'law.' We can pray for the day when we have a majority of Supreme Court justices who respect the sanctity of life.

One thing is for sure: This doctor will snuff out no more life.

What would you say to the writer of this letter if you met him?

CHAPTER FOUR

Sex Morality

We hardly need reminders that in the United States we live in a sex-saturated culture.

Consider the advertisements that enter your living rooms and dens through the sights and sounds of color television. Advertisements for beer, sports equipment, cologne, designer clothing, sports cars, to cite but a few examples, are usually sex-charged. The allure of sex appeal is a dominant note in the promotion of personal hygiene products such as toothpaste, deodorant, and hair products.

Who among us has not been surprised, perhaps shocked, by some explicit scene of nudity or sexual activity in a movie that we were watching either in the theatre or on cable television? Unless we have lived as recluses we have surely heard of the explicitness of movies such as *Basic Instinct* or of the boundaries pushed by in network television by ABC's new 1993 offering, *N.Y.P.D. Blue.*

Since the mid-60s in the United States we have increasingly heard talk about the "sexual revolution" and the "new morality." Almost everywhere, beginning with newspapers, magazines, and the syndicated talk shows, people have been talking about singles bars, casual and recreational sex, one-night stands, open marriages, swinging, cohabitation, public nudity, creative divorce, group sex, teen sex, sexual orientation, and sexual preferences.

Is there an area in the social and cultural life of Americans that has undergone more change in the last two or three decades than in sexual morality? To traditionalists the changes have at best been troubling and at worst have been greatly alarming. A moral decline which is rapidly leading to moral decadence and national disgrace has gained great momentum, argue traditionalists. What is at stake is the future of their children, the sanctity of their marriages and homes, time-honored standards of public decency, and the strength of the American nation.

Advocates and participants in the "sexual revolution" interpreted these lifestyle changes quite differently. In the new laxity about sex they saw new freedoms, new options, new avenues of personal fulfillment and artistic fulfillment.

Unquestionably, human sexual activity and fulfillment is the source of the deepest, most intense pleasure that mature men and women can experience. Sex has also been a source of vexatious trouble and anxiety for the human family since the beginning of Creation. As humans reach and pass puberty they begin the process of resolving who they are and how they shall act as sexual creatures.

Traditional sexual morality, usually but not exclusively reinforced by the church for centuries past, offers strictures and prohibitions to enable people to control that valuable but dangerous force of sexual desire. In order that sexual activity can serve the purposes intended by the Creator, traditional doctrine has specified five mandates:

1. To refrain from sexual activity until marriage.

2. To engage in marital sex without preventing the conception of children.

3. To refrain from sex with anyone but one's spouse.

4. To choose a spouse of the opposite sex.

5. To love one's marriage partner until the death of one spouse terminates the relationship (an exception being for sexual unfaithfulness of one partner).

Christian doctrine emphasizes the positive role of sexual activity in enhancing the bond of love in a committed marriage.

The sexual revolution of the 1960s challenged each of these mandates. Libertarians seriously questioned the traditional doctrine of linking sex with love, marriage, and procreation. They advocated sex outside of marriage, contraception, multiple sex partners (though, perhaps, in succession), sex for pleasure only, homosexuality, and unlimited sexual experimentation. The only valid restriction for libertarians was that all forms of sexual activity and expression must be performed by consenting adults.

Some have contended that because of the alarming rise in the number of incidents of AIDS (Acquired Immune Deficiency Syndrome), as well as the increase in other, though less lethal, sexually transmitted diseases, the sexual revolution is over.

Regardless, there is renewed interest in more traditional values regarding sexuality. The questions and situations you will read in this chapter are designed to provoke thought about your own sexual attitudes and values. However some of these issues get resolved, discussions about human sexuality will no longer be squelched or conducted in private, hushed tones in the interest of propriety.

(Note: Though love will be referred to in the questions to follow, the topic of this chapter is not love in general. Our topic is sexual love or, more broadly, sexual activity with or without love. No one questions the right of anyone to love others in the sense of agape, the unconditional high regard and acceptance of others that was first modeled by God in sending his Son to earth.

Because homosexuality is such an important topic, it will be lifted from this chapter and be dealt with in a separate unit.)

KEY TERMS

Abstinence — The restraint of one's appetites or desires. In this application, the restraint of sexual activity.

Adultery — A voluntary sexual relationship between a married person and a partner other than the lawful husband or wife. Jesus expanded the meaning of adultery to include cultivation of lust (Matt. 5:28). Under the Mosaic law, when a couple was caught in the act of adultery, both parties were to be killed (Deut. 22:22). Paul included adultery in his catalogue of sins which would exclude a person from the kingdom of God (1 Cor. 6:9).

Asceticism — A doctrine or theory supporting a lifestyle which renounces the comforts of society and leads a life of austere self-discipline, especially as an act of religious devotion. The belief that the ascetic life releases the soul from bondage to the body and permits union with the divine.

Celibacy — The condition of being unmarried, especially by reason of religious vows, thus customarily refraining from sexual relations.

Fornication — A voluntary sexual relationship between two persons who are not married to each other. In popular usage, adultery involves married persons while fornication involves unmarried persons. However, the New Testament uses the term *(porneia)* in a general sense for any unchastity (between unmarried persons; between married persons; sexual relations with harlots).

Sexual Libertarianism — The belief in freedom of action and thought in regard to sexual relationships. According to the libertarian, sex is an activity much like any other — golfing, intellectual conversation, fine dining — and what determines the morality and immorality of any of these social activities is whether there is any dishonesty, coercion, or exploitation, and whether the activity violates one or the other partner's obligations (vows) toward others. The doctrine assumes that all participants are adults.

Sexual Traditionalism — The belief that sexual behavior is essentially different from all other kinds of social activity and to treat sex like it is no different from golfing or dining is to miss everything that the Creator intended for sex and its role in our lives. The traditionalist argues that time-honored standards of right and wrong should guide major decisions about sexual conduct. A traditionalist will contend that how we learn to deal with our sexuality is an index to the kind of person we are or are becoming.

KEY SCRIPTURES

Genesis 2:24-25; Matthew 19:3-8; 1 Corinthians 5:9; 6:12-20; 7:2, 9, 36-37; Ephesians 5:3-5; 1 Thessalonians 4:1-8

KEY ISSUES/ARGUMENTS
Arguments for Sexual Libertarianism

1. Sexual choices are private, personal choices; any behavior between consenting adults is nobody's business except their own.

"Why should anyone even care whether Dick and Jane are married or whether Bill prefers sex with Suzy or with Sam? And who cares if Evelyn has fifteen different boyfriends and sleeps with several of them? We all have our lives to live according to our own values and our own needs. Swingers and promiscuous people don't tell you how to live your life. Why should you tell them how to live theirs? And even if people care, they should simply 'back off.'"

2. Curbing sexual freedom is unfair. While many people are comfortable living by and advocating a traditional morality, for others such restraints can be a straitjacket.

"How can you limit the freedom of people to choose their own lifestyle? Sex is a natural human instinct or impulse. Now that contraceptives are easily available and highly reliable, sex should be seen as a purely pleasurable physical experience. Just as fine food can be enjoyed with another person without deep feelings of love and commitment to each other, so can sex be enjoyed for its own sake without traditional restraints. Also, consider that some adults are totally unsuited for marriage; others are unsuited for monogamy. Do these people not have as much right to fulfilling sexual experiences as you do?"

3. Traditional sex morality is hypocritical.

"Do we want to believe that all those who advocate traditional moral standards are fully committed to them in heart, soul, and body? Give us a break! How many pretend to be faithful heterosexual monogamists in church while they do whatever they want on the sly? And how about those traditional-minded parents who advocate premarital chastity, pretending to see the real world through rose-colored glasses, all the while knowing that their teenagers are experimenting sexually?"

4. Sexual repression is unhealthy.

"Any knowledgeable psychiatrist or clinical psychologist can tell you that a great deal of neurosis traditionalists suffer is from unresolved guilt over natural desires and impulses in their sexuality. Repression of any human desire that is normal and natural always leads to maladjustment, in some cases insanity, and we have only Victorian ethics and fundamentalist Christianity to blame for the lives of guilt and frustration that many people live. Free sexual expression is healthy as millions have learned; therefore, please don't turn back the clock on the sexual revolution."

Arguments for Traditional Morality

1. The Bible clearly condemns sexual activity outside the realm of monogamous marriage.

"Admittedly, we are living in an age that seems to reject biblical authority, but there are millions of people in the western world who honor, respect, and follow the commandments of this ancient book. Both testaments clearly condemn fornication and adultery. Christians who respect biblical authority will take these divine commands seriously, regardless of the cultural mores of their time and however imperfect their attempts at obedience."

2. Sex without love is an empty, meaningless experience.

"Libertarianism places a cheap view of the link between sex and love. With someone you love, sex is a rich, meaningful, perhaps ecstatic, experience. That's because sex between a loving couple is both depth sharing and communication; it expresses deep affection and caring. Apart from a love commitment, sexual relations become about as routine as satisfying your appetite for food in the presence of someone else. Just talk with adults who tried the "singles bars" for a while and arranged many "one-night stands" — just ask how they felt about themselves and their partners the morning after."

3. Sexual libertarianism undermines marriage and family values.

"Although marriage has worked wonderfully as an institution since the beginning when God created Eve as a companion for Adam, a highly permissive attitude toward sexuality will undermine commitment to lifetime, monogamous marriage. Since sex will be freely available when restraints are abolished, unmarried people have one less major reason for getting married. We already live in a society where there is no stigma to conceiving, bearing, and raising children outside of a marriage relationship."

4. Sexual libertarianism undermines public morality and the social fabric of our society.

"Our nation has honored, however imperfectly, a sense of decency and discipline in interpersonal relations. If there is widespread failure in private relationships, the entire social fabric is weakened. And once you encourage disrespect for sexual morality, you encourage disrespect for all of morality. Look at the amount of lying, cheating, and corruption that exist in our society. Could it be that people have been taught that in our most basic relationships loyalty and honesty are no longer cherished values, no matter what vows they have taken?"

5. What is wild, uninhibited behavior is not necessarily good.

"All decent societies have discerned an imperative to place boundaries on behavior that seemed uninhibited and natural. The Apostle Paul described the Roman world which discarded both restraints and conscience in its decline to a morally weak and decadent society [Rom. 1-2]. In our contemporary society, unwanted pregnancy has reached an all-time high; in our urban areas, babies are being born to children. The largest percentage of abortions are obtained by unwed women. Sexually transmitted diseases, including the deadly AIDS, are at epidemic proportions and those engaged in casual, uncommitted sex are at the highest risk. We have sown the wind and reaped the whirlwind!"

SELECTED QUOTATIONS

It is through sex . . . that each individual has to pass in order to have access to his own intelligibility . . . to his own identity . . . . Hence the importance we ascribe to it, the reverential fear with which we surround it, the care we take to know it. Hence the fact that over the centuries it has become more important than our soul, more important almost than our life.

— Michel Foucault

Although sexuality is a good, it is a limited good. A limited good treated as a final good becomes an idol. Sexual fulfillment as an end in itself, separated from other concerns, becomes idolatrous and, therefore, demonic.

–John B. Cobb, Jr.

Sexuality has to do with much more than genital sex. People cannot live by orgasms alone, nor even by exquisitely sensuous love-making. Any two persons who are living a full life together as persons know that their sexual relations cover a lot more ground than the few moments of intercourse. Sexuality is involved in the quiet hours of communication and contemplation as much as in the volcanic moments. . . .Sexual fulfillment is achieved when a personal relationship underpins the genital experience, supports it, and sustains a human sexual relationship after it.

–Lewis B. Smedes

Christian sexual morality, like the rest of Christian morality, is based on human nature, on the kind of thing we are and the kind of thing sex is. It is not the changeable rules of a game we designed, but the unchangeable rules of the operating manual written by the Designer of our human nature.

–Peter Kreeft

Fidelity is the ethical element which enhances natural love, and only by its means does the natural become personal. It is therefore the only quality which can guarantee the permanence of the marriage relation. Through the marriage vows the feeling of love is absorbed into the personal will; this alone provides the guarantee to the other party which justifies the venture of such a life companionship.

—Emil Brunner

The orgasm has replaced the Cross as the focus of longing and the image of fulfillment.

—Malcolm Muggeridge

The ultimate erotic challenge lies not in racing from bed to bed, shirttails aflame, but in the quest of what I call High Monogamy: a long-term relationship in which both partners are voluntarily committed to erotic exclusivity, not because of moral or religious scruples, not because of timidity or inertia, but because it is what they *want*. Because they seek excitement and adventure through the love of another person.

—George Leonard

The decision of whether affairs are right or wrong for you is a personal one. I certainly can't make such a choice for you, but I think that affairs are healthy. If you're lucky enough to find a warm and sensitive man, the affair can be joyous. A good one has the power to pull you out of despair, even if just temporarily. An affair can turn into a marriage or a friendship— or at least a pleasant memory. Of course, the other side of the coin is that affairs end, but even with an awkward or painful ending, I wouldn't give up the affairs I've had. They were fun, difficult, infuriating, exhilarating, sad, and passionate, and they made me feel *alive*.

—Lynne Caine (writing as a widow and giving advice to other widows.)

Marriage is a great institution, but I'm not ready for an institution.

—Mae West

Human sexuality should be — self-liberating, other-enriching, honest, faithful, socially responsible, life-serving, joyous. . . . Where such qualities prevail, one can be reasonably sure that the sexual behavior that has brought them forth is wholesome and moral. On the contrary, where sexual conduct becomes personally frustrating and self-destructive, manipulative and enslaving of others, deceitful and dishonest, inconsistent and unstable, indiscriminate and promiscuous, irresponsible and non life-serving, burdensome and repugnant, ungenerous and un-Christlike, it is clear that God's ingenious gift for calling us to creative and integrative growth has been seriously abused.

—*Human Sexuality: New Directions in American Catholic Thought*

QUESTIONS AND CASE STUDIES

1. The Old Testament's Song of Solomon is a treatise extolling the pleasures and virtues of married love between a husband and a wife; it portrays the passionate, tender eroticism of lovers without reference to procreation.

Do you think of human sexuality is a good gift from God? If so, why does the church do so little to mention, much less celebrate, this good gift from God? Should preachers, teachers, and church leaders say and do more to communicate a sense of sexuality as grace and goodness from God?

2. "True love" is the theme of innumerable novels, plays, poems, songs, essays, and paintings, as well as the subject of much thought and musing. The New Testament has a great deal to say about love and, in fact, employs three different words in the original language that are translated "love."

Taking one of those Greek words, *eros*, can you put into words your conception of true erotic love? Include in your discussion a response to the following questions:

(a) Is true love something that has to last a lifetime, or can it exist for a few years and then end?

(b) Can a person love two people at the same time?

(c) To what extent does genuine love require sharing the interests of one's lover?

(d) Is true love purely altruistic, that is, completely selfless? Or does it involve a strong element of self-concern or self-love?

(e) In what sense, if any, does true love require equality?

(f) Must true love be based on mutual understanding, or does it admit to large degrees of illusion and error about one's partner?

(g) Do we "choose" to love, or does love "happen" to us?

3. Do you think of sex as "dirty?" While most would answer categorically that sex is not "dirty," why does the presence of sexual behavior as a story line or the punch line in a joke render the conversation a "dirty story" or a "dirty joke?" Could a joke involving someone's false testimony in a court of law or of a banker embezzling funds or of a farmer abusing a stubborn mule also be considered a "dirty joke?" What is the difference?

4. Does the Bible address the issue of masturbation? Is masturbation an abuse of the body or is it a normal, almost instinctual function? Could masturbation be right or wrong for an individual depending on the circumstance?

When President Clinton's controversial Surgeon General Dr. Joycelyn Elders suggested during a question-and-answer session at the United Nations that masturbation might be taught in public schools as an alternative to other potentially dangerous sexual choices, there was an outcry from many quarters for her dismissal. While other incidents factored into the decision, Ms. Elders was thereby fired by the White House in 1995. Despite the fact that masturbation is not discussed officially in schools, surveys tell us that it is practiced by 90 percent of teenage boys and 65 percent of teenage girls. In modern times we have debunked the myths about masturbation that linked the practice to mental illness or distorted physical features. Now, should masturbation be urged upon adolescents as a form of safe sex or is it be best not to mention the subject with them?

As you begin to answer the first question on biblical direction, consider that historically many people have misappropriated the "sin of Onan" (Gen. 38:8-9) as a divine prohibition against masturbation. In some states, Onanism has been a legal term for masturbation. A correct interpretation of this incident is Onan's refusal to fulfill an ancient rule that if a man dies without children the brother must impregnate the widow to perpetuate the family line. Onan's real sin was not masturbation, but voluntary *coitus interruptus*. We are not told of Onan's motivation.

5. How have attitudes toward sex changed, if at all, since the days of your adolescence? Has there been a sex revolution since the 1960s in this culture? If so, what are the factors which have ushered in this shift in our culture's attitude toward sexuality?

6. Does the Bible contain a uniform, consistent sex ethic or is it more accurate to say that sexual ethics evolved over the centuries? Consider that Hebrew males were allowed to practice both polygamy and concubinage (Gen. 16:1-4; 30:1-13). Levirate marriage was commanded to raise up heirs for a deceased family member (Gen. 38:8; Deut. 25:5-10). A liberal divorce policy was permitted during the Old Testament period (Deut. 24:1-4; cf. Mal. 2:14-16). Is there a clear condemnation of polygamy in the Bible? Has the meaning of "adultery" undergone change from the prohibition in the Decalogue until Jesus' ethical teaching centuries later?

7. When people talk about "sex and marriage" or "sex without love, " etc., by sex they usually mean "sexual intercourse." Is it unfair to use "sex" to have such a limited meaning?

8. Do you view sex to be sacred, as it is considered to be by

some theologians and moral philosophers? Don't most of us consider it to be a matter of libido (or instinct)?

Consider three factors: First, procreation is sacred because it procreates, under God's divine and natural laws, an immortal soul. Second, sexual intimacy partakes of the sacred because it powerfully symbolizes and expresses God's spiritual intimacy and love for his own people. Third, erotic pleasure may be seen as the natural analogy of mystical experience, the self-forgetful, self-loving, "lost in the wonder of you" experience which typifies the eternal ecstasy of a soul in communion with God. Does any of this make sense to you?

9. How much self-serving rationalization goes on in people's moral decision-making about sex? Is it not easy to define any intimate behavior in the throes of romantic passion as true love? Are not sexual passions and impulses almost too powerful to control once discipline and restraint are relaxed? Consider Tim Stafford's quip about sexual passion: "It is like walking a lion on a leash. Sometimes he goes where you want him to go. Sometimes he will not. Sometimes he turns around and devours you."

10. In days past sexual maturation took place within marriage. It was customary for people to become betrothed and marry in their teenage years without extensive experience in courtship. Several trends have emerged in our contemporary society which have bearing on the issue of premarital sexual relations: First, there is the postponement of the age of marriage, especially for women. Both males and females are encouraged to complete college, graduate, or other professional training before committing to a lifetime union. Second, sexual activity can occur largely free from the danger of pregnancy and disease; while both remain serious problems, they result more from the failure to assume available precautions. Third, premarital chastity is no longer considered to be the rare and cherished gem of character as it once was; no stigma regarding marriageability seems to be attached to a single person who has enjoyed sexual experience. Sexual intercourse for committed singles is deemed to be intrinsically good and enjoyable rather than to be suspiciously viewed as a weakness of will or flaw in character.

Now that the triple fears of "detection, conception, and infection" are removed from the list of reasons for premarital chastity, from a strictly logical and humanly rational point of view, would it not be difficult to condemn sexual relations between an unmarried man and woman who have a deep, meaningful relationship? Would occasional sexual relationships between partners in a serious, mature relationship be considered fornication? Does the Bible define fornication? What Scriptures can one use to condemn premarital sex?

11. Ideally, sexual intimacy tends to bond a male and a female. Do you think that premarital and extramarital sex may overcommit two people to each other before they have, in the case of premarital relationships, explored all the dimensions of their relationship and, in the case of partners married to other mates, considered possible consequences of their action on existing relationships?

12. Situation: Imagine that you and your mate are parents of a 21-year-old son who is a college senior. This son, "John," has enjoyed a serious, ongoing relationship with "Rebecca" for almost two years. Rebecca is a junior at the same university. Both openly claim they are in love with each other and that they are planning to announce a formal engagement in the near future although marriage is out of the question until both complete their plans for graduate and professional training which could be four or five years away.

John and Rebecca sign a lease on an apartment and set up housekeeping together. The arrangement, they claim, not only enables them to share expenses and divide domestic roles, but gives them opportunity to explore their relationship in depth. Both assert that sex is not the most important part of this living arrangement.

How do you feel about this arrangement? Do you consider it to be sinful? As parents of one of the two young people, would you offer any unsolicited advice to your son? Would you urge the pair to get married?

When the Christian ideal of premarital abstinence before legal union is not upheld perfectly, is it possible to distinguish between healthy and unhealthy patterns of premarital sex? Is John no more "moral" and responsible in this context than if he were a promiscuous college male who attempted to woo and seduce a different college coed nearly every weekend? Consider that devoted "live-ins" have all the dynamics of marriage in their relationship except for the presence of a legal document.

13. Will a young man or woman who has pleasured himself/herself with numerous sex partners before marriage find it more difficult to remain sexually faithful to one partner after marriage

than someone virginal and sexually inexperienced prior to marriage?

14. In Hempstead, Texas, in 1993, high school officials were forced to reverse a decision last month to bar pregnant girls from the cheerleading squad after several students protested that it was punishment; the National Organization for Women threatened a lawsuit against the district. In Chelsea High School in Manhattan two years earlier, the president and the secretary-treasurer both became pregnant and were encouraged to remain in the elective posts. In an Eau Claire, Wisconsin, high school, the principal and three staff members were disciplined for tampering with a student election which made a pregnant student homecoming queen.

In the old days (40s, 50s, early 60s), pregnant teenagers were banished from schools, ostracized by their peers, or scurried out of town to deliver under the cloak of privacy and secrecy. Not only are pregnant teenagers no longer shunned or ridiculed, but supported and embraced in their decision to give birth, keep their babies, continue their education, and participate in all extracurricular activities. Today, 30.1 percent of all babies in this nation are born to unmarried women, a dramatic increase from the rate of five percent or less two or three generations past.

If you were the parent of teenagers, given the fact that unmarried and expectant youth are presented even as role models for their peers, what would you tell your own children? And what would you tell your children about role models in the news and entertainment media whose lifestyle is not rooted in Christian ethics?

15. Celibacy and abstinence are extolled in Scripture. Jesus acknowledged that some people prefer to remain single for religious reasons (Matt. 19:12), and Paul preferred that single persons remain in that status (1 Cor. 7:8). At no point, of course, did biblical writers require celibacy and among the Jews marriage and childbearing were considered honorable duties.

Is celibacy a higher calling? Should the church at least be reminding its membership of the values of celibacy? Should parents urge their children to remain single? Does the historical context of persecution and belief in the imminence of a new age mitigate scriptural advocacy of celibacy? Consider also the fact Paul contended that the celibate enjoyed an environment conducive to greater spiritual service and growth (cf. 1 Cor. 7:32-35).

16. Are not extramarital sexual affairs understandable in today's

American culture? Consider these propositions:

(a) An erotic love that lasts forever is generally considered to be an incoherent ideal riddled with inconsistent demands and illusions that inevitably lead to frustration and unhappiness. Can love endure forever ("until death do us part") and simultaneously be ecstatically exciting?

(b) Society has become more humanistic and secular in moral orientation; the Bible is simply not accepted as the "final word" in all moral matters.

(c) Women have achieved major strides in terms of equality with men in the workforce; while the "glass ceiling" is still in place, it has become less of a barrier to occupational and career advancement for women.

(d) Men and women are placed together in all kinds of situations away from home — the office, company picnic, weekend conference, private luncheon, special assignment, etc. — which can provide occasions for bonding and temptation for various levels of intimacy.

Given these factors, what kind of message should church leaders and teachers present on this vital issue to non-Christians and to marginally committed members?

17. Situation: You work as an accountant for Miller and Jones Accounting Firm, a successful agency in your hometown. You and Frank Miller, one of the major partners, have formed both a close working partnership, but also a healthy friendship that extends beyond the office. You, as well as a few others in the firm, have traveled with Frank to out-of-state conferences, workshops, and seminars.

Even though Frank seems to be a happily married man and father of three children, you notice that he is careless about his behavior around the opposite sex when he is out of town. At the social hour which almost inevitably follows the day's last workshop session, Frank enjoys seeing old women friends who have traveled to the sessions and meeting new women.

Frank always reserves a private room for each of the two of you, something that is not deemed unusual. However, early in your association you observe that Frank has invited a woman he has met to his room on nearly every night that he is away on business. You hope that the woman who visits his room does not stay the entire night, but then you chastise yourself mentally for even making it your business. After a few instances of inadvertently discovering a woman leaving Frank's room just in time for breakfast the follow-ing morning, you realize that most of Frank's female visitors have been sexual partners for the entire night.

After much discomfort you squelch your reluctance and confront Frank as non-judgmentally as is possible for you, begin-ning by reporting your observations about his behavior and the disappointment and discomfort that you have experienced from these observations.

"Yes, you are quite perceptive about my behavior but, truth is, I've never tried to hide any of my life from you," Frank begins his reply. "I don't have any ethical absolutes to guide my behavior, so whatever happens 'just happens.' I don't feel like I am using these women, any more than they feel 'used.' Any woman I invite to my room is a person I truly like and she is not forced at gunpoint to stay in my room — she is free to leave at any time."

Frank's manner was one of calm confidence as he continued in an almost philosophical defense: "Intimacy is something you can't program. It's like a chemistry between two people. It may happen or it may not. It may last for a lifetime or, because of circumstances and prior commitments, it may last for only one night. Ever heard Bob Seger's song, "We've got tonight. Who needs tomorrow? Let's make it last. Let's find a way. Turn out the lights . . . ."?

"Yes, that's a song about a man attempting to seduce a woman he probably has just met," you reply. "No wonder you like the song."

"Well, let's not force sex into one of two extremes," Frank continued: "that sex is either loving in a marriage or it is a degrad-ing indulgence for sinful, selfish reasons. There's a middle ground. Sex can express simple affection for some woman colleague in this profession I've known since college days. It can express liking or friendship or sheer delight in the beauty of another person. Or it can express the desire to have fun based on the consent of two adults."

Now that you have heard Frank Miller's defense of extramarital sex, do you agree with him? If not, what do you say to him? Is this part of his lifestyle a matter of private, personal choice that you need to respect by your silence?

18. Can good sex save a troubled marriage? Does less sex mean bad sex in a marriage? Does high frequency of intercourse and orgasm guarantee sexual satisfaction?

19. Handling issues of sexuality is difficult for single people who

have been married previously. Such women and men have had sexual experiences and, regardless of how satisfying these experiences, usually miss longingly the experience of physical intimacy. What advice would you give single-again adults who seek a social life and may even develop a romantic relationship with a "significant other" but cannot consider the remarriage option for a number of practical reasons?

20. *Seduction* is a process whereby one person attempts and succeeds to get another person to engage voluntarily in sexual relations. Seduction should be clearly distinguished from rape, where the element of voluntariness is absent. Seduction employs persuasion rather than force or coercion. What kind of moral judgment should be rendered about seduction?

Consider that strategies of seduction include not simply the wearing of provocative clothing or scents, the setting of a romantic atmosphere (candlelight dinner, romantic music, etc.), and the giving of gifts such as candy and jewelry, but may include making loose promises of undying love and respect and/or exaggerated compliments to the intended seductee. What about the devices of deceit and dishonesty in seduction attempts? The old adage "all's fair in love and war" suggests that effectiveness is the only test of seduction strategies and that there are no moral limits to what some people will do in order to coax another person to have sex. What is your response to this? Does seduction exist within a marriage? Should it?

21. Is it possible to erotically love more than one person at the same time? This question has been contemplated by millions of adults whose lifestyles and schedules put them in the social environment of interesting and attractive people of the opposite sex.

Consider first what you consider this question to mean. Are we asking whether one person could experience certain emotions at the same time toward more than one person? Are we asking a practical question about whether there is enough time and energy to pursue more than one relationship at a time? Or, are we asking a value question concerning which kind of relationships have the highest value?

22. The claim is made that AIDS is "changing sexual morality." Do you think AIDS is either a divinely sent punishment for the human race's moral laxity in sex or that it is a natural consequence of people's violating God's natural laws? Or is it neither? Can Christians rejoice because concern about AIDS and other sexually

transmitted diseases provides practical reasons for faithful, monogamous relationships, or do we contend that such a motivation for the return to traditional morality is less than admirable?

23. Scripture clearly teaches that disciples committed to experiencing the new life in Christ will not consort with prostitutes. "Shall I then take the members of Christ and unite them with a prostitute?" Paul asked. "Never! Do you not know that he who unites himself with a prostitute is one with her in body?" (1 Cor. 6:15-16a). Besides committing fornication and placing his health at risk, is there any other reason for a man not to purchase the body of a prostitute? What is a man doing to females when he purchases commercial sex services, whether he is attending sex shows or hiring a prostitute?

Has Hollywood greatly distorted the reality of prostitution, for example in movies such as *Pretty Woman*? How many prostitutes look and think like the role played by Julie Roberts? Studies have revealed some startling facts about females in the commercial sex business: (a) Eighty percent of the prostitutes have been physically assaulted and many have been killed; (b) 55 to 90 percent of prostitutes were sexually abused as children, often by more than one predator; (c) many were recruited as children into the commercial sex business; (d) some came out of poverty and homelessness into commercial sex; (e) prostitutes have severe personality problems, and an estimated 75 percent have attempted suicide. One psychologist and researcher declared: "In my clinical experience, all prostitutes suffer from serious psychological damage." Females in commercial sex have abysmally low self-esteem which turns into self-loathing and to work as prostitutes must shut off emotionally and sexually; when they want to get sexually involved in a serious relationship they find it is usually impossible to get turned on. Many are addicted to drugs to deaden their terrible reality.

Isn't the subsidizing of the commercial sex business a highly moral consideration as opposed to a simple diversion or "small vice"? What about a man who once or twice a year enjoys the diversion of an adult film or a visit to a topless bar? Isn't this at least a small contribution to sexual and emotional abuse of other people?

24. What do you think about flirting? Is it dangerous? Flirting may be defined as "acting amorously without serious intent. Being playful. Having fun." But is there a double standard? If a woman flirts, she may be branded as a tease; if a man flirts, he may be cast as a tomcat on the prowl. Is flirting a dangerous, misleading form

of communication between the sexes or is it a fun, safe, and sane form of attracting someone's attention and offering a compliment without asking for greater intimacy?

25. More than one million teenagers will get pregnant within one calendar year; about one-third will be age seventeen or younger. Teenagers will give birth to a half-million babies — 70 percent born out of wedlock. Teen mothers are less likely to finish their education, less likely to earn a decent wage, and more likely to spend years on welfare. The use of contraceptives and the legal alternative of abortion have served to keep teenage parenting rates as low as they are.

What do you see as factors contributing to high teenage sexual activity? Does a role model such as Wynona Judd, one among many entertainers who openly conceived and delivered a baby out of wedlock, contribute in a major way to the problem? Is there any way that adults can be more effective in teaching adolescents to say "no" to premarital sex without their feeling like an outcast? How do you answer people who say, "Kids will be kids and you can't really stop them from doing what they want to do"?

26. The summer of 1995 brought the Hollywood's release of *The Bridges of Madison County*, a movie version of the Robert James Waller novel by the same name. The movie features Clint Eastwood and Meryl Streep as lead characters Robert Kincaid, traveling photographer for *National Geographic* magazine and Francesca Johnson, the wife of an Iowa farmer. The two, as older adults away from other members of their family, succumb to a intense affair that is short-lived due to circumstances.

Both the book and the movie version have been hits. Therefore, we may appropriately ask some questions. Given the fact that sexual affairs are rather commonplace, does the story honestly reflect reality?

Consider the way a sexually conservative and traditionalist might report this movie: "A man and a woman cheat on their mates, to whom they had pledged to be faithful, meaning, they had vowed to be sexually exclusive. These two people had a chemistry that made them lust after each other, but prior to their adultery they did not know each other very well. The woman connives to encourage the affair, lies to hide it, and holds her heart essentially apart evermore from her husband and family. She spends the rest of her life pining for what might have been.

"The story glosses over reality in its glorification of adultery.

Marriage is an honorable estate, not to be entered lightly. Adultery betrays, devastates, and destroys. Marriage partners suffer because of adulterous affairs and so do children in such a family. Adultery is not romantic or beautiful and neither are its consequences — broken homes and broken hearts."

Consider the way a libertarian might report this movie: "There is more to this story than the momentary transgression of adultery. The depth of the story is in its portrayal of the fulfillment of missing parts of people's lives and of the fleeting nature of ecstasy, fulfillment, and deep insight about human nature. Sometimes the strangest gifts can come to you when you are dying inside. For the briefest of days Francesca Johnson and Robert Kincaid were allowed to step out of the humdrum of ordinary existence and experience what could/should have been if they had met under different circumstances.

"While technically these two were guilty of adultery, lust had nothing to do with what they found. There was a genuine connection of hearts and souls into one beautiful, compassionate experience. There was no intention to hurt anyone else. Neither gave or expected anything from the other except love. These two people were respectable people who cared about their own families. They were strong people who proved weak only when facing sexual temptation. This weakness did not make them immoral — only human."

Which of the two reviews of *Bridges of Madison County* do you believe more accurately depicts reality? Do you know of another book or movie which more realistically depicts the dynamics and impact of adultery? Read on to the next question.

27. The 1987 movie *Fatal Attraction*, starring Michael Douglas and Glenn Close, stirred a lot of discussion among moviegoers, perhaps because so many people could relate to the characters of Dan Gallagher or his wife.

The screen story develops the character of a married man, Dan Gallagher, who has a brief affair with a provocatively attractive woman, Alex Forest, one weekend while his wife is out of town. Gallagher's wife is more concerned with being a good mother to their little girl, therefore their marriage is one of intimacy and friendship but not much sex. Gallagher is quite content to move on with his normal business and family life and thus allow the weekend affair remain a closed chapter. Alex is not. She begins to move in on the family, claims to be pregnant (perhaps truthfully), and demands that Gallagher take responsibility for his actions. Her persistence becomes so unnervingly intimidating to him that he seeks another place to live with his family, but Alex suddenly appears as a prospective new tenant of the apartment they are vacating and makes friends with his wife. Alex's plan seems at first to be to persuade him to tell his wife the truth and leave her; she begrudges his wife the life she has with Dan and their child. When Alex realizes Dan is not going to leave his wife, her plans change and she becomes intent on destroying him, even if it means destroying his family. A shocking moment emerges when Dan's wife suddenly realizes that Alex has gained access to their house and lawn and has cruelly tormented and killed a family pet. Those who have seen the movie will remember the ending.

Do you know personally of someone like Dan Gallagher whose brief affair brought great personal risk, perhaps not of his life, but of his reputation, his influence on others, his marriage and family? Is jealousy an evil character trait? Is there any limit to the revenge a jealous person might take? Did Alex have a right to be jealous? Who is worse in *Fatal Attraction* — Alex Forest, who hounds and torments the family or Dan Gallagher, who began it all by cheating on his wife? If you were Dan's wife, would you forgive him? What do you see as the difference between retribution and revenge?

CHAPTER FIVE

Crime and Criminal Justice

Almost everyone who knew Susan Smith said that she was a good mother. So when the Union, South Carolina, mother took her two sons, Michael and Alexander (ages three years and fourteen months respectively), for a ride on the evening of October 25, 1994, she was careful to strap them into their car seats. Later, she pulled up to a boat ramp at John D. Long Lake, opened the door and stepped out onto the concrete-and-gravel ramp as the maroon Mazda sedan began to roll off into dark waters. For the next ten days the nation agonized with the young mother as an intensive nationwide search continued for an alleged black carjacker as described by the young mother. After Susan Smith's confession, millions of Americans wondered if there was no demonic act, no heartless cruelty, to which some people would not stoop.

Since the 1960s, one of the most serious issues facing our nation has been the rising wave of crime, particularly violent crime. According to FBI crime reports, there were 1,911,770 violent crimes in the United States in 1991: 24,700 murders, 106,590 forcible rapes, and 687,730 robberies.

Some violent crimes are so heinous as to shock our sensibilities. The Susan Smith case captured the nation's attention, at first because it played on every father and mother's fear of a stranger abducting an innocent, beloved baby. In this case, that fear proved unfounded. The real explanation was even more terrifying because it was closer to home and stifled the imagination: What could prompt a mother to murder her own helpless flesh and blood? The Smith case is not isolated. According to one estimate, approximately 1,300 children are killed by their parents or close relatives each year — including about two thirds of homicide victims younger then ten. Of course, in the vast majority of cases it is not a deliberate, premeditated act, but the final episode in a long pattern of violence.

This chapter could be filled with story after story of some of the most vicious, cruel acts against human beings of all ages — drive-by shootings, cold-blooded murders, "heat of passion" murders, terrorism, gang rapes, abductions, torture. Every newspaper is filled with accounts of sordid behavior. Many residents have become fearful to leave their homes at night and would be traumatized to have to walk city streets or be stranded in an automobile at night. Millions have purchased guns for self-defense and many houses are virtual armed camps.

What is the appropriate punishment for the worst of crimes? Many people believe that the only appropriate punishment for those who commit such monstrous crimes is death. Although almost all industrialized societies and a majority of nations around the world have abolished the death penalty, support for the death penalty in the United States has been widespread and passionate. As of 1992, 36 states have the death penalty for premeditated murder (although not all of them have resumed execution) while only 15 states (and the District of Columbia) do not. Since 1977 there have been over one hundred executions in the United States and even now there are approximately 2800 inmates on death row awaiting executions, pending the outcome of appeals.

The morality of capital punishment is one of those perennial issues which has been debated for generations. Does the state have the right to take life in an act of retributive justice? How severe should punishment be? For Christians, it is important to ask what the biblical texts teach about punishment for evil-doing. As we shall see, responsible Christians have interpreted and applied certain texts in varying ways.

No one moral principle is of paramount validity, decisively favoring one side or the other of the controversy. Consequently, one's view of the morality of the death penalty typically is influenced by one's philosophy about punishment generally and how one fleshes out such values as the sanctity and dignity of human life. The whole issue forces us to weigh the value we attach to human life against the horror in which we hold heinous crime.

The legal setting for modern discussion of capital punishment was established in the 1970s with two court cases. In *Furman v. Georgia* (1972), the high court ruled that the death penalty as it was imposed and carried out constituted "cruel and unusual punishment." In *Gregg v. Georgia* (1976) the court reversed the earlier ruling because: (1) capital punishment accords with contemporary standards of decency; (2) capital punishment may serve some deterrent or retributive purpose that is not degrading to human dignity; and (3) in the case of the Georgia law under review, capital punishment is no longer arbitrarily applied. Before proceeding, it is instructive to consider the elements that compose punishment and then to ask about the aims of punishment.

Generally, philosophers discuss punishment in terms of five elements: (1) Punishment must involve unpleasant, undesirable consequences, such as pain or loss of rights and privileges; (2) be administered for a violation of a common sense law or rule which has been clearly stated; (3) must be administered to someone who has been judged guilty; (4) must be imposed by someone other than the offender (people "punishing themselves" is insufficient); and (5) be imposed by rightful authority (a legal system which represents "the people") and according to due process of law.

PURPOSES OF PUNISHMENT

No one disputes the moral acceptability of punishment for criminal wrongdoing. What people do not always agree on, however, is the aim of punishment. The aims of punishment related to two categories: (1) giving offenders what they deserve and (2) creating a desirable social and political environment. There are four purposes of punishment:

1. Prevention. This view of punishment holds that society should punish offenders so that they do not repeat their wrongdoing (or a worse offense) and further erode the fabric of society. A murderer who is locked away will not kill anyone again (unless, of course, he kills an inmate or guard).

2. Deterrence. This view holds that people will be discouraged from committing crime in the first place if they are threatened with punishment. Society assumes that people's fear of being punished for criminal behavior will deter them from engaging in criminal wrongdoing. When potential vandals see that other vandals have been punished for their crime, they are less likely to vandalize. Deterrence is perhaps the most common argument made on behalf of capital punishment.

3. Reform/Rehabilitation. This idealistic view holds that the criminal will emerge from his time served with a renewed desire to conform to the standards of behavior that a society wants followed.

Rehabilitation may involve counseling, job training, recreation, and education to prepare inmates to function usefully upon reentering society.

4. Retribution is a major purpose of punishment, independent of other considerations. Retribution is the principle of justice — some people simply deserve to be punished for their wrongdoing. By this doctrine, the moral order is unbalanced because of a person's evil conduct and can only be put back into balance by appropriate punishment of the evildoer. Additionally, punishment should be proportional to the evil committed if the scales of justice are to be balanced. When the state administers capital punishment to someone who unlawfully takes the life of another citizen, the punishment is viewed as an attempt to restore this disrupted balance, to reaffirm society's commitment to fair treatment for all. Failure to punish appropriately is disrespectful for all citizens, even to criminals who are denied responsibility and spared consequences of their actions.

The Christian is committed to political and social justice; for him/her, there is no uncertainty about the role of justice in restoring and maintaining the sense of human community. Indeed, justice is community in the full sense of the word. While the preamble to our Constitution and certain of its amendments summon us as citizens to justice and make explicit its minimal demands, the church, informed and inspired by the good news of Jesus Christ, possesses a unique perspective that reaffirms the centrality and efficacy of justice in interpersonal and societal affairs. And, as Reinhold Niebuhr has declared, the role of politics in a sinful world is to establish and maintain justice.

H.L. Mencken once wrote that every night he thanked God for the Bill of Rights and then thanked God that he was too prudent ever to try to use any of them. The sarcasm has an element of truth — there is a wide gap between the rights the Supreme Court finds in the Constitution and the rights a person can in fact exercise. Christians may not always take claims based upon justice as seriously as they should and hence, need reminding of the biblical resources of political and social justice:

Old Testament (or Jewish Ethics) Sources for Justice

1. *Chesed* — lovingkindness.
   Leviticus 19:18; Micah 6:8; Mishnah Makkot 24b.

2. Respect for inherent human dignity.
   Leviticus 19:17-18.
3. Community of mutual dependence.
4. Special responsibility to guard the poor and weak from injustice.
   Deuteronomy 24:12-13, 17.
5. Requirement of precise, publicized laws.
6. Avoidance of overburdensome laws.
7. Presumption of innocence.
8. Strict rules of evidence.
   Deuteronomy 17:6; 19:15-19.
9. Reinstatement of punished offenders.
10. Restitution to victims.
    Exodus 22:1-17; Leviticus 6:1-7; 24:18.

New Testament Christian Ethics

1. Love and respect for all persons.
   Matthew 22:37-40; Luke 10:29-37; 1 Corinthians 13:13.
2. Seeking to nurture and maintain community.
   John 17:11, 21.
3. Due humility and restraint.
   Matthew 7:1,3; Hebrews 4:12-13.
4. Special care for poor and weak.
5. Forgiveness and mercy.
   John 8:3-11; Luke 15:11-30; Matthew 6:14-15; 18:23-35.
6. Community of responsibility for sin and righteousness.
   Romans 5:12-14, 21.
7. Law for persons, not persons for law.
   Matthew 2:27; Luke 6:6-10; Luke 14:1-4; Galatians 3:23-26;
   1 Corinthians 8:1.

KEY TERMS

Ahimsa — a principle of nonharming in Hindu and Buddhist religious traditions which creates a strong presumption against the death penalty. Hindus and Buddhists are urged to refrain from taking life, even animal life.

Abolitionists — those who oppose capital punishment, believing it is never morally justifiable, even if they do not agree among themselves on the reasons for their opposition.

Capital crimes — those wrongdoings that are punishable by death; these vary from nation to nation and across time but have generally included: (1) crimes against the government (treason, perjury); (2) crimes against property (train wreck, arson, burglary); and (3) crimes against people (murder, kidnapping, rape, lynching, conspiracy to murder).

Death penalty — the legal punishment of a person who has been found guilty of a crime by depriving him/her of life.

Deterrence — the act or process of deterring crime or discouraging criminal activity.

Efficacious — producing the desired results; effective.

Eighth Amendment — The provision in the U. S. Constitution which prohibits cruel and unusual punishment.

Incorrigible — so firmly fixed in evil ways or bad habits that reform or change cannot be expected.

Ineffectual — not able to produce the effect wanted; powerless.

Recidivist — one who relapses back into crime; a habitual criminal offender.

Retentionists — those who support retaining or reinstituting capital punishment. Retentionists do not always agree on the arguments supporting capital punishment or the conditions under which it is imposed, but they agree that under circumstances it is morally justifiable.

Vengeance — a compensatory and psychologically reparatory satisfaction for an injured party, group, or society.

KEY SCRIPTURES

Genesis 9:6; Exodus 20:13; 21:12-25; Leviticus 24:20; Matthew 5:38-39; John 8:7, 10-11; Romans 12:19; 13:3-4.

KEY ISSUES/ARGUMENTS
Arguments for Capital Punishment (Retentionists)

1. Capital punishment balances the scales of justice. Because murder is the ultimate crime, simple justice requires that the murderer pay the ultimate penalty.

"Murder is the ultimate crime. The murderer takes away something that only God can give. Prevention and deterrence are not

138

the only purposes of punishment. Justice must be exacted by taking moral retribution. That's why citizens insist that punishment must fit the crime. The Bible teaches 'an eye for an eye and a tooth for a tooth.' If moral outrage is not expressed through legal executions, then private citizens will take the law into their own hands and exact their own brand of justice."

2. Biblical tradition has always sanctioned the authority and expedience of the state to exercise the death penalty.

"God himself instituted the death penalty. In the first book in the Bible, God declared: 'Whoever sheds the blood of man, by man shall his blood be shed' [Gen. 9:6]. Capital punishment was intended by God as a penalty for those who take law and justice into their own hands or who for personal gain willfully take the life of another person. God gave to civil government the legitimate authority to use capital punishment to restrain murder and punish murderers [Rom. 13:1-5].

"Those who oppose capital punishment on religious grounds will often quote Jesus' admonitions in the Sermon on the Mount about loving our enemies and turning the other cheek. These commandments, however, relate to interpersonal relationships and say nothing about how a government should respond to those who break the laws of the state. If the state did not punish, or use the threat of punishment, criminal behavior, we would see the collapse of a decent and orderly society.

"When Jesus stood before Pilate, he was silent during some of the Roman's questions. Annoyed at his silence, Pilate declared: 'Don't you realize I have power either to free you or to crucify you?' Jesus' responded: 'You would have no power over me if it were not given to you from above' [John 19:11]. Jesus' point seems to be that Pilate had been granted the right of imposing the sentence of death, but only because God had granted civil government such a right. Otherwise, Jesus might have declared: 'The right to impose the death penalty on anyone is beyond the scope of any civil government.'

Not to inflict the death penalty for the most evil and depraved behavior is a flagrant disregard for God's divine law which recognizes the dignity of human life as the crowning handiwork of God's creation. Life is sacred and precious, and that is why God instituted the death penalty — for the protection of human life.

3. Capital punishment deters crime.

"Common sense tells you that capital punishment is a greater deterrent to crime than the threat of time in prison. The greater the risk, the more reason for a person not to commit a crime. Many people obey the law primarily because of the fear of punishment — the more severe the punishment threatened, the greater the fear and therefore the greater the deterrent value.

"This is not to say that every potential murderer is rational enough to weigh all the factors before deciding whether to kill, but it stands to reason that some are. 'Killers for hire,' like bosses in organized crime, are rational enough to weigh the risks for any decision to kill a person. So long as that's true, capital punishment serves its purpose — protecting at least a few innocent lives."

4. Capital punishment keeps the convicted murderer from killing again.

"How many times have you read about a convicted murderer who is released and then he kills again or rapes a person? Or how often have murder convicts killed a prison guard or another inmate? Capital punishment of a murderer assures society of one thing — we do not have to worry that an executed murderer will kill again."

5. Society should not have to pay the economic costs of life sentences for murderers.

"Everyone knows that there are sociopathic killers who cannot be reformed. If they are only sentenced to life imprisonment, that means the taxpayers must pick up the tab for maintaining the worst, most depraved criminals in a maximum security prison until they eventually die. That's a little unfair, asking the innocent to provide lifetime institutional accommodations and food for convicts who have no respect for human life or society's laws."

Arguments Against Capital Punishment (Abolitionist)

1. Because every human life has dignity and worth, there is a moral principle that deliberate and premeditated taking of human life is wrong.

"Whatever crime a person has committed, that person is still a human being and not an animal of the field. Capital punishment is nothing more than legalized cold-blooded, calculated murder. A civilized and humane society does not deliberately kill human beings. Every human being possesses in some form the image of God. Every human being has worth and dignity.

To oppose capital punishment is not advocating leniency toward malevolent offenders. It is not to feel sentimental and sorry for those convicted of murder. On the contrary, murderers should be condemned for their lack of respect for human life, but life imprisonment without possibility of parole should be sufficient retribution and deterrence. To strap a person to a table or chair and then give him a lethal dose of electricity, gas, or drugs is unworthy of a humane society. The death penalty is nothing more than a relic of the earliest days of criminal justice when slavery, branding, torture, and mutilation were common legal practices; like those other barbaric practices, it must be considered morally unacceptable in a civilized nation."

2. The noblest Christian tradition advocates love, mercy, non-retaliation and human rehabilitation.

"In every person is the image and presence of God. As children of God, even the vilest offender can find grace and forgiveness. We are all redeemable. Followers of Jesus are 'pro-life' in the fullest sense of the term, siding with any victim of violence, always resisting death, and promoting a human life with respect and dignity. The New Testament places emphasis on the themes of grace, forgiveness, reconciliation, and rehabilitation. Admittedly, these are theological concepts, but surely they have some application in the civil order.

"The law of Christ is love. Believers are enjoined to love and serve their neighbors [Matt. 22:37-40; 25:31-46; 1 John 3:18; 4:12, 20]. Jesus challenged his disciples to love rather than execute their enemies [Matt. 5:43-44]. Revenge is forbidden [Rom. 12:17-19; 1 Pet. 3:8-9].

"There are many powerful biblical examples of mercy and forgiveness. Both David and Moses murdered intentionally, most premeditatively in the case of David, and God extended forgiveness and restoration to these great leaders of Israel and they proceeded to live noble and productive lives for the Lord. At the least, these examples show that even if capital punishment is permissible, it is neither mandatory or necessarily advisable.

"In the life of Christ, mercy is also dramatically demonstrated. The religious men of his time brought to Jesus a woman whom they were about to stone to death, legally, for having committed the crime of adultery [the story is told in John 8]. Jesus does not deny that the Mosaic law condemned her, but he questioned the moral authority of those who stood ready and eager to execute her ['Let him who is without sin cast the first stone']. Jesus' words must have made the Pharisees realize their own guilt. If there were ever a time for Jesus to declare something good and useful about the death penalty, this would have been the time and occasion. His silence is eloquent."

3. Capital punishment does not really deter people from committing violent crime.

"True enough, the popular notion that executions are a deterrent to murder appears to be as strong as ever. Regardless of what common sense tells you, however, there is no hard evidence that the death penalty deters serious criminal activity any more than the threat of a long prison term. States which have enacted the death penalty find homicide rates to be just as high or even higher than states which do not impose the ultimate penalty; states which abolish the death penalty do not show an increased rate of homicide after abolition. Do you believe that the vast majority of criminals pause to calculate the pros and cons of a serious crime before they commit it? The murderer probably believes that he will not be apprehended in the first place or he may have a 'death wish' and not care whether he is caught or not."

4. Capital punishment is imposed with class and racial bias.

"Our American system is supposed to provide 'equal protection of the laws' and yet studies reveal some highly disturbing facts: First, there is a strong bias toward the convict who is white, wealthy, and influential; the poor and underprivileged are far more likely to be executed than an individual with money and influence.

"Second, the death penalty is more likely to be administered when the victim is white rather than a member of a minority group. Only a small proportion of first-degree murderers are ever sentenced to death, and even fewer are executed. Such a random and discriminatory application of the ultimate penalty violates the highest concepts of justice and fair treatment.

"From 1976, when executions resumed, until 1994, 254 prisoners have been put to death — a tiny fraction of those convicted of murder and just a tenth of those sentenced to die. What determines the identity of the few convicts who will die for their transgressions?"

5. The innocent man or woman may die; since the death penalty is irrevocable, no reparations can be made to the wrongly convicted and sentenced citizen.

"Innocent people are sometimes accused and convicted of crimes, even with all the safeguards of due process of law. As long as human beings pass judgment on other humans, there will be mistakes. Faulty police work, overzealous prosecution, inadequate defense counsel, a defendant's previous criminal record, a harried jury, seemingly convincing circumstantial evidence — these and other factors undermine any assurance that justice will never miscarry.

"Unlike all other criminal punishments, however, the death penalty is uniquely irreparable and irreversible. Although some proponents of capital punishment will contend that a few innocent lives is not too high a price to pay for retention of the death penalty, the possibility of executing only a few innocent persons should haunt any right-thinking citizen."

6. Capital punishment compromises the judicial system.

"When conviction of first degree murder carries a mandatory death penalty, juries have been known to skew the evidence to convict defendants of lesser charges [or even acquit them]. A capital trial usually takes much longer than one in which the death sentence is not involved, and lengthy appeals almost invariably follow. The appeals which follow the sentence of death involve great cost as well as time. Thus, justice is delayed, subjecting victims' families as well as convicts themselves to extended and unnecessary agony."

7. State-sponsored executions set a dehumanizing example of brutality that only encourages violence.

"True enough, capital punishment is intended to set an example for everyone about the seriousness of criminal activity. However, this much-publicized spectacle of severe justice provides an example of official homicide, inculcating young and old alike with the principle that it is possible to kill people to solve social problems. This is the worst possible example to set for citizens, for when the state murders its own citizens there is always a price to be exacted, no matter how vicious the condemned offenders may be. Executions can bring out the worst in people, as in old England when execution events were scenes of great revelry and celebrated like a holiday. We must teach our young that the taking of human life or the threat of death is never an viable answer to any kind of problem."

SELECTED QUOTATIONS

Whosoever sheds the blood of man, by man shall his blood be shed: for in the image of God has God made man.

— Genesis 9:6

"Vengeance is mine," saith the Lord, "I will repay."

— Romans 14:19

Deterrence should never be considered the *primary* reason for administering the death penalty. It would be both immoral and unjust to punish one man merely as an example to others. The basic consideration should be: Is the punishment deserved? If not, it should not be administered regardless of what its deterrent impact might be. After all, once deterrence supersedes justice as the basis for a criminal sanction, the guilt or innocence of the accused becomes largely irrelevant.

— Robert W. Lee

I have spoken my opposition to the death penalty for more than 30 years. For all that time, I have studied it, I have watched, I have debated it, hundreds of times. I have heard all the arguments, analyzed all the evidence I could find, measured public opinion when it was opposed, when it was indifferent, when it was passionately in favor.

And always before, I have concluded the death penalty is wrong; that it lowers us all; that it is the surrender to the worst that is in us; that it uses a power — the official power to kill by execution — which has never elevated a society, never brought back a life, never inspired anything but hate.

— Mario Cuomo

Nowhere does the Bible repudiate capital punishment for premeditated murder; not only is the death penalty for deliberate killing of a fellow-human permitted, but it is approved and encouraged, and for any government that attaches at least as much value to the life of an innocent victim as to a deliberate murderer, it is ethically imperative.

— Carl F. H. Henry

I was so happy [to learn of Jeffrey Dahmer's bloody death in a prison bathroom]. I was so excited that, finally, the monster was gone. He was just plain evil. . . . That may sound harsh, but when you lose a brother. . . ."

> — Janie Hagen, sister of Richard Guerrer, one of seventeen young men murdered by Jeffrey Dahmer.

The first principle of any society, and especially our own, is the absolute sovereignty of a person over his or her body. People adhere to a society so that they can be protected in their enjoyment of their quiet sovereignty and they give up some of their rights to do and act as they please in consideration for the social contract and to enjoy the benefit of protection.

When imposing the death penalty upon the murderer, society, in the form of the government, is doing only what it must do to preserve the peace and fulfill the contract.

> — Frank V. Kelly

I shall ask for the abolition of the punishment of death until I have the infallibility of human judgment demonstrated to me.

> — Lafayette to the French Chamber of Deputies, 1830

Moralists have traditionally acknowledged that a state may employ capital punishment if in desperate situations it has no alternatives. A country reduced to that expedient would be, however, one in which neither political intelligence nor respect for life were fully developed. On the other hand, abolition of the death penalty contributes to the common good, for it is a step toward a more humane and rational society, one that can resist violence without itself behaving violently.

> — *America*, November 12, 1988

There are three good things about capital punishment. One, the killer gets to experience the same fear and agony he inflicted on others. Two, the recidivism rate for executed murderers is zero. Three, electricity (or rope or bullets or drugs) is cheaper than room and board.

The average time served on a life sentence in the United States is about six years. Murderers can usually find ways to get out of prison. So far, none has gotten out of a grave.

> — Charley Reese

The best evidence that the death penalty has a uniquely deterrent impact . . . is not based on statistics but is rather based on common sense and experience. Death is an awesome and awful penalty, qualitatively different from a prison term. While there is

145

some statistical evidence indicating that it has a deterrent impact, common sense can sufficiently verify that the prospect of punishment by death does exert a restraining effect on some criminals who would otherwise commit a capital crime.

— Charles E. Rice

Punishment is the way in which society expresses its denunciation of wrongdoing; and in order to maintain respect for law, it is essential that the punishment for grave crimes shall adequately reflect the revulsion felt by a great majority of citizens for them.

— Lord Alfred Denning

Perhaps the most harmful cost of the death penalty results from the false assumption that it helps to fight crime. Although the death penalty has no effect on reducing the crime rate, many politicians advocate executions to show they are taking steps to make America safer. This empty gesture distracts society's attention from the difficult challenge of finding effective solutions to the very real problem of violence. Often people who favor the death penalty don't have facts. They would like to believe this punishment is justified by reason, when in fact it results only from helplessness and rage.

— John G. Healey

"Retribution" isn't a dirty word, nor does it signify an attitude that is somehow contrary to a society's moral quest. In fact, only such punishments as are retributive in nature may be considered moral, just, and permissible.

While one may hope that a given instance of punishment has a deterrent effect on others and/or a rehabilitative impact on the offender, it is the theory of retributive justice that exonerates parents who ground their teenagers, educators who penalize students, or a society that punishes one of its citizens.

— Rubel Shelley

State-sponsored executions set a dehumanizing example of brutality that only encourages violence. Allowing the state to kill its own citizens diminishes our humanity and sets a dangerous precedent that is unworthy of a civilized society. Of all the industrialized nations, only the United States and South Africa subject their citizens to capital punishment.

Having lost a husband and mother-in-law to gunmen, I well understand the hurt and anger felt by the loved ones of those who have been murdered. Yet, I can't accept the judgment that their killers deserve to be executed. To do so merely perpetuates the tragic, unending cycle of violence that destroys our hopes for a decent society.

The death penalty provides short-range satisfaction to the very human impulse to seek revenge. In the long run, however, compounding acts of brutality adds to the suffering of loved ones, offenders, and sometimes even victims.

— Coretta Scott King

We surely don't expect to rehabilitate them, and it would be foolish to think that by punishing them we might thereby deter others. The answer, I think, is clear: We want to punish them in order to pay them back. We think they must be made to pay for their crimes with their lives, and we think that we, the survivors of the world they violated, may legitimately exact that payment because we, too, are their victims. By punishing them, we demonstrate that there are laws that bind men across generations as well as across and within nations, that we are not simply isolated individuals, each pursuing his selfish interests and connected with others by a mere contract to live and let live.

— Walter Berns

Capital punishment is society's final statement that we will not forgive.

— Martin Luther King, Jr.

QUESTIONS ABOUT ISSUES AND SITUATIONS

1. How do you define "justice"? Can there be such a thing as perfect justice in an imperfect world? Admittedly, this is an abstract concept, but grappling with the issue may lay a philosophical foundation for formulating our views on criminal punishment.

2. Of all industrialized societies in the world, the United States is among the last still inflicting capital punishment. The community of nations that has abolished the death penalty includes France, Germany, Sweden, Australia, Denmark, Costa Rica, Venezuela, Austria, the Netherlands, Nicaragua, Norway, and the Philippines, according to a recent report by Amnesty International. Some countries, such as Great Britain, Israel, and New Zealand, retain capital punishment only for "exceptional crimes," such as high treason.

What is your personal position on the morality of capital punishment? Is the death penalty a just punishment for heinous crimes, or is it an inhumane and unnecessarily barbaric practice? Is it cruel and unusual punishment, prohibited by the Eighth Amendment, or is it fitting retribution for certain reprehensible offenses?

3. "The sanctity of life." What a beautiful phrase! What a wonderful value to teach and inculcate within our young! Interestingly, abolitionists and retentionists use the phrase in different ways. How is the "sanctity of life" best honored (choose one)?

(a) Some crimes and offenses against the life and uniqueness of another person or other persons are so heinous, so unconscionable, that the only way to honor the sanctity of an innocent life which has been slain is to exact the same penalty on the convicted murderer; or:

(b) Even though a murderer has committed such a terrible crime against an innocent person, the gift of life is so valuable that the state will not take away the life of another person even to punish that guilty murderer.

4. Is retribution a proper motive and purpose for criminal punishment or does all vengeance belong only to God? If you believe in the law retribution *(lex taliones),* would it be fair punishment to exact punishment that is precisely proportional to the crime? Or is it reasonable to aim to provide punishment which is *like* the crime itself? Would you advocate fingers or a hand be severed for an incidence of theft or castration for a rapist?

5. Advocates of capital punishment will often declare, "There is

so much concern about the rights of the accused; we need to hear more about the rights of the victim." Consider: If we speak of murder victims, what rights do they have? Since the victims have been killed, however despicable and regrettable their murder, they are not in a position to exercise or enjoy any rights. Thus, do we speak of the "rights" of friends and family members of the victim? Or does a dead victim still have rights, such as a right to have his innocent blood avenged?

6. Abolitionists often make a charge toward the state about capital punishment: "We're doing the same thing to the criminal that he did to somebody else." Is this a strong argument? Is the statement a correct one? Is the difference between a murder and an execution semantic or ethical?

7. For retentionists: What are the types of crimes that warrant the death penalty? Murder with special circumstances (such as multiple homicide, rape, or extreme cruelty that leads to death), murder during a drug deal, murder of a police officer, murder for hire, and treason or espionage are often considered to be offenses where the death penalty "fits." Are there other offenses for which you would advocate the death penalty? At what age for offenders would you advocate capital punishment? What other exceptions would you propose, if any (for example, diminished capacity from mental retardation or long time drug use)?

8. Let's consider again the Eighth Amendment's protection against "cruel and unusual punishment." Throughout history, there have been a wide variety of methods of implementing a death penalty. In biblical times the guilty party could be pounded to death with stones which broke the skin and bones. Decapitation by sword has a long history. Witches and other offenders have been weighted with a millstone and tossed into a lake or river. The garrote was a method of execution by strangling with an iron collar. The guillotine, invented during the French Revolution and actually employed as a humane measure, lops off people's heads by means of a heavy, sharp blade which goes down grooves from a higher elevation.

In the twentieth century there have been efforts to execute more humanely. Firing squads, electrocution, the gas chamber, and, in recent years, lethal injections (first used in Texas in 1982) have been utilized to make the death penalty more quickly lethal and less painful. Abolitionists have provided graphic descriptions of the emotional and physical anguish endured by convicts subjected to any of these methods. Capital punishment, abolitionists assert, involves wanton pain and violence against a human being and violates all decent human standards.

Should society simply find another way to punish its worst offenders? Would not a life in austere, solitary confinement be more punishing to the guilty one?

9. Do you think the death penalty is really a deterrent to crime? Of course, increasing numbers of people believe that it is. Is it fair to say that statistics cannot prove the case for or against deterrence since a complex web of social, economic, and demographic factors drive murder rates?

10. Have not criminals declared "I deserve to die for my crime!"? Is not this attitude — "I deserve to die for my sin" — a profoundly biblical one? Would not such an attitude be concomitant with genuine penitence over a highly serious and hurtful wrongdoing? Consider that after Nathan rebuked David for his adultery and murder of Uriah, David exclaimed, "I have sinned against the Lord," to which Nathan replied, "The Lord also has taken away your sin; you shall not die." Nathan implied that David, in recognizing his sin, acknowledged also that he deserved the punishment of death. Indeed if "no crime deserves the death penalty," then it is hard to see why it was fitting that Christ be put to death for our sins and crucified among thieves.

11. For abolitionists: If Jesus had to die a cruel and unusual death on the cross for our sins, does this not suggest that for our own sins we deserve capital punishment? If humans cannot sin so grievously as to deserve the death penalty, does not this render Jesus' crucifixion meaningless? Does not the fact that Jesus was put to death as a guilty person, assuming the sentence of guilty persons, presuppose that death is a fitting punishment for the guilty party?

12. Christians are called to be concerned about love, forgiveness, mercy, reconciliation, and moral rehabilitation. Does this mean that we should forgive and show hospitality to the murderer? Consider the case of Saul of Tarsus. If anyone deserved the death penalty for his complicity in the death of many first-century Jewish Christians, would it not have been Saul? And yet Saul experienced conversion on the Damascus highway and Ananias was asked to accept this notorious murderer into his home [Acts 9:10-19]. If Saul had been executed for his crimes against the early Christians, we would have had no great apostle Paul, no masterful missionary to the Gentile world, and no book of Romans or Philippians or other

important documents in our Bible! Does this example instruct us on the issue of capital punishment?

13. Do you find it inconsistent that many Christians who are fervently "pro-life" on the abortion issue are strongly retentionist on capital punishment? Does not a "pro-life" position challenge us on other forms of life issues, such as euthanasia, war, and capital punishment, simply on the basis of the sanctity of all human life?

14. Case study: Flor Cupeles was the kind of a mom who knew everything about her kids: Who their friends were. How they were doing in school. What their dreams were.

There was something else she knew about her son Alberto Ramos, even after he was convicted of raping a 5-year-old girl in a day care center where he worked: It couldn't be true.

She was right — and the authorities who put him behind bars for seven years allegedly knew it, too. Critical documents that undercut the case against him were withheld from the defense during his 1985 trial.

In overturning Ramos' conviction earlier this month, Bronx Judge John P. Collins called the district attorney's handling of the paperwork "cavalier and haphazard."

Ramos charges in a $35 million lawsuit that he was railroaded by a prosecutor who suppressed evidence.

The district attorney's office calls the missing documents a mix-up, not misconduct. The prosecutor, Diana Farrell, says she never saw the documents until two years ago, and complains she has become a scapegoat.

However it happened, an innocent man was convicted on May 20, 1985. He stayed in jail through June 2, 1992, and the charges against him weren't dropped until November 10, 1994.

"I'm just happy to have him back," Cupeles says.

Question for retentionists: Though we can never know for certain, what percentage of convictions do you think have been handed down unjustly? Is the number of errant convictions significant enough to induce you to rethink your position on capital punishment? Is not the execution of the innocent the worst defect to which the death penalty is liable?

15. Case study: On his knees, police evidence expert Daniel Genty crouched across a muddy floor while his flashlight beam highlighted something moving. A small puddle was alive with tiny, squirming red worms. They were feeding on something, Genty concluded.

Genty probed into the muck with a small shovel. He pulled up an arm bone. The date was December 21, 1978. The crawl space was under the modest yellow house of building contractor John Wayne Gacy, a suspect in the disappearance of a 15-year-old boy.

Genty had entered the crawl space searching for the body of one person. In the next few days, twenty-seven bodies were unearthed on Gacy's 60 by 144 foot lot on Chicago's northwest edge; forty-five others had been dumped in nearby rivers. All had been killed from 1972 to 1978. The search was revolting beyond the imagination of the most macabre film.

Gacy stood trial in February, 1980. Jurists heard testimony about sodomy, sadism, and torture, the most chilling from victims who had escaped. Gacy lured teenagers with promises of high-paying jobs; he picked up gay men and male prostitutes with promises of sex. Testimony showed victims were frequently hand-cuffed and repeatedly raped. Most were strangled after Gacy tricked them into allowing him to slip a rope around their necks, then slowly twisted it tighter and tighter with a stick. Throughout the course of his appeals, one attorney felt that Gacy showed no remorse for his evil behavior.

Psychologists who evaluated Gacy traced his problems to a troubled childhood, with a violent father who drank excessively, verbally abused his son by calling him a sissy and demonstrating little love. They conjectured that his crimes were a ritualistic acting out of his childhood demons, with Gacy as the father and each victim the tormented son.

Question for abolitionists: If you were considering the death penalty, would you not advocate it for John Gacy? If you had been a taxpayer in Illinois, would you have felt better about paying for the food, shelter, and clothing of Gacy than about a swift and certain termination of his human existence?

16. If you would not advocate capital punishment for Gacy, would you advocate it for Timothy McVeigh or whoever else a jury might find guilty of the Oklahoma City Federal Building bombing, the worst domestic terrorist event in all of U. S. history?

17. How do you feel about televising executions for the general public to view? With capital punishment gaining favor, isn't it time supporters and opponents of capital punishment view firsthand the consequences of their convictions? In the abstract, capital punishment appeals to many as a tidy way of disposing society's garbage. In the flesh, capital punishment may seem barbaric. Would a tele-

vised version of reality make that case best of all?

18. Dexter is arrested in City X for a series of unsolved rapes and murders. There is enough evidence to convict him of some of these terrible crimes. Psychologists are dispatched to examine Dexter. They conclude that he has homicidal tendencies at least in part because he was severely physically abused by his parents when he was a child; he suffered from beatings and cigarette burns on his young body. Eventually, social workers placed him in a succession of foster homes where he felt neither loved nor cared for. As the years of his adolescence rolled by, the rage and hatred welled up inside his mind and heart. He thought of himself as a loser that no one could ever love. No one taught him proper ways to vent his anger toward his parents. He hated everyone who tried to help him and he hated himself.

Is any of this information relevant to the issue of whether Dexter deserves to be executed for his crimes? If so, how?

CHAPTER SIX

Obscenity, Pornography, and Censorship

In 1991, historians, political scientists, and other thoughtful Americans appropriately focused on the two hundredth anniversary of the Bill of Rights. Seminars, conferences, and new books which celebrated the theme of liberty focused on the purpose and significance of those individual freedoms which, as spelled out in the first ten amendments to the U.S. Constitution, still form the most comprehensive protection of individual freedoms ever written. It was the passage of the Bill of Rights by our Founding Fathers which allayed the deep concerns of opponents of the Constitution, thus leading to the completion of the ratification process.

That bicentennial year was a time of even more challenges to our traditional understandings of the Bill of Rights. Months earlier a strident controversy was stirred by an art exhibit which featured some explicit scenes and images as depicted through pictures taken by the late photographer Robert Mapplethorpe. The National Endowment for the Arts was under fire by certain congressmen and religious spokespersons for having funded certain controversial performances or exhibits. To thoughtful Christians, the vulgarity, violence, and sacrilege which masqueraded as "art" or "entertainment" as in, for example, 2 Live Crew's *As Nasty as They Wanna Be* or in Madonna's photographic collection *Sex*, released the following year, did not deserve the dignity of protection by the U.S. Constitution.

Since the 1950s, at least, the issues of obscenity, pornography, and censorship have elicited strong concern from thinking Christians. "Obscenity" and "pornography" are not biblical terms. The term "obscene," which literally could mean "offensive to the senses," has been traced to ancient Greek theatre, where any act deemed to sensual or too violent for public viewing such as murder or rape always took place "offstage" (*obscenus*). Similarly, "pornography" is of Greek origin, literally meaning "dirty writing" and the

155

word may have been first applied to the writings of prostitutes. One of the two roots for "pornography" is *porneia*, the Greek word in the New Testament which is translated "uncleanness" or "fornication." The ancient Hebrews considered careless public nakedness to be shameful and obscene (cf. Lev. 20:17-19) and biblical writers also condemned prostitution.

The development of institutional concern over obscenity and pornography in works of literature, art, drama, and entertainment has unfolded over many centuries. There were gods and goddesses of sexuality and fertility depicted in the art of several ancient cultures, most notably the Greek. Before the time of Jesus virtually every acceptable and unacceptable sexual practice that we know of today had been etched, carved, sculpted, or painted numerous times.

The one incident of book burning recorded in the New Testament as having been initiated by new Christian converts in Ephesus was not about obscenity, however, but about magic arts and witchcraft (Acts 19:19). The first *Index* by the Roman Catholic Church, designed to prevent "corruption of morals" and the spread of theological heresy, did not appear until 1559. The anemic influence of any Christian opposition to obscenity is obvious from the time of the Reformation through the French Revolution, especially when one examines the writings of Boccaccio, Poggio, Aretino, Brantome, and Casanova, as well as the practices of Marquis de Sade (1740-1814) and the debauchery of the European aristocratic classes.

The development of laws to regulate obscenity began in England with reports of obscenity convictions for public lewdness and exhibitionism beginning around the turn of the seventeenth century. There is little evidence of interest in obscenity by the states in the U. S. just prior and after the American Revolution; indeed, the influence of Puritan thought and practice on sexuality remained strong both in New England and on the frontier. Throughout the nineteenth century there was a small group of men who collected erotic materials and built private libraries, but the relatively secret nature of their interests posed no controversy for American institutions.

In the late 1800s pornography regulation was largely due to the tireless efforts of one person, Anthony Comstock, who, in 1873, organized the New York Society for the Suppression of Vice. Comstock soon became the national leader of a movement which succeeded in enacting laws that, with modification, survived over the subsequent decades. As a special agent for the Department of the Post Office, Comstock spread a wide net to arrest and convict many "offenders," including Margaret Sanger, whose printed materials on birth control led to her arrest and the arrest of her estranged husband. Comstock died in 1915, his movement lost fervor, and charges against Sanger were dropped.

THE LEGAL INTERPRETATION OF OBSCENITY AND PORNOGRAPHY

Prior to the 1930s, the Anglo-American principle concerning obscenity and pornography held that a publication could be banned solely because of the sexual content of the work, even of isolated passages. This principle held until a federal court ruled against the suppression of a work which was destined to become a modern classic, *Ulysses*.

In 1957 Samuel Roth, a distributor of non-traditional books such as the writings of D.H. Lawrence and Balzac, appeared before the Supreme Court to appeal his conviction for mailing obscene materials. The Court upheld Roth's conviction, ruling that obscene materials are those that are "utterly without redeeming social importance" and that, according to community standards, "the dominant theme of the materials appeals to prurient interests."

The decision did not end the debate. Controversy has risen over such works as *Fanny Hill* by John Cleveland, *Tropic of Cancer* by Henry Miller, *Lady Chatterly's Lover* by D.H. Lawrence, *The Story of O* by Pauline Reage, and even *Portnoy's Complaint* by Philip Roth. In the early '70s the pornographic X-rated movie *Deep Throat* received national publicity and stirred even more debate about defining and dealing with obscenity and pornography.

The First Amendment clearly protects works of serious literary value, all citizens concur, but can works that are totally obscene and/or pornographic be defined so as to be excluded from the broad umbrella of legal protection? The federal court system continues to apply a definition of obscenity laid down in a 1973 decision *Miller v. California*. In Miller, three standards were established to test materials for obscenity:

1. The average person, applying contemporary community

standards, would find that the work, taken as a whole, appeals to the prurient interest [in sex]; and

2. The work depicts or describes, in a patently offensive way, sexual conduct specifically defined by the applicable state [or federal] law; and

3. The work, taken as a whole, lacks serious literary, artistic, political, or scientific value.

In 1982 the Supreme Court ruled in *New York v. Ferber* that the standard of obscenity bears no relevance to child pornography. Since child pornography involves the sexual abuse of real children, the Court upheld a New York statute "prohibiting the distribution of material which depicts children engaged in sexual conduct without requiring that the material be legally 'obscene.'"

GOVERNMENT STUDIES OF PORNOGRAPHY

An eighteen-member commission, appointed in 1968 by President Lyndon B. Johnson, studied the issue of pornography and obscenity and presented its findings to the Nixon administration in 1970. The findings of the commission were highly controversial, as three members rejected the majority decision and filed sharply-worded minority dissents.

The commission's overall conclusion was that "empirical research designed to clarify the question has found no evidence to date that exposure to explicit sexual materials plays a significant role in the causation of delinquent or criminal behavior among youths or adults. The commission cannot conclude that exposure to erotic material is a factor in the causation of sex crime or sex delinquency." The minority report, believing that the majority decision was a "Magna Carta for the pornographer," claimed that the commission ignored or underrated important studies in its final report, such as the one that found a definite correlation between juvenile exposure to pornography and precocious heterosexual and deviant sexual behavior.

Given the controversial nature of the first presidential commission on pornography, it was not surprising when President Reagan's Attorney General Edwin Meese III in May 1985 established a new commission charged with the objective of determining the nature, extent, and impact on society of pornography in the United States. Meese noted that since the previous commission on pornography that its content had radically changed, with more and more emphasis on extreme violence; moreover, pornographic materials were more easily accessible, especially with the advent of videotaped materials and cable television.

For one year the commission gathered information, including testimony presented at public hearings in key U. S. cities. The controversial *Attorney General's Commission on Pornography Final Report* (July 1986), a report which had two thousand pages and ninety-two specific recommendations for a wide-ranging crackdown on pornography, concluded that exposure to some forms of pornography does lead to sex crime. Substantial exposure to sexually violent pornography, the commission reported, "bears a causal relationship to antisocial acts of sexual violence." Exposure also "leads to a greater acceptance of the 'rape myth.'" As defined by the commission, the rape myth is a complex of attitudes. These attitudes include: (1) sexual violence is less serious than other forms of violence, (2) victims are responsible for their victimization, (3) offenders are not fully responsible, and (4) "no" means "yes." The report offered similar findings about non-violent pornography that degrades women by treating them as sex objects, though it admitted that the evidence was "more tentative."

What are concerned Christian citizens to make of these studies, whose findings often point to varied conclusions regarding the effects of pornographic materials? Does a Christian really need some presidential commission or other reputable studies based on statistical research to buttress a strong stand against pornography?

Building a case against pornography on the basis of any link between erotica and sexual deviance and sexual violence may not be productive. The world is complex and most consequences we deplore are "caused" by numerous factors. One can adduce studies and "evidence" for both sides of this debate and, though it seems counterintuitive, there is strong evidence that people who are exposed to sexually explicit materials, be they art or pornography, are less rather than more likely to become sexual abusers or other deviants.

We should consider that a statistical correlation between two phenomena does not of itself establish a causal connection between them, and simply because one event follows another does not necessarily mean that the first caused the second. On the other hand, this is not to say there is no causal connection between erotic material and sexual behavior.

Simply stated: Christian ethics does not depend on the studies and research conclusions of any political or social organization.

THE COMPLEXITY OF MORAL CONCERNS ABOUT OBSCENITY AND PORNOGRAPHY

Obscenity and pornography raise numerous moral questions. Two of those general issues concern us here. The first issue may be phrased: Are sexually explicit and/or pornographic materials in and of themselves morally objectionable? Has a Christian acted immorally upon viewing and finding approval and pleasure in pornographic materials? We will state as clearly as possible the case against the use and support of pornographic materials from a Christian perspective. In an effort to be objective on all these issues we will state as fairly as possible the arguments offered by individuals who favor the use of pornography but, in all candor, it seems impossible to imagine that Christians could contend that use of hard-core pornographic materials was anything but morally objectionable.

The second issue concerns the legality of pornography. This issue may be stated as: Regardless of one's view of the morality of using obscene and pornographic materials, is it right for the any governmental agency to limit any adult citizen's access to such materials? In seeking an answer to this question, we will present "Arguments for Censorship" and "Arguments against Censorship."

These issues are separate and distinct. One could validly argue that the use of pornography is morally wrong and sinful and yet still believe that the government or any other organization has no constitutional leverage to deny consenting adults access to it. The two issues are often fused in the minds of many citizens who believe that arguments against pornography are used to justify censorship and arguments favoring pornography are used to protest censorship. Thoughtful Christians will make a distinction.

A BEGINNING POINT

The thoughtful Christian will begin with the biblical texts. Admittedly, there are biblical narratives and statements which, if explicitly dramatized or depicted, would seem violently pornographic or degrading to women. Stories such as Amnon's rape and defiling of Tamar, his brother Absalom's sister (2 Sam. 13:1-22) or a certain Levite's treatment of his concubine (Judg. 19:11-21:25), to cite just two examples, would make cinematic depictions of Joseph's temptation from Potiphar's wife, David's adultery with Bathsheba, or Delilah's seductiveness with Samson seem "PG" rated by comparison. The Old Testament's Song of Solomon has certainly elicited a wide range of emotional response over the centuries.

Since the Bible does not refer specifically to pornography, it is essential to examine the issue with a wider, more expansive perspective. Let's begin with several foundational declarations:

✦ God is the Source of human life and human dignity.

✦ Created goodness and beauty reside in the human being, both male and female.

✦ Sexuality is positively a gift from God to be treasured and enjoyed.

✦ Created by God and called by God to be his children, human beings are asked to refrain from hurtful and demeaning behavior (sin).

✦ God summons human beings into wholesome expressions of mutual affirmation and commitment, the most fulfilling of which is the lifetime union of a man and a woman in respectful, faithful marriage.

✦ Human flesh in all its forms, shapes, conditions, and colors is essentially good and provides a dwelling for the Spirit of God.

✦ Humans have been created with a distinct sexuality which gives them the exalted privilege of placing meaning and value in their reproductive and other sexual acts.

✦ Humans are created with the possibility for finding much joy and celebration in the expression of their sexuality.

✦ God demands responsibility in humans' sexual attitudes and behavior and warns them of the perils of abusing or distorting sexual responsibility.

✦ Christians especially are called to love others and to model positive, wholesome relationships for the world at large.

✦ Human love and and sexuality are appropriately celebrated within marriage, although individuals are free to seek the noble calling of remaining single.

✦ Our purpose in life is to seek and know God and live in relationship with God.

Do not these theological declarations and affirmations provide the foundation for moral consideration of sexual obscenity and pornography as well as other issues in human sexuality? Though we are created to be whole and healthy, our human nature leads us to act in ways that bring alienation from God, from others, and from ourselves. Biblical theology speaks out against such practices as lust, immoral sexual behavior, and public lewdness, and directs us to avoid any environment which renders us vulnerable to evil influences.

Pornography is indeed a serious, concrete manifestation of the fallenness of humankind and the pervasive nature of sin in all humanity. From a Christian perspective, it must be clearly opposed in public forums, pulpits, classrooms, and in private family teaching and modeling because it is essentially anti-human and anti-love, as well as anti-female.

KEY TERMS

Art —The process or the product of creative endeavor, as in painting, sculpture, music, dance, literature, and so forth. Art traditionally refers especially to making or doing things that imitate life, elucidate truth, or appeal to a sense of beauty. An artist may be financially rewarded for his/her artistic efforts, but such remuneration is not the only, or perhaps even the main, purpose of artistic endeavor.

Censorship —An act of official (governmental) suppression or deletion of any materials deemed to be objectionable and harmful either to individual citizens or to society as a whole. Censorship constitutes the legal imposition of restraints upon the production, publication, and sales of objectionable materials or productions.

Control —The practice of restraint or suppression by those who have no legal right to censor or threaten to censor but use persuasion and even coercion to restrict freedom of speech; it follows that those who control have no legal right to prosecute those who are deemed offenders. The objectives of censorship and control are the same but the means are different.

Exhibitionism —A perversion marked by the tendency to personal indecent exposure; it involves the intentional exposure of the genitals to members of the opposite sex under inappropriate conditions. In a broader sense, strippers and other "performers" who disrobe for cameras or live audiences may be considered exhibitionists. Exhibitionism may be connected with personal immaturity, interpersonal stress, or with some other psychopathology.

First Amendment—The first of our political society's famed Bill of Rights. The sparse language of the First Amendment seems perfectly clear: "Congress shall make no law . . . abridging the freedom of speech, or of the press. . . ." Yet a majority of the Supreme Court have never agreed that this "most majestic guarantee" is absolutely inviolable. Obscene material is basically excluded from the umbrella protection of the First Amendment. This exclusion rests on the Supreme Court's review of historical evidence surrounding freedom of expression at the time of the Constitution's adoption. The Court observed that blasphemy, profanity, and obscenity were colonial crimes, but obscenity was not a developed area of the law at the time of the adoption of the Bill of Rights. The difficulties which have arisen related to determining what is obscenity and pornography and what is not.

Obscenity —Words, depictions, or materials which are offensive to one's taste, disgusting, abominable, degrading, and/or loathsome. Ordinarily, people employ "pornography" and "obscenity" synonymously, yet there are depictions and materials which debase and dehumanize individuals but do not focus on sexual explicitness (there is an obscenity in gratuitous violence in the entertainment media, for example, or an obscenity of extremely bigoted or racist behavior toward others).

Pious Pornography —Explicit, yet "soft-core," depictions of sexuality or violence, often in more "respectable" media, which ostensibly have serious artistic or communicative intent but in reality intend to gain attention or exploit for commercial reasons.

Pornography —In general, pornography refers to any erotic and explicit representation or material that is intended primarily for the purpose of creating sexual arousal and curiosity and is produced solely for the purpose of profit or pleasure. The legitimate artist who paints or sculpts erotic pictures or figures which elicit an emotional response is not a pornographer because of the artist's artistic intent to depict truth or beauty rather than to exploit and dehumanize sex. Pornography separates the wholeness of one's person into different segments, mainly different body parts, and is therefore contrary to real enjoyment and acceptance of life. Violent pornography may attempt to glamorize and eroticize violence, power, humiliation, degradation, dominance, or mistreatment of any person, female or male.

Prior Restraint — Censorship before publication or exhibition.

Profanity —An act of debasing or defiling something that is holy; an irreverence or sacrilege, as in profaning the name of God.

Voyeurism —Broadly, the act of seeking sexual gratification by visual means; more specifically, the act of obtaining sexual gratification from seeing or witnessing nudity, seeing sexual organs, and seeing sexual activity. Often voyeurs are prying invaders of others' privacy.

KEY SCRIPTURES

Leviticus 18:22,23; Proverbs 23:7; Matthew 5:21, 27-30; Romans 1:24; 12:1-2; 1 Corinthians 6:15-20; Ephesians 5:1-9; Galatians 5:16-21; Philippians 2:5; Colossians 3:1, 5, 17; 1 Peter 2:2.

KEY ISSUES/ARGUMENTS
Arguments against Pornography

1. Pornography offends the right of privacy and each person's sense of individuality.

"Human beings were created as animals with a difference. They have a unique sense of individual privacy and a capacity for shame and embarrassment when this privacy is violated. Humans almost instinctively employ habits of behavior or dress to make certain their "private parts" are indeed private. This may vary from culture to culture, but in practically all primitive tribes male and female alike cover their private parts and do not engage in intimate sexual behavior before public gaze.

"As fellow humans we respect the individuality and privacy of others. Eating may not seem to be such a private act, but we do not stare at someone who is eating alone. We do not want television news cameras focusing on the final act of dying or on dead bodies.

"Obscenity consists in making the private public, in exposing to public view intimate and personal experiences of life for the sole purpose of arousing lust, inducing shock, or exploiting morbid interest. And in no area is this privacy violated so much as in sexuality.

"If we value individuality and the right to privacy — especially in an age when our burgeoning population and the electronic inroads into our daily lives make real privacy less attainable — then we as Christians must deplore the way in which the most intimate aspects of human life are denigrated by over-publicity."

2. Pornography distorts a basic healthy approach to sex.

"Pornography sends the wrong messages to everyone involved in the sordid business, whether producer, performer, or consumer. Rather than being "pro-sex" in a highly explicit way as some advocates of pornography would lead us to believe, pornography is actually "anti-sex." The pornographer's message: sex can be separated from a loving, caring relationship. To make sex totally impersonal is to dehumanize and cheapen it."

3. Pornography is the antithesis of Christian attitudes.

"True enough, the Christian church over the centuries has not always fostered candor on issues of sexuality and positive, wholesome attitudes toward sexuality. However, such an admission should not lead Christians to push the pendulum to the other extreme and offer uncritical endorsement and even celebration of every book, film, or play produced under the banner of 'new freedom.'

"In addition to distorting a basic healthy approach to sex by compartmentalizing it into a loveless activity, pornography also promotes an un-Christ-like attitude toward other people. The New Testament makes clear that the Christian life is a radically new life and that our hearts and minds are to be transformed away from worldly patterns of thought and behavior.

"Few demands of the new life in Christ are made clearer than God's expectation that we keep our minds and bodies from the impurities of fornication and lust. Certainly what we see and what we hear influences our behavior. One who frequently enjoys pornography will find his/her moral stamina to remain pure greatly diminished. No doubt different people react in different ways, but one thing is certain: pornography offers no deliberate encouragement to moral purity or steadfastness. No one can enjoy pornography and 'have the mind of Christ.'"

4. Pornography degrades and dishonors human dignity, especially of women.

"Pornography poisons our minds against other persons, degrades and dishonors the uniquely human dimension of life, and eventually cuts off lines of genuine communication. The Bible teaches us to love other persons and not use them for selfish purposes. And those who consume pornography come away cheapened and slighted in spirit, perhaps moving closer to self-loathing and self-disgust.

"As for the pornographic photographer, artist, or film producer, the focus is zoomed in for intense concentration on the genitals and accessory sex organs. The pornographer is concerned with ways these sex organs can be used to titillate, stimulate, or be stimulated. These sex organs are devoid of any other meaning — the other parts of the body, the personality, the mind of feelings have no place. Such views as are rarely seen by a near-sighted gynecologist are by their very nature created for the voyeur, or for supplying masturbatory fantasies to those who may feel deprived of, or dissatisfied by, normal and healthy stimulation.

"Pornography depersonalizes sex and exalts it for its own sake. It represents and feeds upon compulsive sexual occupation. Nothing of the sacramental dimension of sex is communicated. Pornography also ignores even the procreative aspects of human sexuality. It is not interested in the language of love, mutual commitment, or mutual revelation. In fact, the role of emotion must be completely divorced from the experience of the moment — it is sexual *activity* as opposed to *feeling* that is exalted. The experience of love is reduced to an interplay of sex organs.

"Pornography is especially degrading to women. Most pornography is produced by men for men and the central message is that women exist as sex objects, as playthings whose only purpose is the pleasure of men and that women actually enjoy rape; and other sexual aggressiveness. When women are treated as sex objects, all of society loses. Pornography is anti-feminist. It is anti-sex. It is anti-human."

5. Pornography is a factor leading to harmful personal behavior.

"All of us are affected by what we see and read, sometimes for the better and sometimes for the worse. Common sense and intuition tell us that the effects of pornography are for the worse.

"'No woman was ever seduced by a book' is an oft-repeated assertion by people who believe that pornography is harmless. That's true, of course, since books in the literal sense do not do anything, including seduce women. Books do, however, instill in their readers ideas and attitudes that later give birth to action, either good or evil. To claim that one's regular ingestion of pornography does not alter a person's attitude and perception of humanity in such a way as to be displeasing to his Creator is to claim something else!

"Yes, it's true that evidence linking antisocial and criminal behavior to pornography is open to varying interpretation, but it is sobering that child molesters and rapists have been discovered to be mass consumers of hard-core pornography."

6. Pornography can only contribute to a lowering of public morality within the nation.

"Among the most libertarian of us, few would grant that pornography and obscenity are harmless. To argue that artistic endeavor can lift up a society and give it renewed spirit and taste and then to deny that any prostitution of artistic expression has cultural consequences must be the height of inconsistency.

"Even if criminal behavior is not our only concern, consider the impact of increased promiscuity and sexual irresponsibility in this nation. The rate of premarital sex has never been higher. The same is true for adultery. Unwed teenage pregnancy has been near epidemic proportions in some urban areas. Consider the wide-ranging scope of sexually transmitted diseases. Not that pornography has caused all of these conditions, but it is clearly a part of a larger problem which has led to devastating consequences for our society."

Arguments for Pornography

1. Pornography can be beneficial as sex education for young people or uninformed older people.

"Everybody needs good sex education. Not everyone is going to purchase a dry, boring manual on sexual physiology and technique. Sexually explicit materials are readily available and are highly interesting. People can learn a lot from pornography."

2. Pornography can add excitement, enrichment, and new openness between married partners.

"Like it or not, a lot of respectable, church-going married couples purchase or rent sexually explicit materials and videos to add interest and excitement to their marriage. When boredom sets into the marital bedroom, something is needed to enhance discussion of sexual matters and liven up the action. Pornography has even been used by sex therapists to treat various sexual dysfunctions."

3. Pornography provides harmless pleasure and entertainment.

"There's one fact that moralists tend to forget: pornography brings pleasure to millions of people or else they would not spend money on it. Everyone needs a little pleasure and happiness in life. That's not to say that everything which brings pleasure is moral, but we can say that anything that brings millions of people harmless pleasure cannot be objectionable without clear and convincing evidence of physical and emotional damage."

4. Pornography is morally neutral since there's nothing morally objectionable about human sexuality.

"There's absolutely nothing immoral or sinful about the human body. All things that God has created are good in and of themselves. Human sexuality is good, both for human reproduction and human pleasure. Pornography is nothing more than sexually explicit material. Unless a book or movie advocates murder or rape or depicts such crime in a favorable light, then why oppose it on moral grounds? If you are uncomfortable with the frank and explicit nature of the material, then viewer discretion is advised. Your comfort level is no reason to raise a moral objection to anything."

5. Pornography provides a catharsis for sexual interest and energy which might otherwise be directed in unhealthy or anti-social behavior.

"There's some evidence to believe that sexually explicit materials prevent sex crimes by providing potential offenders with an outlet or catharsis for people who would otherwise act harmfully. If young adolescents had their curiosity satisfied by explicit sexual materials they would have less reason to learn more about human anatomy by exploiting others' bodies. Ideally, this learning comes through effective sex education, but pornography can perform the same function."

Arguments for Censorship

1. Constitutionally-guaranteed individual freedoms are not unlimited in this political society.

"None of us can be a pure, uncompromised civil libertarian. In several instances the government can play a paternalistic role in our lives. The government can tell us which drugs we can use and which are illegal. The government also compels working people to set aside funds for their retirement and the benefit of other citizens. It enforces safety regulations on employers. Public drunkenness, gambling and prostitution and even littering are still illegal most places. Motorcyclists are usually compelled under law to wear helmets for their protection in a crash. On and on we could go.

"Yes, drawing the line is a difficult thing to do. But obscenity and pornography that are patently offensive have no place in our society. We already have laws against child pornography. Women need protection as well. It's one thing to protect the right of others to voice dissent and unpopular views, but obscenity and pornography are about standards of human decency and not about social or political dissent."

2. Censorship of obscenity may protect us from crime.

"However strong the link between rape and other sexual abuse and pornography, common sense tells you there is some connection. The increase in reported rape in the last ten to twenty years is dramatic. Given the terrifying nature of sex crime, a society would be irresponsible not to censor obscenity as long as there is some kind of link.

"No society can afford to be utterly indifferent to the ways its citizens publicly entertain themselves. Bear-baiting and cock-fighting are outlawed only in part because of humane compassion for innocent, suffering animals. The most important reason such entertainment forms were abolished was because they debased, brutalized, and hardened the folks who gathered to witness such spectacles. Since pornography — especially performed pornography — is just as debasing and brutally destructive of human relationships, it too should be outlawed."

3. Laws serve an instructional and symbolic function in any society.

"Public opinion polls reveal that the majority of Americans favor tough controls on hard-core pornographic materials. Decent people are fed up with the glut of trashy sex on the newsstands and on the airwaves. They believe that such exploitation of sex will undermine Christian values. And until more convincing scientific proof is available to convince the majority of citizens that their

169

fears are ill-founded, majority views should prevail. Put simply, if the majority thinks censorship guards the quality of American life, the laws need to be on the books.

"Government can surely take a hand in the formation of public character. And why not? Laws must reflect the standards of any community. Censorship laws can teach a society that the organized community draws a line between art and pornography, the decent and the indecent, the permissible and the non-permissible. Exploiters and abusers may step over this line, but at least they are fully aware that a line exists. And even if censorship cannot be fully enforced, laws that reflect majoritarian ethics should remain on the books to teach upcoming generations what society values and what society instructs others to honor and respect."

Arguments against Censorship

1. Censorship is unjustifiable infringement of liberty.

"Censorship by its very nature implies that one group is superior to all other groups. It implies that one person or one group can exert their beliefs and values on other people. Few, if any, adults are willing to give censorship rights to some other person. We don't mind being someone else's censor, but we do not want someone else being our censor.

"America is the land of freedom and opportunity. The First Amendment to our Constitution is our most important amendment and it gives us several rights. Among our freedoms is the freedom to choose, to create, to learn, to view or read, even to make bad choices. In the hands of most people, pornography is harmless.

"Even though alcohol leads some people to do abusive and dangerous things, especially endangering the lives of innocent motorists and passengers, society does not ban drinking. Why should society censor books, films, and magazines, especially when the right to free expression is guaranteed in the Bill of Rights and is far more important than the right to drink?"

2. Censorship of obscenity threatens non-obscene material.

"When Christians get into the business of censoring or controlling, they run the risk of silencing an important message of an artist, even if it comes to them obscenely packaged. Some of the art forms are truly anti-religious and offensive to many Christians; on the other hand, to feel angry at God, angry toward religious authorities, or toward religious institutions is a fairly intense and widely shared emotion and as such deserves artistic depiction.

"While I may not appreciate certain depictions of Jesus, Mary, or the cross, as in the photography of Robert Mapplethorpe, one may understand them. True, there are performances that masquerade as art but are only charades. There is art that grabs attention but neither warms the heart nor addresses mind or spirit. One person's art is another person's poison. But I had rather err in generosity on the side of the artist than in caution on the side of the censorious public."

3. Censorship of pornography would not impact the most dangerous threats to the moral fabric of our society.

"True, adult magazines and X-rated videos are seen by increasing numbers of our citizens, but only a minority of Americans will be exposed to some of the more controversial publications and exhibitions.

"On the other hand, millions of our citizens will be exposed to gratuitous violence and sexual exploitation in general release motion pictures, movies which later make their way into our homes via cable or videotape. How many 'acted out' murders, shootings, rapes, and fist fights do you think the average American child will have seen by the time he/she reaches eighteen years of age? What about sex in advertising? Have you ever seen an ad for Calvin Klein? And what about all those tabloids and soap operas and romance novels and on and on? Don't you think that such 'pious pornography' influences sexual attitudes, behavior, and values far more than hard-core obscenity and pornography?"

"There's a lot of hate literature out there — material printed and circulated by the Neo-Nazis and the Ku Klux Klan, just to name two groups. Such 'literature' is protected by the First Amendment. Pornography such also be protected by the First Amendment."

SELECTED QUOTATIONS

We may define pornography, cross-culturally, as words or acts or representations that are calculated to stimulate sex feelings independent of the presence of another loved and chosen human being.

—Margaret Mead

I can't define it, but I know it when I see it.

—Justice Potter Stewart

Pornography, like rape, is a male invention, designed to dehumanize women, to reduce the female to an object of sexual access, not to free sensuality from moralistic or parental inhibition. . . . Pornography is the undiluted essence of anti-female propaganda. . . . It promotes a climate in which the ideology of rape is not only tolerated but encouraged.

—Susan Brownmiller

It is often asserted that a distinguishing characteristic of sexually explicit material is the degrading and demeaning portrayal of the role and status of the human female. It has been argued that erotic materials describe the female as a mere sexual object to be exploited and manipulated sexually. . . . A recent survey shows that 41 percent of American males and 46 percent of females believe that "sexual materials lead people to lose respect for women." . . . Recent experiments suggest that such fears are probably unwarranted.

—Presidential Commission on Obscenity and Pornography

The arts cannot thrive except where men are free to be themselves and to be in charge of the discipline of their own energies and ardors. The conditions for democracy and for art are one and the same. What we call liberty in politics results in freedom of the arts.

—President Franklin Roosevelt

Human freedoms are essentially subordinated to good morals and are safeguarded by them. A campaign for good morals is not an infringement upon freedom, but a preparation for the enjoyment of true freedom.

—Thomas J. Fitzgerald

We use a most unfortunate idiom when we say, of a lustful man prowling the streets, that he "wants a woman." Strictly speaking, a woman is just what he does not want. He wants a pleasure for which a woman happens to be the necessary piece of apparatus.

—C. S. Lewis

Until we look at pornography for what it is — not a First Amendment issue but a commercial product that violates the rights of women — and until we address this violation of women's civil rights, we will continue to have the mainstream culture affected by pornography.

—Norma Ramos

I wholly disapprove of what you say but will defend to the death your right to say it.

—Voltaire

If we truly believe in decency . . . surely the least we can do is protest the use of taxpayer's money to reward and subsidize utterly filthy, so-called art.

—Senator Jesse Helms

Where does it end? When do these people reach into the Bible and ban the Song of Solomon?

—Representative Major Owens

The misuse of any gift from God is to be denounced, and especially the sexual gift, which in most instances involves the rights and dignity of other people. Any misuse of sex that injures, demeans, or reduces another person to a mere tool for one's own satisfaction is clearly contrary to the Christian concept of the sanctity of personhood.

—Robert Bruce McLaren

The worst of all obscenities is the glorifying of war. War is the most dehumanizing of all human enterprises, not only in its effect upon those who are killed and wounded, but also in its effect upon those who do the killing and wounding.

—Kyle Haseldon

To vest a few fallible men — prosecutors, judges, jurors — with vast powers of literary or artistic censorship, to convert them into what Mill called a "moral police," is to make them despotic arbiters of literary products. If one day they ban mediocre books as obscene, another day they may do likewise to a work of genius. Originality, not too plentiful, should be cherished, not stifled. An author's imagination may be cramped if he must write with one eye on prosecutors or juries; authors must cope with publishers who, fearful about the judgments of governmental censors, may refuse to accept the manuscripts of contemporary Shelleys or Mark Twains or Whitmans.

Some few men stubbornly fight for the right to write or publish or distribute books which the great majority at the time consider loathsome. If we jail those few, the community may appear to have suffered nothing. The appearance is deceptive. For the conviction and punishment of these few will terrify writers who are more sensitive, less eager for a fight. What, as a result, they do not write might have been major literary contributions. "Suppression," Spinoza said, "is paring down the state till it is too small to harbor men of talent."

—Jerome Frank

I think that it can start the machinery going for change. I do in a way see myself as a revolutionary at this point. I think it will open some people's minds for the good, and that's enough, as far as I'm concerned.

—Madonna, commenting on her book *Sex*.

In a free society, it will often be appropriate for Christians to tolerate — even while witnessing against — what is highly offensive and an affront to themselves, others, or their God. But toleration is one thing; the government's imprimatur is something else.

—Stephen V. Monsma

DISCUSSION QUESTIONS AND BRIEF CASE STUDIES

1. "Pornography" is from Greek derivation, meaning "dirty writing," or low erotic art, or sexual obscenity. One person once defined pornography as "anything either written or in pictures which arouses sexual feelings." Such a definition is misleading and untenable, for it certainly does not take pornography to excite a lot of people, nor would it be easy to prove that excitation per se is wrong and shameful. By such a definition, art could be pornographic, e.g., Rodin's *The Kiss*, the *Venus de Milo*, and Michelangelo's *David*.

As noted earlier, the Supreme Court has offered three criteria for defining pornography: (1) The "average person, applying contemporary community standards, would find that the work, taken as a whole, appeals to the prurient interest." (2) The work "depicts or describes, in a patently offensive way, sexual conduct specifically defined by the applicable . . . law." (3) Taken as a whole, the work "lacks serious (artistic), political, or scientific value." By the Court's account, then, a work is obscene if, considered in terms of its appeal to the average person, it offends community standards because, taken as whole, it appeals to prurient interests and is without serious, artistic, political, or scientific value.

Are these definitions operational? Do all of our definitions about pornography leave room for a great deal of subjectivity? How do you personally define pornography?

2. Is it possible for a film or literacy work to have "serious value" but also to be pornographic? And, is it possible for a movie to depict nudity and sexual immorality while presenting a message that is morally good and positive? Consider, for example, Steven Spielberg's classic, and 1994's Oscar-winning, movie *Schindler's List*. Were the nudity, violence, and verbal profanity in this movie obscene to you? Were these elements pornographic? Should only adults see this movie?

3. Are parts of the Bible pornographic? Read the story of how Lot's two daughters seduced their father into an incestuous episode on consecutive nights in Genesis 19:31-36. Or read the poetry of the Song of Solomon that celebrates the joys of sexual love. Some Bible scholars believe this was addressed to the Queen of Sheba. Conservative and fundamentalist Christians have tried to de-eroticize the poetry and make it an allegory about Christ and the church. Whatever one's view, do you agree the Song of Solomon is

seldom used as a basis for preaching and teaching in the church?

4. What is obscenity? Is obscenity synonymous with pornography? What relevance does a cultural context have in defining obscenity?

5. What is art? What is the artist attempting to accomplish by his/her writing, painting, sculpting, photography, etc.? In what ways is the purpose of the artist at odds with the purpose of the pornographer?

6. Do you agree that no historical event or human experience should be "off limits" for treatment by the legitimate artist?

7. What is the essential message in pornography in general? What messages, for example, does pornography present about the relationship between sex and love? The dignity of individuals? The purpose of sex?

8. Explicit "hard-core" erotic materials can be easily labeled as pornographic. However, are there other kinds of material that are more easily available, which seem less offensive, but are pornographic in a subtle way? For example, state how you feel about the following:

(a) *Playboy* magazine?

(b) Romance novels?

(c) Men's magazines in fields of crime detection, hunting, motor sports, etc.?

(d) *Sports Illustrated* annual swimsuit edition?

(e) TV commercials for certain labels of perfume, jeans, beer?

(f) Television serial dramas (soap operas)?

(g) "Trash TV" talk shows that deal with sexual themes (aberrations, perversion, etc.)?

(h) Tabloids such as *National Enquirer?*

9. The presidential commissions on obscenity or pornography seem to be uncovering mixed data as to the impact of erotica on consumers. There is some evidence that pornography is a contributing factor to a criminal anti-social behavior, although establishing a causal link between pornography use and sexual abuse is a complex issue. There is other evidence that pornography provides little or no stimulus toward a person becoming a sex criminal. Is it reasonable to make a connection between pornography and sex crime? Can we trust our intuition on this issue? Is this data important to Christians in determining the moral status of pornographic materials?

10. Pornography is often criticized as treating women (and

sometimes men) as "mere sex objects." What do you think is meant by this expression, and is it a valid complaint? (Consider what Kant has said about treating other people as means to our own ends.)

11. Is the use of sexually explicit materials ever morally permissible? Consider differences in the following scenarios:

(a) A man purchases a *Playboy* magazine because he is interested in reading an interview with Rush Limbaugh.

(b) A married couple rents an explicit video which tapes a lecture and demonstration on sexual technique by another couple who happen in real life to be married.

(c) An adult man or woman purchases photographic art magazines containing nude pictures that art critics would consider in good taste.

(d) A young woman reads a romance novel which has a great deal of sexual explicitness.

(e) A single, middle-aged man subscribes regularly to several hard-core pornography magazines because they feature close-up pictures of female genitals, thus providing fantasy material for his masturbatory experiences.

12. Do you believe that objectionable sexual materials should be censored by government authorities? Who should be in a position to censor books, movies, music, photographs, and paintings?

13. Do you think the Founding Fathers had pornography in mind when they drafted a Bill of Rights which protects free speech? Does it really matter what they had in mind when they wrote the First Amendment?

14. How do you define "profanity"? Is it possible to delineate objectionable speech into words which are "profane" and others which are [merely?] "vulgar"? That is, are certain types of objectionable words worse than others? Why?

15. Laws prohibiting pornographic behavior and publications have been difficult to write and enforce. Is there any value in having a law that is difficult to enforce?

16. We turn now to a discussion of lust and fantasies. "Lust" is used both as a verb and a noun in the New Testament and the word is found about twenty-five times in New Testament Scripture. The key question is: What is lust? Should we define it as:

(a) evil and sensuous desire?

(b) unrestrained passion?

(c) mental approval to adultery? (i.e., the desire to sin, but lacking the opportunity.)

(d) "the first look is temptation, the second look is lust" (an old definition).

(e) Other? _____

17. Do you think that lust is such a commonplace and natural experience that all adults have lusted frequently, or have we defined the term too loosely?

18. Jesus spoke of a man lusting after a woman. Can only men lust? If one assumes that nearly all men have lusted, is there a woman who has not lusted?

19. Can we imagine that Jesus ever lusted? (If we label lust a sin, then can we not conclude that Jesus never lusted?) On the other hand, do you imagine that Jesus experienced sexual desire?

20. Is lust one of the "works of the flesh"? Are all works of the flesh related in some way to sex?

21. Are lust and adultery the same experience? If one knows he/she has lusted for someone, is there any reason why he/she should not proceed to physical adultery? Is the degree of guilt the same?

22. Is it lustful to be physically attracted to a person who is not your spouse? If we thank God for the beauty of the earth (hills, rivers, streams, flowers, trees, animal life, etc.), why can we not be grateful for the physical beauty of other people?

23. Is lust an experience of erotic stimulation and sexual desire in a context not involving one's spouse? Are feelings of being "turned on" a gift from God for us to enjoy life or are they a ploy from the devil to lead us down the path to perdition?

24. Most of us married men would concede that marriage did not wave a magic wand over our brain to speed fantasies away. Do sexual fantasies constitute lust? Would not repression of a fantasy be mentally unhealthy? Should not fantasies be brought to the fore-front of our consciousness as aids to understanding ourselves?

25. Are some fantasies, sexual or otherwise, inherently immoral — even though they do not lead to immoral actions? For example, what if a man frequently brings to his mind rape fantasies, even though he never has any strong urge to rape (and never does so)?

26. Would Philippians 4:8 have any relevance to our dealing with the issues of lust and fantasy?

27. Jesus urged us to take radical measures to correct this prob-lem. "If your eye offends you, gouge it out. . .If your hand offends you, cut it off." Of course, this is not literal. Surely Jesus is saying for us to dispense with the source of a major moral problem, what-

ever it may be. Provide a modern paraphrase that applies Jesus' words to a person's problem with lust.

28. Case study: On April 7, 1990, Cincinnati's Contemporary Arts Center and its director, Dennis Barrie, were indicted by a county grand jury. The Center was charged with two counts of obscenity, one for the pandering of obscenity and the other for the illegal use of a minor in nude photographs. The offending exhibit, a collection of photographs by the late Robert Mapplethorpe, had gained notoriety the previous summer when Washington D.C.'s Corcoran Gallery had withdrawn from a commitment to exhibit the collection.

Most of the exhibit's 170 photographs were favorably reviewed and uncontroversial. Seven others, however, had already created a national furor. Five black-and-white photos depicted homoerotic and sado-masochistic acts, including one of a man urinating into another man's mouth and one of a whip handle protruding from a man's anus. Two others depicted nude children in nonerotic poses. Obviously, many people were offended, even at the thought of such a display.

Philadelphia's Institute of Contemporary Art had organized the exhibit; it was shown in the City of Brotherly Love without incident. Had it not been funded by a grant from the National Endowment for the Arts, it probably would have been shown by the Corcoran Gallery without incident as well. The director of the gallery, however, concerned about the political impact of exhibiting the federally funded exhibit in the nation's capital, hoped to avoid controversy by pulling out. When artists objected, controversy erupted. While artists and their supporters claimed that the gallery was guilty of censorship, other groups objected to federal funding of works they considered obscene. Soon afterward, the Institute of Contemporary Art was denied further NEA grants. Later, artists seeking grants were required to pledge not to use the money to create, exhibit, or perform obscene works; and several controversial performance artists were denied grants on the basis of past works. Senator Jesse Helms has taken the lead in calling national attention to federal funding of controversial art.

(a) If you had an opportunity to see the controversial Mapplethorpe collection, would you view it? Why?

(b) Would there have been as much public outrage about this exhibit if Mapplethorpe had photographed explicit heterosexuality rather than homosexual themes?

(c) Does denying federal funds to controversial artists

amount to censorship, or is it just a matter of responsible overseeing the expenditure of taxpayer dollars?

(d. The law violated by the two nude photographs of children was intended to ban child pornography. Since the poses in the Mapplethorpe photographs were non-erotic and the photographs were taken with the permission of the parents, who were pleased with the results, should the law apply to them?

(e. Who should decide how NEA grants are distributed? Should it be peer review panels of artists? Should it be the taxpayers through their elected representatives? What about a blue-ribbon panel of professionals from various fields?

29. All Christians can become actively involved in stemming the tide of objectionable sexual materials. Below are some of the measures that could be taken:

(a) A public vow and commitment never to produce, present, distribute or consume pornographic material.

(b) Support family and sex education of children and adolescents.

(c) Pray for the individuals directly involved in the battle against pornography in all its varied forms; for the many innocent victims; for those who sell, produce, and distribute pornographic material;

(d) Educate themselves to become more aware of the impact that pornography is having on society;

(e) Withhold patronage from establishments that deal in or support pornography;

(f) Be actively involved in the public debate over pornography by contacting public officials, writing letters to the editors of magazines and newspapers, and speaking openly with friends, neighbors and family members, and in so doing, holding forth the biblical standards for sexuality.

Which of these strategies do you believe to be the most useful? Can you think of other strategies?

30. In April 1991 the author was invited to address a conference in Cleveland, Ohio, which was organized to discuss the theme "Beyond the First Amendment: Censorship, Art, and Moral Responsibility." The conference was sponsored by Case Western Reserve University's Center for Professional Ethics and the author was asked to address the audience as a member of the clergy.

The following four-paragraph excerpt provided the conclusion for this address:

"Christians have no simple and easy answers to the complex issues related to First Amendment rights of free expression. Who among us can formulate a plan of action which can be claimed as the Christian solution? While Christians are called to preserve, perpetuate, and share moral values drawn from their families of faith, as well as issue prophetic judgment against severe threats to those values, they may also believe in zealously guarding the open American marketplace of ideas and free expression.

"Christian citizens should be informed, discuss moral issues, and take action which, in ways either real or symbolic, will clearly communicate their opposition to objectionable performances, materials, and exhibits. The entertainer who conscientiously withdrew from a "Saturday Night Live" production which featured a comedian notorious for lewd and sexist remarks is one example of such personal, positive protest.

"Perhaps the best solution for concerned Christians is merely to ignore that to which we object. If, for example, a publisher is exercising poor judgment in publishing a book which unnecessarily offends, the best way to register disgust would be to ignore the book. To be ignored is more painful for an artist than to be banned. A call for a boycott or demonstration can become self-undermining, sending unsympathetic readers or viewers straight to bookstores, theatres, or museums to buy the book or see the production or exhibit.

"We can truly vote with our dollars for works of art which celebrate and advance humane values rather than desecrate and undermine human worth and dignity. And we can make wise personal choices for ourselves and for our families which move us even closer in the direction in which our Lord is leading us."

Do you agree that Christians can vote with their dollars? Do you believe that demonstrations and publicly-announced boycotts may become counter-productive by enhancing curiosity and even support for an objectionable exhibit, movie, or performance? Is it best to simply ignore the phenomena that we object to or will that only make matters worse?

CHAPTER SEVEN

Work: Vocation, Corporate Responsibility, Personal Responsibility

Ivan F. Boesky was once notorious as Wall Street's best known speculator in corporate takeovers. At the same time, Michael R. Milken was Wall Street's biggest behind-the-scenes junk bond chief at Drexel Burnham Lambert Inc. Before the decade of the '80s had ended, a "decade of greed" according to many observers, both Boesky and Milken had been thoroughly discredited with the American public and sentenced to jail terms and to pay hefty fines.

Boesky was often behind the scenes during those boom months in the stock market, pulling the strings and making deals that enhanced his own personal wealth. After exposure of his illegal insider trading, Boesky was soon telling shocking tales of corruption of Wall Street financiers and disclosing wrongdoing by a number of major securities firms. In December 1987 Federal Judge Morris Lasker sentenced Boesky to three years in jail; additionally, the former tycoon had already paid a $100 million civil penalty and faced scores of lawsuits.

Milken played a major role in transforming the world of American business and finance by making junk-bond financing the tool of choice for corporate raiders. Through his manipulation of the market and destruction of the records of his shady transactions, Milken made himself fantastically wealthy and turned his firm into a Wall Street giant. In 1988 the Securities and Exchange Commission brought civil complaint and criminal charges against his firm. Due to his heavy involvement in illegal deals and market fraud, Milken felt the full force of federal racketeering law against him. In April 1990 he pleaded guilty to six felonies — including conspiracy, securities fraud, mail fraud, and filing false tax forms — in return for federal prosecutors dropping the remaining ninety-two charges and granting immunity against further prosecution. Milken was given a prison sentence and a record $600 million in penalties.

While Americans were exposed to the names of Boesky, Milken, and other Wall Street scandals, millions were surely perplexed about the nature of business laws, the complexity of business scandal, and the demands of business ethics. How vastly different our world of work and vocation from biblical times in which families lived simple lives, enjoyed no luxuries, and six days a week watched their men head to the pasture to tend sheep, to the field to tend a crop, to the lake or sea to catch fish, or to some shop to craft a product or provide a service!

There can be no doubt: Work is the defining principle in most adults' existence and identity. Whenever we meet someone for the first time, the next question after "Your name is . . . ?" is most likely to be "And what do you do?" Work is a vivid sign that there is life in us. Work expresses our character and our personality. While generations past labored with sweat and soreness for the sole purpose of being able "to eat," work for current generations has acquired new meanings and significance. Most of us do not work simply for the basic necessities of food, clothing and shelter — indeed, we can accomplish that in a few hours a week — but we work for fulfillment, for the good life for ourselves, for the good life for our mates and children.

Of another fact there can be no doubt: one's work site can be the environment where some of the toughest ethical choices of one's life must be made. In most jobs, ethical decisions are made each day, most being made almost unconsciously and others being made after much careful deliberation and reflection.

Consider your own job or profession and place of employment. Do you interact with other people? Do you supervise the work of other people? Do you make decisions about material goods and services? Do you have input into decisions about hiring and firing? Do you gather and have access to confidential information about some of your co-workers? Do you attempt to maximize profits? Do any habits in your personal and private lifestyle impact the quality of your work life? Does your company provide supplies that you or your family could find useful? Have you ever had charges regarding discrimination in hiring and firing or sexual harassment leveled against you? Have you ever given or received disciplinary action?

Enough. "Yes" to any of these questions means that we bring our moral values and principles into the work place and into our professional life. Sometimes the issues are easily resolved. At other times the issues are as stressful and gut-wrenching as anything we have ever faced. But they must be faced and resolved.

Business ethics is now a well-established academic subject. Most colleges and universities offer courses in business ethics and text-books abound in the subject. Some cynics scoff at the idea of business ethics, jesting that the concept is as much an oxymoron as "jumbo shrimp" or "government efficiency." Our concern in this chapter is to broaden the scope of business ethics to work in general, but only to provide an overview of some basic concepts, issues, and definitions.

AN OVERVIEW OF WORK AND PHILOSOPHY ABOUT WORK

In a general sense work is any form of producing something of value, whether or not one is compensated for it. We often declare that we "have to work for a living," and conclude, grudgingly on many Monday mornings, that work is one of the necessities of life to "keep body and soul together." There is always the fantasy of being rich from birth and "not having to work one day in a life-time" and that such an existence would be paradise. Such daydreaming misses the place of work in our lives, our happiness, and our character development.

The concept of work is taught in the first narrative of Holy Scripture. Arduous work, not work per se, was the punishment leveled by God for the sin of Adam, the prototype for the entire human family. Unfortunately, the notion that work is a curse upon the human family is mistakenly accepted in popular culture as an idea that is rooted in biblical theology.

The geographical setting for the biblical treatment of vocation is far away and long ago. Work life in the Garden of Eden and in generations afterward was carried on in a primitive rural setting, a simple agricultural economy, bleak and grim, where men eked out of dry soil an existence at the level of bare subsistence. God called the human family to cultivate the earth and exercise dominion over all life forms. Generations later, the exalted view of work was encoded into the Decalogue: "Six days you shall labor and do all your work. . . . You shall not steal. . . . You shall not covet. . . ." (Exod. 20:8-11, 15, 17). Consequently, the Bible is filled with stories about peasant workers — their toils, their troubles, their needs, their anxieties, and their triumphs. Thus, one reads about prayers for harvest, prayers for rain, prayers for nets filled with fish.

Evidence of trading exists in the Middle East as far back as the

Sumerian civilization, which flourished almost three thousand years before Christ. Weapons, jewels, household goods, and slaves were offered for barter. In ancient Greece, Aristotle, the most influential philosopher and writer of antiquity, theorized about the rules of trade and the nature of "distributive justice." He made a distinction between ordinary household trading, which he called *oecinomicus* (from which we get "economics") and trading with the idea of making a profit, which he called *chrematiske*. In ancient civilizations the principle that those who produce the wealth should keep it was not known. Instead, the wealth would go to military generals and powerful statesmen, to religious leaders, and to others who do not "produce" anything at all; in essence, those who toiled were rarely the ones who reaped.

In the New Testament there are stories of men who were scribes, rabbis, tax collectors, tentmakers, teachers, statesmen, and military leaders as well as farmers and fishermen. In many ways, Christianity has always been the religion of the working classes. The people of Jesus' day were astonished that an apprentice carpenter could become such an authoritative teacher ("Is not this the carpenter . . . ?"). The Apostle Paul, a tentmaker as well as a missionary, summed up the ancient world's philosophy of work concisely: work or starve (2 Thess. 3:10). In another epistle this tentmaker-missionary comments that not many high and noble by the world's standards answer the summons to Christian faith (1 Cor. 1:26-27). Interestingly, next to none of the leading New Testament figures earned their living in a church job.

In the Middle Ages the ancient prejudice against business affairs become more deeply rooted because of the religious ideology which supported it. The real calling of life is the salvation of souls and business was but a temporary matter, and even a danger, compared to personal salvation. Medieval thinkers considered what moderns call "ambition" to be avarice and what moderns call "business sense" to be greed. Trade was permissible, of course, but an attempt to reap profits was considered usury. Spiritual callings were considered the noblest professions of all, and wealth was suspect for "it is easier for a camel to pass through the eye of a needle, than it is for a rich man to get into the Kingdom of Heaven."

The distinction made in the Middle Ages between "sacred" callings and "secular" callings came under serious critique by the Protestant reformers. One implication of Martin Luther's exposition of justification by faith is that such faith is bestowed by God's grace regardless of one's merit or station, whether one wears a clerical robe and collar or overalls and flannel shirt. Grace comes to anyone, not just to "sacred" workers, just as God's announcement of the Incarnation was announced first to shepherds in the fields rather than to priests and scribes in the temple. Any common needful work becomes the occasion for the fulfillment of one's calling to God and, according to Luther and Calvin, all callings were "sacred" callings. Calvin contended that one need not enter a monastery to serve God, for the entire world is God's monastery.

In modern times the industrial and technological revolutions of Western Europe, the United States, and Japan have overturned the mode of work by substituting machines for the hand, the factory for the farm, the sprawling urban complex for the village and small town. Products of every conceivable usage are produced in mass quantities. Productivity has increased enormously. In recent years the philosophies of "Total Quality" and participative management have affected systems of work and styles of interaction on the job.

The Industrial Revolution was undergirded by the Protestant work ethic, an ideology which attempted a marriage between capitalism and Protestant doctrine. The "ethos" or spirit of capitalism was expressed in the virtues of initiative, individualism, hard work, thrift, self-discipline, accumulation, and investment. Such beliefs and values were characteristic of middle-class entrepreneurs and had been forwarded to the early industrial period as duties by such popular philosophers as Benjamin Franklin.

The gospel of work, calling for strenuous effort, frugality, shrewdness, and rugged individualism, soon became the gospel of wealth, adopted in the nineteenth century by a Scottish Presbyterian named Andrew Carnegie, who felt it his vocation to make money hand-over-fist to the glory of God. A popular slogan of wealthy business leaders at the turn of the twentieth century was "Make all you can, can all you make, give away all you can." With the latter part of the slogan, many capitalists were convinced that the good ends of philanthropy would justify whatever hard bargains and ruthlessness were required as means of getting money.

RECAPTURING A BIBLICAL SENSE OF VOCATION

Is it possible to recapture a biblical sense of the vocation? Regrettably, the word "vocation" or calling has come to mean no more than a way of describing how a man or woman earns a living, what one does when he/she is not on vacation. The word "vocation" is the latinized form of the Teutonic-English word "calling." "To call" has two principal meanings: (1) to give a name to something or somebody, and (2) to summon. Both of these usages appear in the Bible (cf. 1 John 3:1; Isa. 43:1; Hosea 11:1; Isa. 49:1-3). The Apostle Paul employs both senses of the word when he writes, for example, of "the prize of the high calling of God in Christ Jesus (Phil. 3:14), or of the peace of God "to which you were called in one body (Col. 3:15). To the Ephesians the same writer admonished that Christians "walk worthy of the calling" in which they were called (4:1).

In view of the many Scriptures on calling, does this mean that God calls us to some special vocation such as plumbing, farming, teaching, selling, or engineering? Few would contend that their present employment is the only job they are capable of handling or the only job in which they could find fulfillment and contentment. Fewer still would contend that they entered their present vocation through a sudden and vividly clear revelation from God who told them what work field to enter and that they had an instant impulse to answer and obey. Even a good many who settle in Christian ministry will admit they tried other professional careers first and eventually entered pulpit ministry with much uncertainty and skepticism.

The vocation to which Christians are called is much more general, more encompassing, and more noble, than the calling to any specific form of employment, such as mechanics, law, medicine, carpentry, and so forth. God calls us through his Word to be his children, his friends, and to seek to bring others into this realm of fellowship through a witness in the world of words and deeds. Once we have been able to accept this higher calling, our specific employment in a community is merely a means of furthering in the best way we can the goals of the higher commitment. Paul was employed as a tentmaker, but his higher vocation or calling was to the faithful dissemination of the good news.

THE WORK ENVIRONMENT

Because most work is performed for financial compensation and is done outside the home, we tend to think of the morality of business and work as simply doing a job honestly — a fair day's work for a fair day's pay. Yet the work environment now provides a context for interpersonal relationships with supervisors, colleagues, clients, and members of the general public. With the movement in the United States away from a production toward a service economy, with blue collars exchanged for white collars, greater numbers of people will find themselves in close proximity and frequent interaction with other men and women.

Collegiality is a virtue that is essential for successful and highly satisfying work relationships. Collegiality means more than refraining from certain harassing or insulting behavior toward one's colleagues. Collegiality is basically a special kind of connectedness which is strengthened by bonds of mutual respect and cooperation for the people with whom one works. These bonds are nurtured and strengthened by integrity and sincerity in communications between parties, by words of encouragement and support between work partners, by a willingness to work together and support one's colleagues in pursuit of a worthwhile goal, and by little acts of good will and kindness toward one's colleagues.

The issue of loyalty raises serious ethical concerns. Basically, loyalty begins with fidelity in discharging one's assigned duties and expands to include a sincere affection or sentiment for one's employing firm or organization and for one's colleagues. Loyalty may also entail "going the second mile" or devoting extra time and energy to company goals or assignments, as well as taking special pride in services rendered or workmanship. Loyalty seems to be inherently good, and thus a virtue, but its practice must be placed in the context of corporate mission, company expectations, and standard operating procedures.

Collegiality and loyalty can have negative consequences. One can spend more time socializing with co-workers than handling work assignments. Combined with a legitimate interest in keeping a job, one can do whatever the supervisor orders, even if it is dishonest, unethical, or at the expense of the public good. Loyalty also presumes the morality of institutional or organizational goals; for example, one might not imagine "loyal pimps" or "loyal racketeers" or "loyal drug suppliers," even "loyal Nazis," since there is no moral obligation to traffic in public vice, corruption, or to serve Hitler.

KEY TERMS

Bribe — Remuneration for the performance of an act that's inconsistent with the work contract or the nature of the work one has been hired to perform.

Capitalism — Ideally, an economic system in which the major portion of production and distribution of goods and services is in private hands, operating under a profit or market system. A capitalist system is in contrast with socialism, an economic system characterized by public ownership of property and a planned economy. The key features of capitalism: existence of business companies; a profit motive as the reason for the company's existence; open competition among business firms in the free market; private property and private control over basic economic assets and productive resources.

Collegiality — A relationship of colleagues who share almost equally in authority and responsibility. In a work place, collegiality might involve a basic respect for colleagues, mutual appreciation for each other's work, a sense of connectedness by shared mission and common commitment, and a spirit of cooperation toward achieving common goals.

Corporation — An organization owned by its stockholders — interested individuals or other organizations who contribute capital to the corporation in return for shares (partial ownership) in the corporation. Corporations are legal persons with rights and obligations; they can own property and enter into contracts; they can sue and be sued in civil court, and they can be tried in criminal court. Stockholders control over a corporation is usually indirect.

Corporate Culture — A general constellation and mindset of shared beliefs, values, mores, customs, behavioral norms, and standard ways of conducting business that are unique to each corporation. Corporate culture may be both explicit and implicit, and its nature is determined more by the beliefs and decisions of high-level managers than by any other party within the corporation. Corporate culture may be a factor that makes one company work while another one languishes.

Kickback — A percentage payment to a party who is in a position to influence or control a source of income.

Laissez faire — An economic policy which opposes any form of government interference in business; the French phrase means "let [people] do [as they please]." Libertarians typically agree with Adam Smith that unregulated capitalist behavior best promotes everyone's interests.

Loyalty — A faithfulness and allegiance to any of the following: one's calling, one's employer, one's company or corporation, one's colleagues, or one's clients. One's loyalty leads to faithfully discharging responsibilities toward these parties.

Nepotism — The practice of showing favoritism in employment practices and employee relations to relatives and close friends. Nepotism raises serious moral concerns regarding both managerial responsibilities and of fairness to other employees or job applicants.

Norm — A working principle that in some way is accepted by all or most of an organization as a standard for decision-making, but may not be written or promulgated officially.

Profession — Professions are occupations assumed by a limited number of people and which require advanced education and specialized training, sophisticated skills, and commitment to service to some vital public good. Usually, professionals develop relationships with clients based on caring, consultation, and consent. Because of the specialized nature of professional services and the wide variety of possible services and courses of action, as well as fees charged for same, moral dilemmas arise frequently for professionals.

Proprietary Data or "Trade Secrets" — Special private information that can affect a firm's competitive standing in the free market. A "trade secret" is any formula, device, pattern, or special information which is peculiar to one business firm thus giving it advantage over competitors who do not know or use it.

Protestant Work Ethic — A philosophy about vocation and work which emerged from the theological writings of the great Protestant reformers, such as Martin Luther and John Calvin. Key elements of the "Protestant Work Ethic" include these notions: (1) All work, not simply the ministry of "holy men," is dignified; even the menial becomes holy; (2) all persons are held accountable for integrity in their work, under the eye of the Lord of the universe; (3) all work thus becomes serious, therefore one must work with diligence and care from dawn to dusk; (4) the virtuous worker demonstrates frugality and simplicity in lifestyle, because nothing should be wasted on sins of the flesh; (5) there is meaning and purpose to work, even work that seems like menial operations; (6) the laborer should give liberally to charity; and (7) the inevitable fruit of one's labor will be material prosperity, for indeed "God helps those who help themselves."

Responsibility — A position of trust which involves accountability, answerability, sometimes liability but also rewardability. Typically it includes authority, benefits, and superior-subordinates relationships.

Vocation — The work in which a person is regularly employed, often with a sense of compelling inclination or divine calling.

Work — In a general sense, any form of expending energy to produce something of value, regardless of whether one is paid for it. In a narrower and more common usage, work is an activity for which the laborer receives compensation, financial or otherwise, and that most frequently occurs outside the family and home.

KEY SCRIPTURES

Genesis 2:15; Exodus 20:8-11, 15, 17; Luke 10:7; Ecclesiastes 9:10; 2 Thessalonians 3:10; Colossians 3:17-24.

KEY ISSUES/ARGUMENTS
Is American business ethical? (Yes!)

1. The image of the unethical businessman is based on stereotypes.

"Businessmen have always had bad press in this country. Business is usually depicted as shady dealings between two dishonest, conniving parties. Think of any movies that have dealt with business, movies such as *Wall Street* or *Working Girl*, to name only two. Don't these movies always depict at least some major roles in the plot development as non-principled, manipulative business operators?

"The businessman has rarely been treated with accuracy and fairness in television or movies, two media which exert strong influence on the popular mind. How many movies or programs have you seen which depicted businesspersons as loving, caring individuals who are devoted to their family and their church? Or who become moral heroes? Or who donate large sums to charity or to worthwhile civic projects? Or who pursued cultural and educational goals as well as profit margins? Or who would choose fidelity to a mate rather than a secret rendezvous with a lover?

"The reason for this unfairness, in part at least, is that the drama and fiction written for production is the product of artists who have little experience in the workaday business world. The lifestyle and values of artists in general places them at odds with businesspeople who make deals and work for profits. How can we expect them to entertain a fair and positive view toward business life?"

2. There is a long-standing but unfair bias against businessmen.

"The stereotypes of businessmen that people see in the entertainment media are merely symptomatic of a much deeper bias against business professionals. Such a bias is rooted in great historical documents.

"The Greek philosophers believed that the truly happy life came in terms of one's intellect, especially dialectic with eager students and quiet contemplation. Jesus himself seemed to view wealthy people with great suspicion, telling one to sell all his possessions and give to the poor and follow him, and then warning all his disciples about the immense difficulty of a rich man entering heaven. In general, the Bible seems to oppose the loaning of money for the price of fair interest. And Karl Marx, whose political and economic doctrines fueled a communist revolution, contended that under capitalism the workers are exploited by unscrupulous bosses and factory owners who reap obscene profits by the sweat of others' brows. Students of American history know about the Rockefellers, the Vanderbilts, the Carnegies, the Mellons, and other wealthy industrialists who became obscenely rich under a laissez-faire system.

"True enough, business organizations are concerned with profit. And true enough again, business corporations can seem to be impersonal because they exist separately from the people associated with them. However, one cannot feature a world that operates smoothly without businesspeople and business corporations. We cannot all be islands with no connection to anyone else or any group. Furthermore, while a corporation is not something that can be seen or touched, it does have prescribed rights and legal obligations within the community it serves. Like you or me, a business organization may enter into contracts and may sue or be sued in courts of law. Both individuals and organizations are subject to the laws of the land. If business affairs, capitalization, and all normal transactions that go with the business world are evils, then they are surely necessary evils."

3. Businesspeople need no more regulation than any other profession.

"If you examine the ledger of sins of which businesspeople are guilty you will discover that, alas, these are the same sins that are committed by people in all other walks of life. There's a theological reason for this — the Bible tells us that every man and woman is a sinner. All of us break either the letter or the spirit of some of the Ten Commandments. Folks who run corporations, own businesses, and invest money have no more monopoly on sin than do folks who teach school, practice law or medicine, or repair automobiles. And, quite possibly, a thoroughly dishonest man could last longer in preaching and teaching than he could in managing a business.

"We need to stop thinking of the quest for profit as evil. Profit in the form of money is the lifeblood of our capitalist system. Sure, there are businessmen who seem to have an insatiable appetite for more and more money, but all of us have economic self-interests. There are people outside the field of business who have an insatiable appetite for power or for control of others or sex or food. What's worse?"

4. The free market system ultimately brings a sense of justice and fairness to all businesspeople.

"Most of us understand how the free market system works. Each of us is free to provide a service or manufacture a product and offer it to the public at a price the producer deems to be fair. Then, each producer will be judged by his/her peers. Our goods and services will be evaluated by consumers who will meet our price if they feel that, given all the other factors (their need, their ability to pay, the nature of competing goods and services, etc.), our offerings make a "good buy." This is the ultimate judgment on the value of the fruit of our labor.

"Is not the general public at times uninformed, biased, ignorant on certain subjects, and easily swayed by advertising? The answer is yes. But that's the way the system works for all businesspeople. Do we have a product or service that other people need or want? If the answer is yes, these consumers will reward us handsomely and render us successful as a businessperson. If the answer is no, it matters not that we have labored long and hard over a product that we dearly adore. The customer renders a verdict. The playing field is level. The rules of the game are fair. The customer calls the shots.

"Consider how the free market system keeps businesspeople on their toes. Free competition, said Adam Smith in his classic *Wealth of Nations* (1776), is the regulator that keeps a society from degenerating into a mob of ruthless profiteers. When all individuals have equal access to raw material and markets, all of us are free to pursue our own interests. As we pursue our own interests, however, we run smack into others similarly motivated. If any of us allow blind self-interest to run unrestrained, we will quickly find ourselves beaten out by a competitor who, let's say, builds a better mouse trap, charges less, or provides a better service. Free competition and the open market are the best regulators of individual economic activity."

5. Corporations realize that responsibility goes hand-in-hand with power and that they owe something back to society.

"Corporations now realize that they do not exist in a vacuum. They exist in a society and they cannot be oblivious to the ills of society. Corporate leaders know that society faces an array of social problems. There are major changes in the work force. There are increasing number of married couples where both spouses work, for example. The stresses of double-income marriages and raising a family certainly impact a business, therefore many companies are providing assistance in child care. Also, the American economy is experiencing a shift from manufacturing to service industries; therefore, some companies have provided for counsel and retraining of employees for new jobs.

"The largest American corporations have become multinational in operation and they take in more money than governments of most countries have to spend. These corporations are beginning to realize they owe something in return to a society which gives them the freedom to function."

6. Business corporations know that social responsibility is in their best interests, therefore they are increasingly becoming more socially responsible.

"Corporations and their shareholders now realize that they have common interests with the remainder of society. They know that we're all in this thing together. Some critics of business have contended that businesspeople don't care about poverty but, truth is, they know if poverty increases consumers will not have the revenue to purchase goods and services. Businesses and corporations have to be as concerned about crime as the rest of us. Corporate leaders know that if they don't treat their employees or the consumers fairly they risk labor organization and strife, consumer boycott, and additional governmental regulations and red tape. No business wants any more of that."

Is American business ethical? (No!)

1. The number of business scandals seem to be rising.

"There seems to have been an eruption of questionable and

sometimes downright criminal behavior throughout corporate America. Sure, all statistics are suspect, but consider the factors that put pressure on today's businesspeople and their employees: plant closings and downsizings, corporate mergers, rise of both domestic and foreign competition, the number of young graduates entering the work force each year, dwindling natural resources which drive costs upward, and the increase in the cost of living, to cite only a few factors.

"The result of these changes in society and the economy: the fear of losing status and/or jobs. Therefore, why not juggle the sales reports to make a better impression? Why not misrepresent product claims to gain more sales? Why not cut corners in laboratory testing? Why not abuse a competitor? Why not falsify an internal audit? After all, time is of the essence. And if you don't look out for 'number one' nobody else will."

2. The interest in business ethics does not guarantee an enhanced moral responsibility in the world of business.

"True enough, there are increasing numbers of business schools offering courses in business ethics and there are companies which have ethics programs and ethical guidelines in place. However, there have been major scandals at corporations which had substantial ethics programs in place for several years. Whether or not ethical programs are in place, all the newly learned ethical guidelines can be shelved when an employee is convinced that he/she must be perceived as a top performer or be laid off. Nobody knows how many high-level managers are intentionally dismissing ethical guidelines when considering questionable acts simply because those actions are paying financial dividends."

3. Much recent corporate restructuring and business decisions have been accomplished with little or no regard for consequences on people.

"Corporate leaders who have been desperate for greater profits have made decisions which have displaced workers and adversely affected families. Many job reductions have been necessary, the result of poor business management, but at least some top managers have axed employees to pump up short-term profits or impress investers. Companies which expect a high measure of loyalty from their employees may be loathe to extend any measure of loyalty to their employees.

"Corporations have turned to exploit emerging markets overseas, often dispatching a management team into a foreign business culture where bribery, game-playing, disregard for patents, and sloppy accounting are a way of business life. We all know automobile manufacturers who decided it was cheaper to risk the lives of innocent motorists and their passengers than to redesign their vehicles. How many companies would really care about the toxic wastes and pollution they create if the government did not keep a close eye on them?"

4. Corporation shareholders believe that corporate social responsibility is both unfair and economically irresponsible.

"Why do people buy stock in the first place? To improve the environment? To solve social problems? To end pollution? Of course not! People invest with a company because they believe it will bring the best return on their money. If investors and shareholders wanted to right the ills of society or improve the environment they could more directly address these concerns by contributing huge sums to such organizations as United Fund, Greenpeace, or Habitat for Humanity.

"Many investors are ordinary working people who buy stocks to prepare for their retirement years or to have a nest egg to handle some unexpected financial setback. To contend that corporate leaders should chip away at the legitimate earnings of ordinary citizens, all in the name of social progress, is grossly unfair to them.

"Furthermore, corporate social responsibility is bad economics. A corporation is like an individual; each has the right to pursue, within the confines of the law, private economic interests without the burden of social responsibility. A social agency should do what it does best, namely help people, and a corporation should do what it does best, namely provide goods and services to profit its management, employees, and investors."

5. Corporate leaders do not know how a socially responsible corporation should act.

"How can American business be more ethical when it does not know how to be socially responsible? A business is not a church. It is not a school. It is not an institute for the study of social problems. It is simply an organization attempting to make a profit.

"Even if a corporation could identify all the social woes of the society in which it conducted operations, how would it know what to do about those ills? Even social scientists and environmentalists cannot agree among themselves. What standards must be met for a "decent living"? What standards must be met for clean air and clean water? How much noise pollution is "too much"? Should the dam project be spared or the tiny snail darter fish? How endangered must northern spotted owls become before forest lands are sealed off from loggers? What standards must be met for product safety? Obviously, people's lives must not be endangered, but how safe is "safe enough"? Who's right? The Sierra Club or the Business Roundtable?

"The burden of these matters is too great for American business leaders. Rightly or wrongly, they will be deferred to market forces or to government bureaucracies."

THE MAGNIFICENT SEVEN AND THE RESOLUTION OF ETHICAL DILEMMAS

The number of ethical dilemmas which the average business and professional person will face in his/her career are myriad. Often there is not time to carefully weigh, analyze, and seek counsel on all options. Decisions so often must be made with haste.

Are there some moral common denominators which will anchor our business lives in something of lasting value and meaning and thus give our business decisions a sense of ethical direction?

The Magnificent Seven represent the distillation of ethical values from moral philosophy throughout the centuries. In their general form they state what most responsible thinkers value, in some way, about life, about others, and about human behavior. Though they are general, they can form a foundation for principled decision-making in any business or career. When wrestling with a difficult ethical decision on the job the thinking Christian can ask, "Will the action I am about to take in this job situation serve to further or to impede one or more of these universal principles?" Such sensitivity to moral concerns at work will render our decisions more value-based than simply business-as-usual based.

1. *Dignity of human life.* Each woman or man has dignity and deserves respect as a human. This principle means that we may not act in ways that harm or injure innocent people. It means that all who labor, no matter how menial their task responsibilities, must be treated with respect. It means that businesses are concerned

198

with the safety and security of their employees and their clients or customers. It means that product-testing is taken seriously.

2. *Autonomy.* All persons are intrinsically valuable and have the right to self-determination. Each person has a right to make choices which affect his/her on career or destiny. Each person is a free moral agent. No employee deserves to be treated as a slave.

3. *Honesty.* The truth should be told to those who have a right to know it. The ethics of business are foremost about integrity, truth-telling, and honor. Honesty pertains not simply to interpersonal relations at the work site, but also to claims about products and services, sales, reports, records, and advertising, to cite a few general areas.

4. *Loyalty.* Promises, contracts, and commitments should be honored. The keeping of pledges and promises, maintaining the public trust, quality service, reliability, keeping of confidences and secrets, respect for company property, honoring just laws, policies, and rules are all a part of loyalty.

5. *Fairness.* People should be treated justly, fairly, impartially, and equitably in all relationships and transactions. Justice is giving to every person his/her due. Fairness tolerates personality, religious, racial, and gender differences in colleagues, clients, and customers.

6. *Humaneness:* Our actions ought to accomplish good and, concomitantly, we should avoid doing evil. Obviously, business affairs are conducted for the purposes of personal and corporate profit and self-interest, but not at the expense of others' welfare. While humaneness is a principle with many possible interpretations, the Golden Rule is an ancient, time-honored standard which points businesspersons in the right direction.

7. *The common good.* Actions should accomplish the "greatest good for the greatest number of people." Company policies and actions impact people in various ways, but ethical decision-making serves to benefit the welfare of the largest number of people, while protecting the rights of individuals. The common good is also served by the pursuit of excellence — opening new lines of both horizontal and vertical communication; developing new skills of employees; providing special training and education; the pursuit of excellence at all levels. No work at *any* corporate level that is less than best can be meaningful and rewarding — or profitable — in the long run.

These principles are general enough to be "fleshed out" and

enacted in most if not all business situations, but, on the other hand, abstract enough to be manipulated by rationalization and unchecked self-interest. The ethical businessperson will continually reflect on the moral dimensions of his/her business life and behavior, remembering always that one's most noble motives and deeds can be tainted with self-interest, and seek the counsel and support of ethical-minded friends and colleagues.

SELECTED QUOTATIONS

Every man's work shall be made manifest: for the day shall declare it, because it shall be revealed by fire; and the fire shall try every man's work of what sort it is.

—1 Corinthians 3:13

You can't eat for eight hours a day nor drink for eight hours a day nor make love for eight hours a day — all you can do for eight hours is work. Which is the reason why man makes himself and everybody else so miserable and unhappy.

—William Faulkner

I like my job and am good at it, but it sure grinds me down sometimes, and the last thing I need to take home is a headache.

—TV commercial for Anacin

Early to bed, and early to rise,
Makes a man healthy, wealthy, and wise.

Then plow deep, while sluggards sleep,
And you shall have corn to sell and to keep.

—Benjamin Franklin

The business of America is business.

—Calvin Coolidge

The business of America is not business. It never was. The business of America is individual liberty, with the law enforcing an even-handed justice among equal persons. When the law provides a free field and no favor — which was the original implication of laissez-faire — the economic order is the free market.

—Edmund A. Opitz

Work is still the complicated and crucial core of most lives, the occupation melded inseparably to the identity; Freud said that the successful psyche is one capable of love and of work. Work is the most thorough and profound organizing principle in American life.

If mobility has weakened old blood ties, our co-workers often form our new family, our tribe, our social world; we become almost citizens of our companies, living under the protection of salaries, pensions and health insurance. . . . all work expresses the laborer in a deeper sense: all life must be worked at, protected, planted, replanted, fashioned, cooked for, coaxed, diapered, formed, sustained. Work is the way that we tend the world, the way that people connect. It is the most vigorous, vivid sign of life — in individuals and in civilizations.

—Lance Morrow

Bowed by the weight of centuries he leans
Upon his hoe and gazes on the ground,
The emptiness of ages in his face
And on his back the burden of the world.

—Edwin Markham

What constitutes the alienation of labor? First, that the work is external to the worker, that it is not part of his nature; and that, consequently, he does not fulfill himself in his work but denies himself, has a feeling of misery rather than well being, does not develop freely his mental and physical energies but is physically exhausted and mentally debased. The worker therefore feels himself at home only during his leisure time, whereas at work he feels homeless. . . .Work is not the satisfaction of a need, but only a means for satisfying other needs.

—Karl Marx

The message out there is, Reaching objectives is what matters and how you get there isn't important.

—Gary Edwards

If God shows you a way in which you may lawfully get more than in another way (without wrong to your soul or to any other), if you refuse this, and choose the less gainful way, you cross one of the ends of your calling, and you refuse to be God's steward, and to accept His gifts and use them for Him when He requireth it; you may labour to be rich for God, though not for the flesh and sin.

—Richard Baxter, 19th Century American Preacher

This book, being about work, is by its very nature, about violence. . . to the spirit as well as to the body. It is about ulcers as well as accidents, about shouting matches as well as fist fights, about nervous breakdowns as well as kicking the dog around. It is, above all (or beneath all), about daily humiliations. To survive the day is triumph enough for the walking wounded among the great many of us. . .for the many there is a hardly concealed discontent. The blue-collar blues is no more bitterly sung than the white-collar moan.

—Studs Terkel, in introducing his classic volume *Working*

As soon as you're doing what you wanted to be doing, you want to be doing something else.

—Lovka's Law of Living

Taxes on unearned income and inheritance are good for the work ethic; over time they return the rich and their offspring to useful toil. It is one of the oddities of our time that we think the work ethic to be particularly ethical for those in the lower income brackets.

—John Kenneth Galbraith

Why doesn't America work? Because for too long too many people have waited for someone else to do something. Change starts with us.

Can we make America work? Yes. Emphatically yes. The key is to restore a high and morally rooted view of work that once again inculcates in the American character those historic virtues of the work ethic: industry, thrift, respect for property, pride in craft, and concern for community.

—Charles Colson and Jack Eckerd

Don't look to corporate America for moral leadership. Too many chief executives share the ethics of a welfare cheat. The welfare cheat breaks the law to chisel the government. Well, many a CEO twists company rules to raise his pay — and bilk the company. Welfare cheats probably need the money and grasp their wrongdoing. The CEOs don't need the money and are oblivious to their wrongdoing. Who's more honest?

—Robert J. Samuelson

Managing only for profit is like playing tennis with your eye on the scoreboard and not on the ball . . . Nice guys may appear to finish last, but usually they're running in a different race.

—Kenneth Blanchard and Norman Vincent Peale

The unemployed haven't "lost" their jobs; they know where they are. The jobs are now overseas or they are one of the balls juggled and dropped in union-contract negotiations. Very often those lost jobs can be found listed proudly as "efficiency accomplishments" in the resumes of corporate executives.

Ending a job relationship is not unlike severing a mortal one. "Losing a loved one" is a gentle phrase; it implies things may be set right again, that if you managed to look in the right place, you might find the person who has gone. I assure you that I didn't "lose" my dear parents. I know exactly where I left them, even if I am less certain about their spiritual whereabouts at this moment. So I haven't "lost" my job. My job *died*.

—Mary Jo Purcell

The view has been gaining widespread acceptance that corporate officials and labor leaders have a social responsibility that goes beyond serving the interest of their stockholders or their members. This view shows a fundamental misconception of the character and nature of a free economy. In such an economy, there is one and only one social responsibility of business — to use its resources and engage in activities designed to increase its profits so long as it stays within the rules of the game, which is to say, engages in open and free competition, without deception or fraud . . . Few trends could so thoroughly undermine the very foundations of our free society as the acceptance by corporate officials of a social responsibility other than to make as much money for their stockholders as possible.

—Milton Friedman

If a young man fathers a child, then it is not unreasonable to expect him to support and nurture that child. There is little argument about that proposition. Yet if a corporate executive makes a decision to close an inner-city factory — a move that will make it more difficult for many young men to support their children — he is likely to applauded as a wizard of corporate restructuring and rewarded with bonuses of millions of dollars. If he can get the same work done in Mexico for one-tenth the labor cost, he's simply a shrewd businessman.

Who will denounce him as irresponsible? In the Candidean world of free-market economics, his pursuit of narrow self-interest ultimately produces public good. Why not see the runaway father's narrow self-interest in the same entrepreneurial light?

—David Moberg

Never invest your money in anything that eats or needs repainting.

—Billy Rose

Hard work fascinates me — I could sit and watch it for hours.

—Bumper Sticker on an old "clunker"

DISCUSSION QUESTIONS AND BRIEF CASE STUDIES

1. Do you think that work has intrinsic value? That is, is there something valuable in work that is worth doing for its own sake?

2. Can a Christian make a distinction between a "sacred" and a "secular" calling? Is it possible to serve God in *all* careers and vocations?

3. Do our jobs and careers define us more than anything else about our lives? How would the Apostle Paul have answered the question, "What do you do?"

4. Does God command us to "work hard"? (See Eccl. 9:10; Col. 3:17, 23.) How do you work diligently and faithfully for employers and co-workers who do not deserve your best efforts?

5. One could argue theologically that God plans everything (e.g., Leaves and snowflakes are unique. God gave special missions to Abraham, Moses, David, John the Baptist, Jesus [cf. John 17:4], Saul, and others). How specific is our calling from God? Does God call all men and women to do something in this world or does he call only select individuals? Is God's calling general, such as a call to accept his grace and live and think as the Son demonstrated, or is the call specific, such as a call to be a physician, an attorney, a teacher, or a clerk? If God calls us to specific vocations, how can we know his call?

6. How do you understand the Protestant work ethic? Do you think it has relevance for our times?

7. Do you think the work ethic of previous generations is now dead? While our fathers and grandfathers and great grandfathers concentrated energy upon plow and drill press and pressure gauge and tort, do not younger workers ask questions about the point of knocking themselves out for corporate bosses who live in another city and state? Do today's workers care about the quality of their product or service?

8. What features of business are definitively part of the practice of business, that is, without which business would no longer be business as we know it in this culture? Name some familiar features of business that are not essential or definitive aspects of business. Is the making of profits an essential part of business? Is advertising and public relations a part of business? Are company social gatherings an essential part of business? Are business lunches an essential part of business? Why or why not?

9. Is "bluffing" in business unethical? Is bluffing a kind of lying?

How much should you relate to a competitor? (Pick a particular competitive situation from your own experience or reading.) Would competition in business be possible if everyone involved was completely "open" and had complete knowledge of everyone else's activities? If you hold to the highest standards of integrity, how might you fare in representing a multinational corporation in negotiating in a foreign country where deceit and bluffing are expected in their corporate culture?

10. How would you define a "workaholic"? What drives the workaholic? How can a workaholic overcome his/her addiction to work?

11. Does an employee owe his/her company loyalty? What is employee loyalty, anyway? When is a contract or commitment no longer binding? What if loyalty endangers your job or a promotion? Are "whistle-blowers" acting loyally to their employer? What information can you take to a new employer from your old organization? Could you maintain loyalty when your company does not care about you and would dispose of you if such dismissal were advantageous/profitable to the firm?

12. Are there certain jobs which involve greater ethical choices and moral dilemmas than most other positions? Are there certain vocations you could not enter because of the moral temptations inherent within the occupations? Cite examples.

13. What would you do as a Christian if you found yourself working in the following situations?

(a) You were asked to produce useless products or sell luxury items that did not benefit anyone but the wealthiest of people.

(b) You were asked to lie continually and fabricate good press about company services and products.

(c) A small amount of the products you distributed to retail outlets included adult sexual materials and alcoholic beverages.

(d) Your supervisor, salaried at twice more than you are paid, received her position because of race and gender, but appears to you and your colleagues to be totally incompetent, inept, half-hearted in commitment, and biased against you.

(e) Your company flagrantly violates EEOC standards.

(f) Profanity, lewdness, and discussion about extramarital affairs continually pervaded your office environment.

14. How do you handle the frustration of not being in an ideal job, being qualified for a much better position, but finding yourself passed over for others who seem to be less qualified?

15. How many of the Ten Commandments are relevant and applicable to business ethics? Would it be possible to rewrite some of these Ten Commandments with an emphasis toward merging biblical theology and business ethics? For example, the first commandment could read: "I am the Lord thy God. The organization shall not become the director of people's lives but only of their activities within it. The organization shall always become a means to an end, not an end in itself. The manager shall not give to either his/her job or company more than his/her activities, functions, and work." Do you agree with this rendition? Could you rewrite other commandments for the business environment or corporate culture?

16. Do you think that pulpit ministers and other salaried, professional church staff should labor under a professional code of ethics? If so, who should devise the code? Should it be enforced?

17. "All good work has a combination of excitement, drudgery, boredom, and challenge. Our personality, attitudes, and predispositions are crucially important in how we feel about what we are doing." Do you agree?

18. The federal court system sets the legal context in which business acts and lets employers know what they are and are not legally permitted to do. But legal decisions per se do not exhaust the relevant moral issues. For example, the morality of affirmative action programs is still an issue for reasoning and debate.

"Affirmative action" means programs taking the race or gender of employees or job candidates into account as part of an effort to correct imbalances in employment that exist as a consequence of past discrimination, either in the corporation itself or society as a whole. Critics of affirmative action often label it "reverse discrimination." Are there strong moral arguments for affirmative action? Are there strong moral arguments against affirmative action?

19. Does it pay for a corporation or business to be honest and ethical? Obviously, there is a perceived short-term gain for a business organization to jack up prices unfairly, to skimp on quality, to add work and demand more of employees, and to exaggerate product or service claims in advertising. Laying morality aside for a moment, does it "pay" a company in the long run to operate according to high standards of ethics? Consider, for example, the impact of unethical business practices on employees. Consider the long term impact on company reputation within the business community.

20. *Case study:* Kerry Lambert is a sales representative for a company which issues a wide variety of insurance policies and retirement plans. He travels throughout the state of Tennessee, usually with his colleague, to make presentations to various groups about the benefits of his company's policies.

Kerry comes to you with a dilemma. His colleague and traveling partner has developed a system of making extra money from their company in ways that Kerry considers unethical. For example, his partner might report expenses for meals which he did not purchase. Quite often his partner has spent the night at a friend's home in the town in which he was working but later collected expenses for a motel room which he did not use. This colleague has also been charging long-distance phone calls to the company for several years. All of this activity is against company policy.

Should Kerry "blow the whistle" on his colleague, who otherwise is a congenial person and highly capable sales representative? Kerry has already confronted his colleague about the unethical activity, but his only response was to "blow it off" and instruct Kerry not to worry about it. It's obvious, Kerry reasons, that their company should more closely monitor their agents' activities and that it should require meticulous documentation by receipts, but that is not the point. Does collegiality obligate Kerry to say nothing about these violations of policy to their employer? Does loyalty to the company obligate Kerry to report the infractions? What should Kerry do?

21. You do not have to work for an organization very long, at a management or non-management level, to realize that your interests and desires are often on a collision course with the interests and desires of the organization. If the stakes are important enough to both parties, then a serious conflict of interest has arisen.

When a person is hired, he/she commits to discharging contractual obligations in exchange for salary. Thus the employee performs the specified job assignment and devotes energy within the framework of prescribed hours in exchange for pay. Implicit within any work agreement is the principle that employees will not use the business organization for personal advantage. Of course, one may gain status and ego satisfaction from employment with a firm, but that employment is not intended to provide unauthorized personal gain at the expense of the company.

Below are listed several common unethical practices. (Some of these terms have been defined already under "Key Terms.") As you consider each one, can you provide personal illustrations of having observed the practice? Are any of these practices morally justified? Which of these practices, in your opinion, is more common? Which of these practices is more reprehensible and inexcusable than the others?

(a) Employee theft of supplies or equipment
(b) Falsification of time records or expense allowance reports
(c) Unauthorized invasion of confidential employee records
(d) Improper use of sick leave
(e) Improper use of patented or copyrighted materials
(f) Theft of a company's proprietary data or "trade secret"
(g) Bribes and kickbacks
(h) Gifts and entertainment to influence business decisions
(i) Insider trading

22. Consider these two oft-quoted maxims for maintaining sanity and progress: One is "Don't get mad — get even!" and the other is "Go ahead and do it. It's easier to ask forgiveness than to get permission!" Does either maxim provide good advice when it comes to ethical situations?

23. What do you think that companies can do to enhance ethical standards in the work place and to raise the level of sensitivity to ethics at all levels of employment? How can managers foster rather than impede ethical conduct? One sure way would be by rewarding admirable and morally excellent behavior. How could that be done in the company for which you work?

24. *A Final Question:* How can you use your career position or professional training to convert your talents into gifts in order to minister to others and glorify God?

CHAPTER EIGHT

Euthanasia/Suicide

For centuries and centuries it was different. Until our modern age, major life events such as birth and death occurred in the home within a small community of family and friends. Women rarely went to a hospital to deliver their babies, and those who were dying expired in their own homes. In previous generations, of course, hospitals had so little to offer critical patients by comparison to what is available in modern times.

Today, seventy percent of elderly Americans do not die at home; they die in hospitals and nursing homes. In hospitals the drama of the congested emergency room, heroic resuscitative efforts, and efficient life support machines are all taken for granted. Emerging from all of these special care scenarios is renewed interest and concern about several issues: How should human life end? How should life be terminated? Where should the suffering patient die?

Euthanasia, like abortion, is another of those vexing and morally ambiguous issues in bioethics in which both private citizens and public policymakers must make decisions about life and death options. The dilemmas that citizens face in bioethics defy easy answers and simple solutions. Like the debate over abortion, there has been a sharp and intense polarization between the proponents and the opponents of euthanasia.

Death is the inevitable termination of human life on earth for everyone, sooner or later. What was once the simple act of dying, as noted at the outset, in modern times has been complicated by the dramatic changes in medical technology as well as in the cultural milieu of American life.

In the twentieth century vaccines and inoculations were intro-duced which eliminated many of the devastating plagues which killed or crippled millions. Life support equipment has been invented to sustain human existence for months. Respirators, artifi-cial kidneys, dialysis machines, intravenous feeding, new drugs — all have made it possible to sustain life artificially (i.e., long after a person has lost the capacity to live independently). The expected life span of modern Americans has been extended in this century by three to four decades.

CATEGORIZING EUTHANASIA: THREE WAYS

Euthanasia is derived from two Greek words, *eu* meaning "good" or "happy" and *thanatos* meaning "death." Terminology regarding euthanasia can be divided into three different categories, each approaching the issue from differing actions or perspectives:

1. Voluntary/Nonvoluntary. Voluntary decisions about death refer to cases in which a competent adult patient requests or gives informed consent to a specific course of medical treatment or nontreatment. Informed consent means that the patient understands what he/she is agreeing to and voluntarily chooses it. A nonvoluntary decision about death refers to cases in which the decision about treatment is not made by the person who is to die. Such cases would include patients who are incapacitated by age, mental impairment, or unconsciousness and, therefore, a person's family, in consultation with physicians, would make strategic decisions for the patient.

2. Active/Passive. These terms focus on the kind of action taken to induce death. Active (sometimes called positive) euthanasia refers to the act of painlessly putting to death persons suffering from incurable conditions or diseases; for example, injecting a lethal dose of medication into a terminally ill patient would constitute active euthanasia. Passive euthanasia, by contrast, refers to any act of withholding or withdrawing treatment to sustain human life; for example, not providing a severely ill person the needed antibiotics to survive acute pneumonia or disengaging a ventilator which sustains the breathing of a brain-dead patient would constitute passive euthanasia.

Later we will question whether there is significant moral difference between active and passive euthanasia. Suffice it to say that many consider the difference to be between killing a person and allowing a person to die. Presumably, "killing" a person is taking a definite action to end another's life (a commission), while in contrast, "allowing a person to die" is simply a matter of omission.

3. Direct/Indirect. These terms relate to the role played by the person when his/her life is terminated. Direct euthanasia refers to cases where the individual patient carries out the action of death. Indirect euthanasia refers to situations where someone else carries out the death wish.

The much celebrated case of Karen Ann Quinlan in the mid-1970s brought to national attention the ethical and legal dimensions of euthanasia. On the night of April 15, 1975, Ms. Quinlan, for reasons still unclear, ceased breathing for at least two fifteen-minute periods; she also failed to respond to mouth-to-mouth resuscitation as administered by her friends. She was rushed to a hospital in New Jersey and was placed on a respirator. Though physicians characterized the patient as being in a "chronic, persistent, vegetative state" with no form of treatment available to restore her to cognitive life, there were legal barriers to disconnecting the respirator. As medical costs mounted, the patient went from 120 pounds to 60 pounds and lay in pre-natal position with vague responses to pain, bright light or loud noise. Eventually, the Supreme Court of New Jersey granted Joseph and Julia Quinlan's request to turn off the respirator and their daughter remained alive but comatose until June 11, 1985, when she died at the age of thirty-one.

In recent years there is one person who has dramatically monopolized news coverage and headlines on the issue of mercy killing: Dr. Jack Kevorkian, often called by his media moniker, "Doctor Death." Kevorkian, a retired pathologist from Pontiac, Michigan, gained notoriety as well as jail time by educating and providing death machines and education about their use for patients with interminable or such chronically painful diseases that they sought the ultimate release from such pain and suffering. After several cases of Kevorkian-aided suicides, several states passed laws that, in one way or another outlaw physician-assisted suicide. Undaunted, Kevorkian continued his crusade and in June 1995 opened a clinic in Michigan for the sole purpose of administering death.

Kevorkian has appeared to the general public as a kind of fanatic who could prompt people who share his views to change their minds. The "death doctor" appeared on television after each new death, invoking a higher moral authority and ignoring court orders and judges' instructions. Kevorkian's assistance in death decisions for people who were chronically but not terminally ill seemed to confirm conservatives' concerns about where lines would be drawn if active euthanasia were legalized.

In the early 90s several hundred thousand copies of *Final Exit: The Practicalities of Self-Deliverance and Assisted Suicide for the Dying* were sold to an American public which had learned that dying in America was no longer a simple matter. Authored by Derek Humphry, president of the Hemlock Society, the volume addressed growing concern over how to end one's life in a way that ensures a dignified, humane death.

DEATH, PERSONHOOD, LIFE: THREE KEY ISSUES

Three major considerations form the core of this ethical issue. The first is *a definition of death*. Contrary to traditional wisdom, which regarded death as specific moment when life ceases, many of our contemporaries will not die "all at once." For them, and perhaps us, death in medical terms is a gradual process, a sequence of stages: "clinical" death, when vital functions of breathing and heartbeat cease; "brain" death, when there is no discernible brain wave activity (determined by a flat electroencephalogram); and "biological" death. In current legal and medical practice, brain death is accepted as the point at which a person is officially dead.

The concept of personhood is also at the center of the euthanasia issue, just as it is in the abortion dispute. What are the criteria for personhood? Should an organism be considered human because it possesses certain biological properties? Or does personhood depend additionally on a complex listing of psychosocial traits, such as the capacities for consciousness, rationality, memory, communication, self-determination, and moral decision-making? Was Karen Ann Quinlan, while lying in a vegetative state, a human being?

And, finally, for Christians there is *a wide range of deeply theological and philosophical questions* to be answered: What is the purpose of life? Is a person's life exclusively one's own? Does a person have a right to dispose of one's life at any time and in any manner? May one enlist another's assistance in this process? Are extreme pain and physical suffering always evil? Can the concept of mercy and grace be extended to the point of killing another human? Is there a "fate worse than death"?

None of these philosophical-theological questions carries with it a transparent answer. Nor will they be answered in a medical school textbook. Our faith, our understanding of life, our understanding of Scripture, and our values will determine the answers we construct to these questions. But the kinds of answers we give to these questions, as well as our understanding of both death and personhood, will determine whether our attitude toward euthanasia is positive or negative.

A WORD ABOUT SUICIDE

Ernest Hemingway. Abbie Hoffman. Vince Foster. Marilyn Monroe. Kurt Cobain. What does this motley mixture of humanity have in common? The answer, of course, is that they chose a road of self-destruction which may have started with depression and but eventually led to the grave.

If one searches Scripture, not much will be located on suicide from the point of view of moral judgment. Six cases of suicide are recorded in the Bible: Samson (Judg. 16:30), who pushed the pillars of a house until it fell; Saul and his armor-bearer, who killed themselves in battle (1 Sam. 31:4-5); Ahithophel, who hung himself in despair after his counsel was rejected (2 Sam. 15:31; 17:23); Zimri, the failed monarch who burned the house over him (1 Kings 16:18), and Judas, the well-known traitor to Jesus (Matt. 27:5). Neither the Old or New Testaments offer any specific judgment or prohibition about suicide; nor is there any indication that suicide is condoned in Scripture. There is at least one case of assisted death, active euthanasia, in Holy Scripture. Abimelech, king of Israel, battled against the city of Thebez (Judg. 9:50-57). The text reveals ". . . a certain woman threw an upper millstone upon his head, and crushed his skull." Rather than suffer death at the hands of a woman, Abimelech persuaded his armor-bearer to kill him with a sword. The ". . . young man thrust him through, and he died." There is no biblical record of condemnation for this action.

A number of biblical characters grappled with the question of self-termination — men such as Moses, burdened with the problems of the Hebrews and wishing to die, but the Lord offered an alternative plan to ease his administrative burden (Num. 11:5-23); Jonah, depressed over the penitence of Nineveh and wanting to die, but God asked if he was justified in his anger (4:8); and Elijah, desiring death when he considered the threat issued by Jezebel (1 Kings 19:1-20). The Philippian jailor was admonished to ". . . do thyself no harm" when it appeared that he would take his own life (Acts 16:27).

Today, there are as many mysteries to suicide as there are weapons to perform it. Some facts we do know: There's as much suicide among the rich as there is among the poor and middle class. Fame does not exempt one from suicide. White males are more likely to commit suicide than any other group (some 18.0 per 100,000). Firearms are the suicide weapon of choice, used four times as frequently as the second most common method of hanging and strangulation. Suicide can be triggered by a wide range of sad events — loss of employment, death of a loved one, betrayal of a loved one, aging, severe impairment of health, loss of status — but underlying almost all cases is an underlying psychiatric illness, usually depression. Females, by around three to one, attempt suicide more than males, but males usually employ more lethal means and are four times more likely to die.

Suicide among youth is particularly alarming. In the vast majority of youthful suicides, a young man or woman has employed a permanent solution to a temporary problem.

The good news: 99.9 percent of Americans do not kill themselves. For better or worse, they stick to life. Perhaps the vast majority of us have made an unspoken covenant with ourselves and others that we will affirm life in all its problems and frailties — our own life and the lives of people we care about most.

KEY TERMS

Cruzan v. Missouri Health Services **(1990)** — This was the first time the Supreme Court ruled on a right-to-die case. The Court denied the right to remove the feeding tube to a patient in a permanent vegetative state because authorities did not have evidence (no living will) that the patient would prefer to die rather than to be left in this state. However, the Court did establish a constitutional basis for voluntary passive euthanasia (or allowing to die) in cases where there is clear and convincing evidence that such action is in accordance with the patient's wishes.

Death Selection — The deliberate removal of persons whose lives are no longer considered socially useful; people in this category need not be ill, but are considered useless and expendable, such as hardened criminals, mentally retarded, or entire ethnic or racial groups.

"Death with Dignity" — Allowing the patient to die a truly human death rather than using extraordinary means to postpone death.

Euthanasia – Good death or happy death, derived from two Greek words – *eu* meaning "well" or "good," and *thanatos* meaning "death."

Hemlock Society – A national society with approximately 25,000 members, along with its political arm, Americans Against Human Suffering, which proposes and lobbies for public acceptance of active euthanasia and for new legislation legalizing same. The organization was founded in 1980 by Derek Humphry (who euthanized his first wife at age 42 because she was ravaged by incurable bone cancer) and is named for the hemlock weed ancient Greeks used to commit suicide.

Hippocratic Oath – The ancient creed to which a physician is bound: "to help the sick, never with a view to injury and wrongdoing;" the doctor must do all possible to preserve life.

Hospice – A homelike facility designed to provide medical, nursing, and supportive care for terminally ill patients but also to allow them to die with dignity, within the familiar and intimate circle of family.

Immortality – A central Christian tenet of faith which proclaims that life is only a fleeting episode in the pilgrimage of the soul. Therefore, death is not an enemy, but the appointed end of a human's earthly existence (Heb. 9:27; 2 Cor. 5:1; 1 Cor. 15:53).

Living Will – A document signed while a person is in good health that states that if a time comes when the individual cannot take part in decisions about his/her future, and if there is no reasonable expectation of recovery from physical, mental, or emotional disability, he/she asks to be allowed to die rather than to be kept alive by artificial means.

"Mercy Killing" – An act with the intent of releasing someone who is suffering excruciating pain and has no other way of escape except death. The action, seen as an act of mercy, may involve using medical technology to hasten or cause death.

Suicide – The act of taking one's own life because of emotional or psychological reasons.

Vegetative State – An extreme physical condition where the patient has no outward signs of life and is unable to live without the aid of life-support equipment; most people recognize this condition as one of "clinical death" and that biological functioning could not continue without the aid of support equipment.

KEY SCRIPTURES

No Scriptures address the issue of euthanasia directly. Numerous Scriptures treat the issues of the dignity of life and purpose of human suffering. The following Scriptures are often employed to show that God cares about life and health: Genesis 1:26,27; Exodus 19:13; 23:25; Job 14:2; Jeremiah 17:14; 30:17; Matthew 9:6-7; 21:22; James 5:14-16; 2 Corinthians 4:16; Psalms 22:24; 50:15; Isaiah 30:19.

KEY ISSUES/ARGUMENTS
Arguments for Voluntary (Active) Euthanasia

1. An individual may lose the essence of personhood, thus becoming only a biological organism; there is no need to maintain biological life that does not sustain personal life.

"Just because an individual is breathing by some means does not mean that the individual possesses personhood. An individual who is in an irreversible coma is no longer a person but is only a biological organism, a 'vegetable' in most people's vocabulary. 'Pulling the plug' on an irreversibly comatose individual does not increase his/her suffering, but it may relieve the agony experienced by close friends and relatives. The mere possession of biological life, at least by one who once possessed life in its fullness, is not enough warrant to sustain artificially one's continued existence.

"Preserving life at all costs is to operate under the false value that any and all life is valuable and must be preserved no matter what the circumstances. Deep inside of all of us we know that the quality of life is more important than the quantity of life and that there is a fate worse than death. Let's face it: when it comes to human suffering as well as any other bad experience, a time comes when 'enough is enough.'"

2. An individual should possess the moral and legal right to decide about his/her own life and death.

"Of all the rights that older people might claim for that time in their lives, what right is more basic than the right to determine the circumstances of one's own death? Whether one dies in an intensive care ward connected to all kinds of tubes in a drugged state or stupor or unconsciousness or in the privacy of his/her home surrounded by a caring family is too important of a decision to be dictated by a court or legislature."

3. People have a right to die with dignity.

"Few people would choose to spend their last weeks and days lying in a hospital bed, wasting away as a human being to the point of being hardly recognizable to even your closest of friends. What's dignified about that? Because we respect others, we allow them to live with the privacy and dignity they want. Why not allow them to die with the privacy and dignity they want?"

4. The Golden Rule requires allowing active euthanasia as an option; to deny this right is unfair and cruel.

"The Golden Rule is the most basic ethical standard of all civilized societies. Now consider: If you were in intense pain and had to be drugged almost to the point of unconsciousness, you'd want some doctor to give you a lethal injection to put you out of your misery, wouldn't you? Then, if you treat others the way you want to be treated, how could you deny that same option to others?"

5. Some families cannot afford the cost of radical and extreme means of medical care.

"It's a simple fact: medical care is very expensive. Some families' insurance coverage may not cover radical and extreme treatment for the terminally ill. The dying patient's misery is made worse when he/she contemplates the burden that his/her illness is placing on the family. That means the greatest cost is not simply financial, but emotional."

6. The sixth commandment ("Thou shalt not kill") is not absolute.

"Appeals to the Sixth Commandment, "Thou shalt not kill," Exodus 20:13, are not valid. Very few people have absolutized this commandment. Christians who are opposed to euthanasia are often people who favor capital punishment for hardened criminals, military action against other nations, and killing in self-defense. The kind of killing that was prohibited by the Sixth Commandment is killing of human life which is intentional, premeditated, malicious, and contrary to the wishes of an innocent man or woman. Voluntary euthanasia is an act of mercy, not of malice."

Arguments against Voluntary (Active) Euthanasia

1. The "sanctity of life" principle means that life must not be taken deliberately except in extreme circumstances.

"Life is precious. Life is valuable. Human life is sacred because God gave it and we are created in the image of God [Gen. 1:26-27]. However wracked with pain, however distorted the body image, however unconscious a person may be — that person still bears the image of God. This theological principle alone counsels extreme caution in decision-making about the treatment of such people."

2. Only God gives and sustains life. People must not "play God" by deliberately terminating it.

"God is the source of all life. The Bible says, 'The Lord giveth and the Lord taketh away.' The human being, as trustee of one's body, acts against God when he/she consents to being euthanized or takes his/her own life. Because life is God's gift we must treat it with highest value and regard and not discard it even in extreme circumstances. To treat human life otherwise is the ultimate act of ingratitude for something that God gave and yet still owns."

3. Once a society becomes comfortable with euthanasia, it gradually becomes indifferent to other abuses of the "sanctity of life" principle.

"Ending the life of terminally ill patients who ask for it is a dangerous step. The term 'hopelessly ill' can be broadened to include all those who might be considered too "ill" to function normally any longer. Does a person suffering from Alzheimer's disease have a right to be put out of his/her misery? How about someone suffering from chronic depression? Severe arthritis? Where is society going to draw a line once it condones active euthanasia?"

4. We can't be certain that consent is both voluntary and well-informed.

"Both medical staff and next of kin both know that the circumstances surrounding most terminally ill patients make voluntary, informed consent nearly impossible. Such patients are in intense pain or they're drugged out of their minds; they are in no position to make a rational, objective evaluation of their situation."

5. There's always the possibility of a mistaken diagnosis, a new cure, a new pain reliever, or spontaneous remission.

"A medical opinion that a person only has limited time to live is not always the last, authoritative word. The diagnosis may be mistaken. A new cure or experimental drug may come along which could be effective in prolonging the patient's life. How many times have you heard of cancer patients going into spontaneous remission?

"Only *death* is the final word about a person's physical condition. And if some doctor kills a patient, then that patient is truly beyond hope. But while there is life there is always hope, however slim that hope may be."

6. Intense suffering, though never sought and never enjoyable, can have a positive function in a person's life.

"Suffering most surely is a terrible thing and no one should consider it flippantly. Christians have a clear duty to provide comfort and support to all people in extreme need and to alleviate their suffering whenever we have the means. However, suffering is a natural part of life — to live is to suffer.

"Suffering also can have positive value in a person's life. Several passages of Scripture speak of the positive functioning of suffering [Rom. 5:3-5; 1 Pet. 1:6-9; 2 Cor. 4:17, 12:10; and the book of Job]. The person who has heroically endured suffered can offer empathy and insights to other people who must suffer a great deal."

SELECTED QUOTATIONS

To everything there is a season . . . . a time to be born and a time to die.

—The Preacher (Ecclesiastes)

It is enough, now, O Lord, take away my life.

—Elijah

The record of a previously noble life is precisely what makes it sheer insult to allow death in pitiful degradation. We may not wish to 'die with our boots on' but we may well prefer to die with our brains on. . . . . I have preferred chloroform to cancer.

—Frances Perkins Gilman, feminist, patient with terminal cancer who took her own life in 1935.

I believe often that death is good medical treatment because it can achieve what all the medical advances and technology cannot achieve today, and that is stop the suffering of the patient.

—Dr. Christian Barnard

The term 'death with dignity' has caught on because of its allit-
erative catchiness rather than because it represents anything based
upon Judeo-Christian moral principles. . . . In a sense the whole
problem of the right to live and the right to die, centering around
one's understanding of abortion and euthanasia, has a significant
analogy to the behavior of Lucifer. We do not know whence his
temptation came, but we do know that he sought to be 'like the
most high.' Our society, having lost its understanding of the sanctity of human life, is pushing the medical profession into assuming
one of God's prerogatives, namely, deciding what life shall be born
and when life should end.

—C. Everett Koop

In our determination to prolong life at any cost, we have forgotten that dying is part of the process of living. These people's bodies
are telling them there really is no purpose in going on, and yet we
make them go on.

—John Paris

Euthanasia concerns the type of society we wish to live in and
bequeath to our children. Established as right, proper, and legal,
euthanasia would be part of a society where all life is subject to
state determination. Equal protection of the laws for any class of
people the state considered disposable would be meaningless.
Mercy for the suffering or elderly could next be 'mercy' for the
deformed, the defective, the burdensome. Those of differing values
and philosophies could then be the subjects of state recognized
'mercy'. No horror against life is impossible once we have allowed
anyone but the Creator to usurp sovereignty over life. Whom the
gods would destroy they first make mad. Legalized euthanasia is
such madness.

—Frank Morriss

It is ridiculous to give ethical approval to the positive ending of
subhuman life in utero, as we do in therapeutic abortions for
reasons of mercy and compassion, but refuse to approve of positively lending a subhuman life in extremis.

—Joseph Fletcher

The true test of a society's faithfulness to the pro-life perspective is not only in its opposition to killing but also in its willingness
to make adequate provision for those who are suffering and
nonproductive. As costs of care increase, individuals in specific
circumstances and society as a whole will be strongly tempted to

sell out both compassion and responsible reverence for life in exchange for economic considerations. If the day comes when euthanasia is established as an economic policy, we will have ceased to be either fully moral or fully human. It is imperative that we oppose every step toward irresponsible euthanasia and also affirm the reordering of the priorities and expenditures of our personal and corporate life in order to provide the compassionate care every human being deserves. If we are not vigilant in opposition to unjustifiable euthanasia, we may one day be haunted by horrors more antiseptic, but no less terrifying, than Hitler's 'final solution.'

—Lowell O. Erdahl

It is silliness to live when to live is torment;
And then have we a prescription to die
When death is our physician.

—William Shakespeare

Why are so many people more readily appalled by an unnatural form of dying than by an unnatural form of living?

—Norman Cousins

We have been placed in this world under certain conditions and for specific purposes. But a suicide opposes the purpose of his Creator; he arrives in the other world as one who has deserted his post; he must be looked upon as a rebel against God. So long as we remember the truth that it is God's intention to preserve life, we are bound to regulate our activities in conformity with it. This duty is upon us until the time comes when God expressly commands us to leave this life. Human beings are sentinels on earth and may not leave their posts until relieved by another beneficent hand.

—Immanuel Kant

The suicide does not play the game, does not observe the rules. He leaves the party too soon, and leaves the other guests painfully uncomfortable.

—Joyce Carol Oates

Health care workers involved in the decision of withdrawing life support should understand that not only do our patients often have different value and belief systems, so do we. To not accept this is to impair our ability to communicate properly with our patients and their family, as well as our colleagues. There is an old saying that when you point a finger at someone you have three pointing back at you. That would seem to apply to the medical profession pointing its finger at patients' families and the legal system in matters relating to withdrawing life support. Perhaps we need to find a way to agree amongst ourselves before we ask others to do the same.

—Frank Boehm, M.D.

Oh, well, whatever, never mind.

—Kurt Cobain

DISCUSSION QUESTIONS AND BRIEF CASE STUDIES

1. In the United States medical personnel perform hundreds of abortions daily. Scores of convicted criminals are sent by the state to their death. Historically, young men have been drafted and dispatched to foreign soil to die for their country. Why is it that the issue of euthanasia seems for many people to be a much more emotional issue than any other life and death issue?

2. In what way, if at all, does a devout Christian approach this issue differently from non-Christians? How would a Christian, or a devout Jew for that matter, answer the following:

(a) What or who is the source of all human life?

(b) Does life have sanctity and a value above all other values?

(c) Is a person's life exclusively his/her own? Is that person free to dispose of or terminate that life at his/her own volition?

(d) What is death? Is death "the last enemy" to be resisted at all costs? Is death a "blessing" to be hastened and gladly received when it seems appropriate? Did not the first and second century martyrs for their Christian faith welcome and long for death? Is death the worst thing that could happen to a person?

(e) What about suffering? Are extreme pain and suffering to be resisted at all costs or are they to be welcomed and counted joyously as the "chastening of the Lord"?

3. We extend mercy to pets and farm animals who are suffering with no hope of a normal life by "putting them to sleep" or "putting them out of their misery." To borrow the title of an old movie, "they shoot horses, don't they?" Why is the same consideration not extended to terminally ill human beings? Why should a society be less merciful to humans?

4. Is a society which legally permits abortion under certain restrictions guilty of hypocrisy and inconsistency when it does not legalize active euthanasia under certain conditions? Aren't the issues of life and personhood the same for abortion and euthanasia?

5. If a state or national government were to legalize active euthanasia with certain restrictions, what restrictions do you believe should be imposed?

6. Cruelty is the complete antithesis of every Christian virtue about love, kindness, and compassion. What is "cruelty" when applied to the care of those who are gravely ill? Is cruelty simply the deliberate infliction of unnecessary pain or harm or should we broaden the definition to include deliberate allowing of harm and pain? Does not the ideal of the Good Samaritan, who not only avoided cruelty but went to great length to help a suffering victim, refute a narrow definition of cruelty?

7. Is the expression "playing God" valid when considering this issue? If so, when does one "play God"? Isn't one "playing God" when inoculations are taken to prevent disease or when medicine is taken in order to prolong life? Don't most people believe in "playing God" even to the extent of killing those who want to live — in military action, in self-defense, and in punishment of crime? Why is the taboo against "playing God" now focusing almost exclusively on terminating a life for other reasons?

Is one "playing God" more when he/she resuscitates and places a patient on life-support equipment or when he/she disconnects the life-support equipment all the while knowing that the person cannot live without it?

8. Although passive euthanasia is now widely accepted as a legal and merciful act, there are strong emotional and legal barriers to active euthanasia. Many Christians feel that doctors may morally refrain from treatments which would unnecessarily prolong the lives of terminal patients, but that they would be acting immorally to administer drugs to kill them. Obviously, it is much easier emotionally to accept the death of a loved one who was mercifully permitted by medical staff to die rather than to accept the death of that loved one by a deliberate killing by medical personnel.

The distinction at first thought appears to be a clear and logical one for moral decision-making. The tough, critical thinking Christian must question if there is truly a crucial moral and logical distinction between the two types of euthanasia. If one simply withholds treatment, it may take the patient longer to die and so he/she may suffer much more pain and agony than if more direct action were taken and a lethal injection given. As for the patient's suffering is concerned, there is more mercy shown in active rather than passive euthanasia. Put another way, the process of being "allowed to die" can be relatively slow and painful, whereas being given a lethal injection is comparatively quick and painless. Is killing really worse than letting die? Are not both "actions"? Is not withholding treating a decision to "do" or "act"? Would not a physician who allows a patient to die, for humane reasons, be in the same moral position as the physician who administers a lethal injection for the same humane reasons? If not, what is the difference?

9. If a person who believes that active euthanasia is immoral is also suffering intensely with an incurable disease, would it be wrong or a sign of spiritual weakness for that person to pray that God would take him/her out of the pain and misery being experienced? Should not the person pray for greater strength to bear the pain and misery?

10. "God wants human beings to trust in his providence, not in themselves, when their own welfare is in question," argues J. L. Lombardi. "Wherefore he commands them never to act on intentions that are purely self-interested. But that is what a person does by committing suicide in a purely self-involving situation. Therefore, God prohibits it." Do you agree with this statement? Is a person who seeks death over intense and prolonged suffering prior to death not trusting in God and acting purely out of self-interest?

11. What does the book of Job teach modern readers about suffering? A traditional interpretation contends that God uses the suffering and affliction of potentially good people to help them mature spiritually and thus suffering should be accepted. Did Job accept his suffering? Did he understand his suffering? Is not the story of Job a dramatic illustration of a man who was tempted to reject God but who refused to yield to rebellion and suicide?

12. Does the euthanasia issue have a "slippery slope"? If a legal door is open to active euthanasia, will certain abuses start appearing? For example: Will the mongoloid (Down's syndrome) be chosen as having a life that is not worthy to live? How about the man who is hopelessly crippled in a wheelchair and, having no living relatives, has become a burden on society? What about the retarded? What about the senile? Would some be calling eventually for the mercy killing of a whole race or class of people because of the need for population control?

13. For proponents of passive euthanasia: If a person continues biological life after medical machinery is disengaged (for example, Karen Quinlan), does the sanctity of life principle require that such life go on?

14. It is a common occurrence in the birthing rooms of large hospitals for a baby to be born, often premature, with severe physical and mental defects. Such defects include Tay-Sachs, a fatal degenerative disease; Down's syndrome, which manifests itself in mental retardation and various physical abnormalities; and duodenal artresia, in which the upper part of the small intestine, the duodenum, is closed off, therefore preventing the passage and digestion of food. Such babies have no chance of a normal life, either in quality or quantity of life.

What are the ethical considerations in allowing the baby simply to die by starvation and neglect because its obstacles to normality are so severe? What factors should be taken into consideration? Are adults in a position to determine what is "meaningless human existence" for a retarded infant?

15. The story captured national attention. On Thursday, June 9, 1994, little Angela Lakeberg, died. Thus ended a ten-month medical odyssey. The costs had been staggering.

This story began on June 29, 1993, when twin conjoined daughters were born in Loyola University Medical Center in Maywood, Illinois, to Kenneth and Reitha Lakeberg. Debate began as to benefits of surgical separation. On August 20, doctors at Children's Hospital in Philadelphia performed the operation, allowing Amy to die and Angela to live. Doctors knew that the chance of either twin surviving was about one in a hundred. The cost of Angela's medical care topped one million dollars.

What are the ethical issues involved in this case? Should doctors make decisions to perform high-risk, long-shot, high-tech operations when there are so many children in the nation who lack basic medical care? Are there not thousands of babies in populated areas which are at risk? Should these two infants have been allowed to die after birth? On the other hand, does not medical science advance with new knowledge when doctors attempt experimental surgery and technicians test new equipment? Also, who pays the medical expenses that this family, nor the funds established for the conjoined twins, could not cover? Should doctors attempt to save as many high risk newborns as possible and pass the tab on to the general public?

16. Case study: Louise is an 83-year-old woman who needs open-heart surgery but refuses because she says she's "too old." A person of vitality, Louise has lost her energy and zest for life as her weak heart gets progressively worse. She refuses to eat, so life-sustaining tubes are forced down her throat, through her nose, and into her veins against her will. She implores you, as her child, to let her die a peaceful death. What do you do?

17. Case study: Robert is a healthy 23-year-old man who enjoys hobbies such as motorcycle riding, windsurfing, and backpacking. Robert was in a motorcycle accident that has left him paralyzed and in a coma for three and one-half years. The doctors say that he may or may not recover. He doesn't need a respirator, but does need to be fed intravenously. You are Robert's parents. Should you ask that food and hydration be stopped to bring about death, or do you wait, hoping that Robert comes out of the coma?

18. Case study: Albert has suffered a stroke that has left him comatose. The doctors say that the 56-year-old man has no recordable brain activity and his brain stem is severely damaged. Since Albert had no health coverage, sustaining Albert's life is a financial burden on his wife, Ruth. She loves Albert but believes that the man she married is now gone; only his body remains. Should Ruth disconnect Albert's life-support system to save herself tens of thousands of dollars?

19. New medicines and new treatments are always under development. Does this point — that a new cure or a new medical treatment might be around the corner — make a strong enough argument to disavow euthanasia in any form?

20. Case study: For nine months in 1988 and 1989 Rudolfo Linares visited his son Samuel in a Chicago hospital. The fifteen-month-old boy, partially brain dead, lay connected to a respirator where he lay virtually lifeless throughout those almost three hundred days. The suffocation which followed after swallowing of an uninflated balloon at a birthday party was the accident which created the crisis.

Both Rudolfo and his wife had been pleading with hospital officials to disconnect the respirator. No pleading or appeal was effective. In exasperation, Rudolfo disconnected it himself, but security officers reconnected it. He was then advised to hire a lawyer and challenge the hospital in court.

The legal process dragged on. In one last visit to the hospital Rudolfo brandished a handgun, which he used to hold off nurses, doctors, and police officers as he disconnected the respirator and cuddled his son in his arms. Weeping continuously, Rudolfo sat with his son for over a half hour, well after hospital instruments verified that he was dead.

"I did it because I loved my son," he said. Prosecutors immediately charged Rudolfo Linares with first degree murder. A storm of national publicity followed. Charges were dropped.

Consider: Who should decide whether to "pull the plug" in cases like this one: the parents, the attending physician, a hospital committee, a special panel of ethicists, or the courts?

Suppose hospital officials refuse to cease radical life-sustaining treatment. Do family members have the moral right to take matters into their own hands, as did Rudolfo Linares?

21. Case study: A moralist might be tempted to say that Mickey Mantle brought his liver problems on himself.

Most American adults, even those non-baseball fans, have heard of Mickey Mantle, the former great baseball slugger who starred in the 50s and 60s with Roger Maris, Yogi Berra, Billy Martin, and Whitey Ford on the New York Yankees. Mantle and Maris set many records. They were American heroes. Along the way, some of those Yankees lived a rather free lifestyle.

In 1995 it was discovered that Mantle had liver cancer. This malignancy may have resulted from a hepatitis C infection he acquired from a blood transfusion years earlier. But Mantle also had been an alcoholic for many years and developed alcoholic cirrhosis, which greatly accelerates the course of virus-initiated cancer. If Mantle had abstained from alcohol, he might never had developed cancer.

Mantle's physicians called for a liver transplant in June 1995. Within hours another liver was available for the transplant. A tearful Mrs. Mantle thanked Americans for their support. Days later, "the Mick" was released to recover at home. Yet many Americans, amazed at the rapid availability of the new liver, wondered openly if the former slugger had received special treatment. Questions:

(a) Why does any doctor give a liver to an alcoholic when thousands of other, more temperate people languish on a waiting list? Can a deference to the celebrity status of the person in need of a life-saving organ be morally justified over some kind of random selection process?

(b) Did someone like Mickey Mantle deserve preferential treatment based on being "an American hero" or a "baseball legend"? Aren't American heroes and legends fairly rare anyway?

(c) Should alcoholics with liver disease, obese people with heart disease, and smokers with lung cancer receive preferential treatment over people needing expensive treatment but who have lived lives of moderation? Shouldn't these people go to the bottom of any waiting list? What is prudent use of scarce money and scarce vital organs?

Though, sadly, Mantle died in August 1995, after the contents of this book had been completed, his personal story has raised consciousness about both the need and value of vital organ transplants as well as the ethical issues associated with donor and recipient decisions.

22. What does the Bible, if anything, teach about suicide?

23. What moral obligation do you have to a person who seems to be seriously contemplating suicide?

24. If you could anticipate a crisis in which you become irreversibly comatose, what should you do in advance of such a crisis?

CHAPTER NINE

Homosexuality

Few, if any, issues are more explosive, or more vexatious and complex in nature, for thinking Christians than the issue of homosexuality.

Homosexuality itself is not a new issue. Homosexual behavior has existed throughout recorded history and among some cultures has been tacitly accepted and approved. The ancient Roman, Greek, Persian, and Moslem civilizations condoned some measure of homosexuality and in later Greece and Rome homosexual prostitution existed openly. Several Greek philosophers reported their involvement in homosexual acts. So prominent were homosexual activities in the ancient Greco-Roman world that the Apostle Paul cited them among the catalogue of sins of the pagans that Christians were to shun. Whether homosexuality was a factor in the decline and fall of these once-great ancient political cultures has been debated by historians and traditionalists. In Elizabethan England, an attitude of permissiveness was taken toward homosexuality without apparent harmful effects. Most western societies, however, have sought, often violently, to suppress homosexuality and have dealt contemptuously and harshly with homosexuals.

Not a few of the notable figures of history — including Alexander the Great, Michelangelo, Oscar Wilde, Peter Tchaikovsky, Gertrude Stein, and Virginia Woolf — are thought to have been homosexuals. In more modern times, such well known public figures as Martina Navratilova, Madonna, Liberace, Rock Hudson, Rudolph Nureyev, Billie Jean King, Greg Louganis, and many others have confessed bisexual and/or homosexual interests and preferences.

Prior to modern times, homosexuality has been viewed exclusively in terms of moral choice and moral behavior. Traditionally, heterosexuality has been viewed as the divinely ordained and appropriate mode and norm of sexual behavior. Homosexual activities have been viewed as a deviation, a perversion, of what is normal and healthy. Homosexuality was regarded as a mental disorder and homosexuals as "sick" persons in need of treatment. Morally, homosexual activities received the most scathing condemnation as blatantly sinful and depraved behavior dooming impenitent practitioners to the pit of hell. Most homosexuals preferred to live "closeted" lives of secrecy regarding their sexual preferences.

Recent developments have spawned broadsweeping changes in the outlook toward homosexuality. For one, the gay liberation movement which gained some clout for the mid and late '60s has forced the issue out of the closet and onto the front pages of magazines and newspapers nationwide. Traditionalists have been forced to examine specifically the morality and immorality of homosexual issues.

Renewed interest and research into the causes of homosexuality has been another major development. Prior to modern times, homosexuality was understood exclusively in terms of choices, behavior, and practices. The contemporary outlook compels us to consider homosexuality as a personal orientation, a sexual inversion based on predisposing factors, and a lifelong pattern. Put simply, whether homosexuals are homosexuals because of "nurture" or "nature" is the real puzzle, but scientific evidence now leans toward the conclusion that it is more a matter of nature than nurture.

While the rise of the modern field of psychology in the late 19th and early 20th centuries brought interest and a shift in the understanding of this phenomenon, more recent scientific studies of the 1990s have seemingly confirmed what many gay activists have claimed for years. Two studies, one by Swaab and Hofman and the other by Simon LeVay, examined and compared the brains of homosexual and heterosexual men and discovered significant differences; LeVay's study concluded a significant difference in the hypothalamus of heterosexual and homosexual men. Researchers caution that their findings should be considered speculative and, furthermore, the results do not provide basis for knowing if changes in the hypothalamus are the cause or the consequences of an individual's sexual orientation.

Does homosexuality begin in the genes or in the nursery? Is it a matter of nature or nurture? If homosexuality is a sin, then who is to blame? Is the blame to be shared with others? These questions are crucially important in dealing with this issue for at least two reasons: First, if homosexuality begins in the chromosomes and is something innate or constitutional, then homosexuals are no more responsible for their sexual orientation than for their eye color or height or dominant hand and arm. Second, this claim has moral and religious ramifications. If homosexuality is a matter of destiny and not choice, how can homosexuals be called sinners? Is not sin a conscious choice, a premeditated rebellion against God and his will?

PRACTICES VERSUS ORIENTATION

Contemporary evangelical thought on this issue has urged thinking Christians to make a distinction between homosexual practices, on the one hand, and a homosexual constitution or orientation, on the other hand. Biblical writers, indeed ancient culture in general, knew only about homosexual choices and behavior and not about predisposing factors, orientation, and constitution. Some ethicists contend that the homosexual orientation is not sinful, for the Bible neither knows nor condemns it as such, but homosexual behavioral choices and practices are sinful, for they are clearly condemned in Scripture. Though a person may have strong genetic blocks stacked against him/her (e.g., an alcoholic or other drug addict), it is possible through the power of God and the Holy Spirit to overcome sinful choices and immoral behavior.

How many people are actually impacted by this moral debate? Establishing reliable data on the number of homosexuals has been understandably complicated. Since the time of Alfred Kinsey's landmark study of sexuality (1948) it was contended that as many as ten percent of American males were homosexual. More recent studies indicate that the number of males must be much, much lower. In the United States it is estimated that three to five percent of the adult male population, and a smaller percentage of females, are homosexual in orientation. Some researchers dispute even these findings as being too high.

Contrary to popular opinion, it is not easy to divide men and women into two clear-cut categories — heterosexual and homosexual. Instead, these labels signify extreme poles on a continuum and in between we find many individuals whose experiences and desires combine both heterosexual and homosexual components. Researchers have found that one-fourth to one-third of adult males have had some overt homosexual feelings or experience, generally between the onset of puberty and sixteen; for the majority, this homosexual fascination was likely a phase to be passed through and not a firm, stable preference.

We will now proceed to consider arguments and contentions on the key concerns of this high voltage issue, as well as hear the voices of others who have written or spoken on the topic. Church leaders, ethicists, church fathers, and other responsible thinkers have grappled intensely with this issue and have not reached universal consensus. Certainly values are in collision here. Deeper values seem to be at stake — values such as the sanctity of the man-woman relationship in a monogamous family; the healthy expression of love and the procreation of children; the integrity of a homosexual relationship; the moral fiber of our nation; the moral authority of the Holy Scriptures; the literal interpretation of the Bible; and last, but not least, the Christian regard for the dignity and worth of all persons, especially the oppressed and victims of prejudice.

Do not expect to find this issue to be an easy one to manage intellectually or emotionally!

KEY TERMS

Bisexual — A person who experiences strong sexual feelings toward a member of either sex.

Gays — Men who experience primary sexual attraction to other men. The term is sometimes employed to describe homosexuals of either gender. Traditionalists lament the takeover of a morally neutral adjective and a wonderful one-syllable name for a female by homosexuals to describe their views and lifestyle.

Homophobia — The irrational fear and hatred of homosexuality, homosexual acts, and homosexuals. Often, homophobia leads to acts of prejudice and persecution: ridicule, discrimination, support of legal suppression and oppression, and violence against homosexual men and women.

Homosexuality — The sexual orientation centered on a primary attraction to members of one's own sex.

Lesbians — Women whose primary sexual attraction is toward other women.

KEY SCRIPTURES

Leviticus 18:19-23; 20:10-16; Ezekiel 16:49-50; Luke 10:10-13; Romans 1:26-2:1; 1 Corinthians 6:9-11; 1 Timothy 1:10

KEY ISSUES/ARGUMENTS
Arguments Against Acceptance and Condoning of Homosexuality

1. The Bible clearly and unequivocally condemns homosexuality.

"Make no mistake: the Bible in both the Old and New Testaments clearly condemns homosexuality. In fact, every time the Bible mentions homosexual acts they are unequivocally labeled as among the worst of sins. Any effort to take the Scriptures which treat this subject and make them read as morally neutral perspectives on homosexuality is to torture the texts in ways similar to how racists used the Bible to defend racial discrimination and segregation.

"The holiness code of the Old Testament made homosexuality an offense against God that was punishable by death [Lev. 18:22; 20:13]. The story of Lot and Sodom [Gen. 19:4-11], as well as the importance given this narrative by other inspired writers [Ezek. 16:49-50; Jude vs. 7; Luke 10:10-13], express God's view of homosexuality. The apostle Paul clearly condemned homosexuality and unnatural uses of the body in his wholesale indictment of the paganism of the Gentile world [Rom. 1:26-27].

"The heart of Christian sexual morality is both simple and profound: God designed sexual union with another human being for one purpose alone — the uniting of a man and woman as husband and wife into one flesh in marriage. The Creation order is our model for all redeemed humanity; God made Adam and Eve and not Adam and Steve. The fact that Jesus never once mentioned homosexuality in his recorded teachings provides no evidence for laxity on this issue — Jesus himself extolled the moral ideal of one man and one woman faithfully committed to one another for life."

2. Homosexuals have made a moral choice about their sexual orientation.

"The idea that homosexuality is unchosen and therefore morally acceptable is nonsense. Sure, there may be predisposing factors and environmental forces which must be dealt with, but individuals still are given by the Creator the freedom to choose their behavior.

"Furthermore, Christian ethics maintains that no person is exempt from moral accountability simply because there are areas in our lives in which we do not exercise full choice. An alcoholic, for example, may not be responsible for the physiological make-up and cravings of his/her body, but he/she is still morally responsible for choices made regarding alcoholic beverages. New Testament theology teaches us that we are enslaved to sin, that we are so easily deceived about sin, and that we are victimized by the evil one who seeks to ensnare us; however, the Bible does not excuse persons on the basis of their not consciously and conclusively choosing to be the way they are. Rather, the New Testament holds out the offer of God's grace and mercy to cover all of our failures, sins, and fallenness — no matter what the mix of conscious choices and predisposing factors."

3. Nature itself teaches that homosexuality is wrong.

"Both nature and common sense tell us that homosexual union is both unnatural and abnormal. To put it bluntly, the shape and position of the male and female genitalia complement each other perfectly. And why is this true? It is because the Creator made man and woman for each other. Homosexual activity is a clear misuse of body parts.

"The Bible declares such truth. Paul says that both men and women of his day had abandoned natural sexual relations and were inflamed in passion for others of the same gender. Such liaisons were labeled by Paul as both unnatural and shameful. Does not nature instruct us that male and female were designed for each other, sexually as well as in other ways? Does it not teach us that each is incomplete without the other? Did not God declare in the first biblical narrative: 'It is not good that man should be alone' [Gen. 2:18]?"

4. It is possible to overcome the desire for homosexual activity.

"Admittedly, the possibility of homosexuals making a change in their lifestyle is a controversial issue. Can a homosexual become a heterosexual? If what we have contended thus far is true, namely that male-female sexual union within marriage constitutes God's moral ideal and command, then surely God gives homosexuals all the strength they need to change their orientation and behavior.

"Yes, change is difficult, but major change in other areas of life is also difficult. When we place ourselves in God's hands and say "Have Thine Own Way, Lord," then we will find, perhaps with the help of Christian psychotherapists, pastoral counselors, and lots of prayer and Bible study, that the change we seek is possible."

5. Even by humanist standards, homosexual pairing is unlikely to measure up to the highest standards of Christian marriage.

"If marriage is a lifelong commitment, terminated only by such radical fractures [death of a spouse or sexual infidelity], then homosexual bonds have little chance of measuring up to this high standard. This is especially true of male relationships. Male homosexuals tend to be inherently promiscuous. A number of scientific studies have been completed which indicate the very low rate of permanence or long-term satisfaction in same-sex unions.

"The reason for same-sex union failure is inherent within a system that is human-justified rather than God-ordained. Because these relationships do not encompass male and female, they cannot serve as ideal models for the community at large, especially for children. Furthermore, even though such relationships can include genital sexual activity, they cannot by nature produce children. Additionally, same-sex unions face the stigma of the community at large. The negative forces, both external and internal to such unions, are so powerful, therefore, that the chances of a fulfilling, enduring "marriage" are minute indeed."

6. Cultural acceptance and condoning of the homosexual lifestyle would undermine traditional American family values and public morality.

"Homosexuals contend they are not harming anyone else by their lifestyle choices; they delight in contrasting the church's stand on this issue with its stand on war and military service. For certain, homosexual activity does not kill, maim, or involve loss of blood. However, a larger issue is what acceptance of homosexuality does to the mind. The human psyche and moral consciousness are such fragile entities that are influenced by seemingly small and inconsequential developments and phenomena. The soul can be wounded in ways that leave no obvious scars. Satan works in such subtle and devious ways to deceive humans and point them in a damnably wrong direction.

"Additionally, adolescence is such a treacherous experience for most youth. There are immense uncertainties and anxieties which surround psychosexual development. While most people may be stable as the Rock of Gibraltar, there are a great many youngsters and young adults whose development has been so complicated and problematic that homosexuality presented to them as a morally neutral and acceptable alternative would be convincingly attractive.

"Finally, since the Bible categorically sets forth the model of committed, monogamous, male-female marriage as God's design for the entire population, as well as the context for the procreation and nurturing of the human race, the condoning of any alternatives undermines the moral fabric of a decent society."

Arguments for Acceptance and Condoning Homosexuality

1. The Bible does not offer a ringingly clear condemnation of homosexuality.

"Despite what moralists hope and expect to find in the Bible about homosexuals, the Scriptures to do not offer the crystal clear condemnation of homosexuality we have been asked to accept. True enough, we must conclude that there are Scriptures which speak of homosexuality in a negative manner, but such texts are open to varying interpretations which preclude a wholesale, definitive condemnation of homosexuality.

"First, a total of only seven brief passages in the Bible, all with negative statements about homosexuality, have formed an almost impassable gulf between Christians over the moral status of gay believers. Second, the issue of Scriptures' reliability and relevance on all social quandaries in our modern culture must be raised — did the Bible speak the final word on this subject or did it offer tentative direction as it apparently did in the cases of slavery or polygamy?

"Isolated passages must be examined on an individual basis. The story of Lot and Sodom comes first to mind. This story is not about sexual perversion and homosexual practice. The story is about inhospitality and attempted rape, as well as [according to Luke 10:10-13] failure to care for the poor. Ezekiel's perspective on Sodom and Gomorrah was a condemnation of abundance of wealth, idleness, and insensitivity to the poor, and not about sexual perversion. To suggest that Sodom and Gomorrah is about homosexuality is an analysis with as much validity as suggesting that the story of Jonah is essentially a treatise on whale fishing.

"The prohibitions in the Leviticus holiness code are admittedly clear bans on homosexual acts. But Leviticus also explicitly bans eating raw meat, planting two different kinds of seed in the same field and wearing garments with two different kinds of yarn. Sexual intercourse during a woman's menstrual period is also condemned. If moralists want to be consistent, why don't they preach out against these other archaic violations? There was capital punishment prescribed for numerous offenses, including adulterous sexual behavior and rebellious children's behavior.

"The apostle Paul's passion was stirred over homosexuality because it blatantly represented the secularism of the Greco-Roman world in contrast to Judeo-Christian idealism. Paul is *surely* not condemning a homosexual orientation in Romans and 1 Corinthians, but is more likely condemning exploitative sex and male prostitution. There is evidence that Paul was greatly vexed over the practice of pederasty, the seduction of boys by adult males. The writer clearly condemns an unnatural use of the body, but a person with a homosexual orientation chooses an unnatural use of his/her body when a heterosexual partner is sought for sexual purposes.

"The story of the Genesis creation of male and female for each other simply describes the reality for the majority of people, rather than provides a scathing condemnation of homosexual unions. For that matter, the Creation story does not address the issue of marriage or the moral obligations of heterosexual partners. The point: traditionalists should take care not to read more into the Bible than each text actually states."

2. Homosexuality cannot be condemned on the basis that it is "unnatural."

"The 'unnatural' contention is foolish for several reasons. First, consider that people get equally disgusted and uneasy at a variety of behavior that is perfectly *natural*. In the United States, we are revulsed by a woman who will not shave body hair on face and legs and in armpits. We have queasy feelings when a mother nurses a young baby in public view.

"On the other hand, we are perfectly at ease with people who do certain 'unnatural' things. It's truly unnatural to place miniature glass lenses on the naked eye simply for the vanity of not wearing larger glass pieces framed and perched on the nose and anyone who has attempted this for the first time can tell you how the entire body recoiled from such an experience. It's not natural to brace and clamp tightly a set of steel wires on one's teeth over a period of time. The same is true for surgically implanting sacks of silicone gel in female breasts that are perceived to be inadequate in size. Eating snails may not 'feel natural,' but it does not follow that eating escargots is immoral.

"Is homosexual activity 'unnatural' because it does not produce children? So is much heterosexual behavior engaged in with contraceptive measures carefully taken!

"One can define 'natural' in terms of 'the *primary* biological function.'

Thus, the natural function of the digestive system and of eating is to provide nutrition for the entire body; however, it does not follow that it is immoral sometimes to eat just for pleasure or for the company of a friend or mate even though one is not hungry or in need of food at the moment.

And the parts of the body that produce speech or vocal music are body parts that are employed for more important biological purposes, such as respiration and eating.

"Does 'natural' mean healthy? Mental and emotional health are important. In 1974 the American Psychiatric Association acknowledged that it had made a mistake and amended the *Diagnostic and Statistical Manual of Mental Disorders* to delete homosexuality as a mental disorder.

"Does naturalness refer to the 'fitting together' of genitals during heterosexual intercourse? Here, 'natural' seems to mean "geometric congruence." Is this sufficient reason for moral objection or does it reflect heterosexist bias and ignorance about homosexual intimacy? Would a moralist employ the naturalness argument to condemn oral sex between married heterosexuals? How about a tongue or finger playfully and gently inserted into the ear? After a while, this 'naturalness' argument gets silly."

3. Strong evidence indicates that homosexuals do not have an easy choice about their sexual orientation; their only choice is about telling the truth.

"Picking the gender of a sex partner is markedly dissimilar from any other of life's decisions, such as choosing between a Ford or a Chevy or in selecting only one flavor of ice cream from the many offered by Baskin-Robbins. If the ice cream parlor were out of your favorite "Pralines 'n' Cream" you would simply choose another flavor. And if people were the objects of sneers, bad jokes, and persecution, as well as living under the threat of loss of employment and career, all because they selected "Fudge Brownie" ice cream, they would surely select another available flavor. That homosexuals abide in their lifestyle even in the face of threats and harmful abuse indicates that being homosexual is not a matter of easy choice.

"The truth is, no one sets out to be a homosexual. Not in the way one sets out to be a mechanic, a lawyer, a surgeon, or a nurse. No one ever says, 'My goal in life is to be a homosexual.' Most homosexuals resist the compelling forces that pull them into open acknowledgment of their basic sexuality. Gradually that orientation must be accepted, at least privately.

"Have homosexuals made the 'wrong choice,' as former Vice President Dan Quayle once said? The only choice they make is between pretending that one is heterosexual, staying in the closet, perhaps even marrying someone of the opposite sex, or, on the other hand, having the courage to admit who one is and live one's life openly and without hypocrisy."

4. The vast majority of people are sexual deviants to some degree.

"Admittedly, this is a radical claim, but it is based on theology. Consider that the Bible teaches that all of us are sinners. The doctrine of total depravity asserts that every dimension of our human existence has been distorted by sin. Since our sexuality is such a major part of our human adventure, it is unthinkable that our sexual activity, both thoughts and actions, would not have been tainted and twisted by sin.

"Could it be that in God's view we are all sexual deviants? Is there anyone who has not engaged in masturbation, looked lustfully on another person, viewed pornography, 'used' even a marriage partner as an object, or engaged in sexual fantasies who has not deviated from God's perfect ideal of sexuality? If homosexuality is perversion, is such perversion different in *kind* or in *degree* from other types of sexual perversion?"

5. Discrimination and stereotyping are basically unfair; the request for protection against such does not constitute a request for "special rights."

"Perhaps no other group of people in history has been more misunderstood and more subject to all kinds of abuse than homosexuals. The most extreme form of 'gay bashing' has led to killing and maiming of innocent people simply because it was discovered they were homosexual. Homosexuals have little legal recourse against even blatant bias. There is no federal law protecting gays and lesbians from losing their jobs, being evicted from their homes or being denied a bank loan because of sexual preference. Only six states and about 110 municipalities have statutes barring discrimination against gays. No state recognizes gay marriage. And we all know the flack that was raised when President Clinton attempted to make good on his promise to admit gays to the military!

"How can Christian men and women be apathetic in the light of such abuse and discrimination? How can anyone hold up a big poster with the message 'GOD HATES FAGS' as did one man in a St. Patrick's Day parade in Boston?

"Are homosexuals demanding special rights? To qualify as a minority deserving legal protection, they must be a 'suspect class' similar to the disabled. To qualify, a group must meet three criteria: (1) Are they subject to historic discrimination? (2) Is that discrimination unfair? (3) Do they lack political power? Consider the number of cases of abuse against homosexuals and the number of cases brought before the courts on this issue. Consider the justice of treating someone unequally who, like the disabled, has a trait or characteristic that is either inborn or environmental? Consider how little impact homosexuals have on presidential policies or the laws of Congress. When the Civil Rights Act of 1964 was passed, blacks and Jews and other classes were not asking for special rights — they just wanted to be treated equally and fairly. So do homosexuals!"

6. Historically, it is impossible to prove that acceptance and condoning of homosexuality ever led to a weakening of the social fabric.

"This whole issue is about liberty of individuals to pursue happiness and seek meaning in life in their own way without the interference of others. You show me a nation that practiced control of the private lives of individuals and I'll show you a totalitarian government that did not care about its citizens.

"Sure, freedom can be abused, but no nation is made weaker because it permitted its citizens to enjoy the rights and privileges of democracy. There are nations in the western world, both now and in the past, who have tolerated homosexuality with no ill effects for others. Those countries seemed to be at peace with themselves and with other nations. The United States will not fall apart at the seams if it takes a tolerant position on homosexual practices.

"If rights and benefits could be extended to gays that are already enjoyed by the dominant culture, this nation would confirm its self-designated vision of a morally progressing nation, a nation serving as a beacon for others in the area of human rights. The words which end our pledge — 'with liberty and justice for all' — are not description of present achievement but a call to future challenge. Such a call led the black civil rights movement to great success and it could do the same for gays when it is consistently extended to others who deserve it."

SELECTED QUOTATIONS ON THE ISSUE

The emission of semen ought to be so ordered that it will result in both the production of the proper offspring and in the upbringing of this offspring. It is evident from this that every emission of semen, in such a way that generation cannot follow, is contrary to the good for man. And if this be done deliberately, it must be a sin. . . . For which reason, sins of this are called contrary to nature.

—Saint Thomas Aquinas

We are all human beings. That is to say, there is no such phenomenon as a "homosexual." There are only people — human persons — made in the image and likeness of God, yet fallen. However strongly we may disapprove of homosexual practices, we have no liberty to dehumanize those who engage in them.

—John R. W. Stott

In a television interview last month, President Bush said that he would still love his grandchild if he found out he was gay, but he wouldn't want him to promote his gay lifestyle. Would somebody please tell me what a gay lifestyle is? One may choose a country-club lifestyle, a Western lifestyle, a city lifestyle, but there is no such thing as a gay lifestyle — just as there is no such thing as a hetero sexual lifestyle. Homosexual lifestyles, like heterosexual lifestyles, run the gamut. They defy classification. And the only way I can "promote" my sexual orientation is to show other gay and lesbian people by my example that you can be homosexual, live outside the closet and lead a full, happy, family-centered life.

—Eric Marcus

If we remove homosexuality from a narrow psychopathological

setting and give it a wider connotation. . . it has many positive aspects as well. Homosexuality gives the individual a great capacity for friendship, which often creates ties of astonishing tenderness between men, and may even rescue friendship between the sexes from its limbo of the impossible.

—C. G. Jung

When they act as citizens, Christians have a serious obligation to support basic civil rights for homosexuals. It is unthinkable that men and women should lose jobs, be denied housing, and suffer police harassment for refusing to be bound by rules which most of their neighbors have for all practical purposes abandoned long since. If we argue that what happens in bedrooms is not the public business, we cannot in good conscience keep peeking through keyholes. If we hold that what happens in bedrooms is the public business, we have far more pressing problems to solve than those presented by Gay Liberation.

—William Muehl

It is particularly ironic that many Christians are prepared to set aside the direct and explicit teaching by Jesus on divorce but cling rigidly to obscure and questionable sources as justification for condemning homosexuality. There is nothing "biblical" or responsibly theological about such practice.

—John B. Cobb, Jr.

There are only two ways one can neutralize the biblical witness against homosexual behavior: by gross misinterpretation or by moving away from a high view of Scripture.

—Stanton L. Jones

The real moral problem that exists for parents of a homosexual son or daughter is one of loving acceptance. Parents of a homosexual have no reason to assume guilt for his condition; but parents of a psychologically healthy homosexual have good reason to believe that they have done their difficult task well.

—John McNeill

Even if the homosexual orientation could be shown to be the "natural" inclination for a certain percentage of the population in any given society, that fact alone would not necessitate an acceptance of homosexual activity. Ethics is not merely a condoning of what comes naturally. On the contrary, Christian theology warns us that we dare not always entrust ourselves to what we sense to be "natural." Our natural inclinations are not a sure guide to proper human conduct, but share in our fallenness. Jesus himself warned his followers that evil can proceed from the human heart (Mark 7:21). For this reason, disciples of the Lord are often called to deny what they may perceive to be their natural desires and inclinations, in order to follow the radical ethic of the Master.

—Stanley Grenz

The average man with sexual drives of normal strength, who chooses to accept the homosexual role, will probably seek physical satisfaction through contacts with other men and is destined to increasing frustration and ultimate loneliness.

—Richard Hettlinger

Nowhere in the Scripture is there a clear condemnation of a loving sexual relationship between two gay persons.

—John J. McNeill

The Bible clearly condemns certain kinds of homosexual practice (. . . gang rape, idolatry and lustful promiscuity). However, it appears to be silent in certain other aspects of homosexuality — both the "homosexual orientation" and "a committed love-relationship analogous to heterosexual monogamy."

—Letha Scanzoni and
Virginia Mollenkott

We believe that homosexual activity is sin and that God has called all persons to put away sin in their lives whether that be fornication, adultery, homosexuality, lying, greed, bitterness, etc.. We believe that no person is born a homosexual. Homosexuality is a learned identity and way of life. There is freedom. We believe there are normal legitimate love-needs underlying most cases of homosexuality. As a person is willing to allow God to begin to heal the wounded areas of his/her life and to work at seeing and changing old mindsets and behavior patterns, that person will begin to experience change in his/her view of God, self, and others.

—Christian Coalition For Reconciliation

Could I not stand, alone before my God, and say, "This is who I am. I can be no other." Wasn't this the essence of Christianity — a direct and personal relationship between a human being and God? "Listen, for whatever reason you made me, I am part of your creation. I have found a capacity to love. I do not believe that that is sin."

—Malcolm Boyd

I found myself on my knees, before God, cursing this lot. My curses turned to tears, asking forgiveness of God for questioning His unfolding plan. I asked God to simply, and in His time, relieve me of this undesirable truth.

I began attending a church which proclaimed that God could remove this sinful truth from me if I would seek Him in obedience and prayer. Three years, obedient celibacy, and many prayers later, this sinful truth remained within me. My religious peers claimed that I should be ever more persistent in my prayers. Waiting, patiently, prayerfully, I began focusing less on my truth and more on loving my God unconditionally. It was then that I began to understand my truth in His presence: I am loved and accepted, just as I am, by the One who lovingly designed me. My truth was no longer unbearable, unspeakable, unacceptable, devastating, imprisoning, perverse, undesirable, or sinful. My truth, in His presence, was beautiful.

—Chad Porter

I consider my own position as liberating: I do not have to serve as judge over other people's lives. I am committed to being like Jesus Christ, who said he came into the world not to condemn people but to make them whole: I will accept and associate with all those that Jesus accepted and associated with, and I know of no class of humanity, however scorned and despised by society, that he rejected. This does not mean that he always approved of their lifestyle.

—Leroy Garrett

DISCUSSION QUESTIONS AND BRIEF CASE STUDIES

1. How do you understand what the Bible says about homosexuality? If, most likely, you believe that the Bible labels it a sin, in what sense is it a sin?

Some evangelicals have taken what seems at first sight to be a definite condemnation of homosexuality and offer two arguments to the contrary. They contend that although Paul condemned homosexuality, the inspired apostle knew nothing of the modern distinction between "inverts" (those who are constitutional homosexuals or who have a homosexual disposition) and "perverts" (those who are heterosexually inclined, but indulge in homosexual practices). Paul is condemning the latter, the argument goes, because he describes as serious sinners those who have "abandoned" natural relations with women, whereas no exclusively homosexual male would ever have had them. Second, Paul is portraying the reckless, shameless, promiscuous, depraved behavior of people whom God has condemned and "given up." Why should stern divine punishment be leveled against a loving, committed homosexual partnership?

How would you answer this logic? Can we agree that sin is a serious choice that people make? Do people *choose* their sexual orientation or do they *discover* it? Think back on your own experience in early and middle adolescence.

Would it be fair to say that, since there is so much evidence of homosexuality being caused by varied complex factors beyond an individual's control, the homosexual disposition or constitutional nature is *not* a sin? What is sin, on the other hand, are the homosexual activities of an individual. If this logic is persuasive to you, then does God create an individual with one kind of orientation with its compelling drives and then ask that person to live and behave as though he/she were born with the opposite kind of constitution and orientation? Is the fairness of God at stake here?

2. The word "sodomy" has become a legal term for homosexuality and less typical forms of heterosexuality. The term comes to us from the story in Genesis 19 which tells us "the men of Sodom, both young and old" surrounded the house where Lot was staying and demanded that he send his two house guests (angel visitors?) out to them for the crowd's sensual pleasure. Lot, in pleading with the crowd not to commit such an abomination, even offered to send out his daughters for their pleasure to placate their demands

245

(an offer which raises major ethical issues apart from the homosexual issue). The angelic visitors intervened in the volatile situation, striking the unruly intruders with blindness, and then urged Lot to rescue his family and flee Sodom before its divine destruction.

Can we not conclude that homosexual gang rape was being threatened and that God's judgment was swift and awesome? Or, should we conclude that the real sin of sodomy was inhospitality to out-of-town visitors? On what reasoning do you base your conclusion?

3. Do you think it is possible for homosexuals to change their orientation to a heterosexual orientation? Homosexuals have asked traditionalists to consider how easy it would be for heterosexuals to give up *their* typical sexual attitudes, thoughts, and behavior and to accept homosexual attitudes and thoughts and to engage in homosexual behavior. Is that a fair analogy?

4. How would you counsel a Christian homosexual adult male who had decided to give up the homosexual lifestyle? Would you offer marriage to a woman and sexual abstinence as the only two proper alternatives for persons of same-sex orientation? What advice would you give to help him resist temptation to engage in homosexual activities? Would you recommend a counselor or clinical psychologist?

5. Do you agree that homosexuality should be condemned because it is not "natural"? How do you define "natural" and "unnatural" in ways that have moral significance or relevance? Are all "unnatural" activities sinful to God? If not, how do you make distinctions?

6. Do you know of people who are homophobic? How do you explain their motivation for being homophobic?

Consider: It is one thing to view homosexual practices as sinful; it is another to feel justified in "putting down" homosexual men and women in a wide range of ways, ranging from ridicule and tasteless jokes to opposition to their legal rights.

Does a phobia ever become a sin? It is certainly not immoral to harbor and act cautiously upon phobias about spiders or snakes or heights or airplane travel or closed spaces. Why should it be immoral to hate gays and lesbians? (Is not the obvious answer that homophobia is directed toward real human beings and not animals, spaces, or modes of transportation?)

Is homophobia a prejudice? What if a person said, "I'm not a racist but I have phobia about black people. I just don't want to be around them"?

Is homophobia a form of prejudice equally as evil as prejudice based on race, nationality, religion, or physique?

7. If homosexuals openly acknowledge their sexual orientation and if such orientation and preferences are treated publicly as "no big deal," what impact will this have on the nation? If young children sit at the feet of openly homosexual teachers, or are trained by homosexual athletic coaches or music teachers, will this lead children to become homosexuals (or at least their experimenting with homosexual activity)?

8. One objection raised against homosexuality is, "What if everyone (or most people) became homosexual? There would not be enough children to sustain society." Is this a good argument?

9. Heterosexuals take for granted the legal right to marry in any state in the United States, but homosexuals are denied this right. Is this unjust discrimination? One basis for denying homosexuals the right to marry is that many people understandably consider homosexuality to be immoral. Does this reason suffice for denying homosexuals the right to bond and receive legal recognition and protection for this bonding? Before answering, consider this situation: Historically, many people have believed the use of contraceptives is immoral and there have been laws in the twentieth century prohibiting their usage. Today, those who believe that contraceptives are sinful do not advocate laws which prohibit their use by others or prohibit people who use them from marrying. Is this a fair analogy or is it far-fetched?

The following is an excerpted "three-star" letter from a reader published in the *Tennessean* in response to another reader's letter which implied that "family" is defined by the natural ability of male and female to procreate:

". . . hence, the 'homosexual family' ceases to exist after one generation. Surely it takes little brain power to realize that "family" implies much more than the ability to generate new life. If procreation were the only important definition, then "family" should be outlawed. In one fell swoop we would rid the world of indigent, neglected and homeless children, not to mention over-population in general. A true family is not defined by sexual activity or length of existence; it is a unit which carries with it implications of healthy commitment, caring, nurturing, love and understanding. With these components, a wide variety of families may be defined: Straight couples, gay couples, those with or without children. Without these components, you either have an unhealthy family or not one at all (even though a marriage certificate may imply that you do). Individuals may have or become part of a family unit that may be less traditional, but just as valid, just as important and just as natural."

Do you agree with the basic point of this letter?

10. For several months you have been an energetic and loving teacher for a high school Sunday School class. You have attempted to relate to the teenagers' interests and issues. One young lady, "Sally," who is not a member of your church, has been attending your class and seems interested in your lessons. You have gotten to know more about her personal life and her school work by a few private visits after class. You were not, however, prepared for an issue she raised when she asked to drop by your house one evening.

"I'm sixteen years old and I have a problem," Sally began. "My mom is gay and I live with her and her girlfriend. I haven't told anyone, but I think my friends are starting to suspect what's going on. This is getting so embarrassing for me. What should I do?"

What do you say to Sally? Which of the following statements best describes how you would respond to Sally?

(a) "Wow, Sally, I'm shocked to hear this. I don't know anything about homosexuals and I don't feel comfortable talking about it. Let's talk about your Sunday School lesson for next week. I wouldn't be talking to anyone about this if I were you."

(b) "You need to get out of that deplorable and sinful living situation immediately. *You* can be saved, but God will render eternal condemnation on your mom, I'm sorry to say, as well as her girlfriend, if they do not repent. You can't hang around to learn the outcome."

(c) "According to a recent study there are three million gay and lesbian families in this country and they have a total of eight to ten million children. You ought to get in touch with some of these families and that will help you realize that you are not alone."

(d) "You need to tell your mother just exactly what you have told me. She's made a choice which affects your life, and even if that choice feels completely moral and natural to her, she needs to know that, right now, it doesn't seem so right for you."

(e) "You shouldn't talk about your mother that way. You have undoubtedly misinterpreted what is going on at your house. Children are good observers but not good interpreters. Your mother probably has had trouble finding good boyfriends and perhaps her friend has the same trouble. They're just living together to save money. Housing is expensive, as you know. If your mom were a lesbian she'd never have had sex with your father."

(f) "Sally, you should find a few friends whom you can tell about your home life since I'm sure part of your stress comes from feeling like you have to hide things from people you care about. Start by telling one or two of your closest friends that your mom's girlfriend lives with you and then add anything else you feel comfortable with. Now just remember that the issue of homosexuality can tap some strong emotions, so try to read their reactions as you go along."

(g) "Don't worry about what your friends will think, Sally. Homosexuality is a perfectly valid choice that your mother has made. If your friends are reasonable, they should be able to see that your mom's sex life is (a) her business and (b) nothing to judge you by. Of course, your mom's lesbianism may drive a few of your friends away from you, but in that case they weren't friends you'd want to have in the long run anyway."

11. Some people say that they have nothing against homosexuals, but they morally object to homosexuals "flaunting" their sexuality by holding hands in public, or having arms draped around each other, and kissing. The same people do not object to heterosexuals exhibiting the same affection. Are their views morally consistent? Do such homosexuals who make public displays of affection have a greater problem than homosexuals who remain "in the closet"?

12. We live in an era which has witnessed the emergence and near epidemic growth of incidents of Acquired Immunodeficiency Syndrome. When AIDS first became a public concern, some Christians were quick to label it "the gay disease." A few preachers and other church leaders offered a view that AIDS was part of God's direct interventionist judgment against homosexuals' behavior. Meantime, medical science has cleared the air about how AIDS is and is not contracted.

Is it fair to say that AIDS is caused by homosexuality and homo sexual acts? Is AIDS a gay disease? Has God sent AIDS as judgment on the gay community, perhaps as a continuation of the judgment which was leveled on Sodom and Gomorrah?

13. How should the church respond to the AIDS crisis? Should the church seek opportunities to minister compassionately to AIDS victims in the name of Jesus? Should education about AIDS and its prevention be offered under the auspices of local congregations?

14. Can the story of David and Jonathan in the Old Testament shed any light on same-sex relationships? There is nothing in the Bible to suggest that there was genital activity between David and Jonathan, but clearly a great and good "normal" man like David might love another man more than he loves any woman. Do you think there was something strange about this relationship?

15. The following letter was sent to "Dear Abby":

DEAR ABBY: I'll get right to the point — I am gay, but I don't like being gay. I want a wife and children. I also have a career in which further advancement would be very difficult if it becomes known that I am gay. Psychiatrists and other therapists I have consulted have tried to help me adjust to my homosexuality rather than help me to change. Abby, adjusting to homosexuality is fine for those who have accepted their homosexuality, but I have not. I know I'd be happier straight. Please help me. — UNHAPPY"

The following is Abby's answer:

"DEAR UNHAPPY: Did you choose to be homosexual? If so, you could choose to be "straight." But if you have always had erotic feelings for men instead of women, then face it, you are homosexual — and even though you may be able to change your behavior, you will not be able to change your feelings. Some therapists insist that if a homosexual is sufficiently motivated, he or she can become "straight." Maybe so, but the chances are slim. Marrying and having children may make you happier, but what about the other people you involve? To thine own self be true. Only then will you find true happiness."

Question: Did Abby give good advice? Would you have given different advice?

16. A judge in Richmond, Virginia, ruled that a lesbian is unfit to be a mother, and thus allowed a woman to retain custody of her homosexual daughter's two-year-old son. The woman's daughter, Sharon Bottoms, 23 years old at the time of the court decision, lived with a female lover. Since we cannot know all relevant facts in this case, an issue still emerges: are homosexual couples morally and emotionally fit for parenting? If you were a judge or human services social worker with the responsibility of placing two or three young children in a home, which of the following homes would you select: (a) A married man and woman who had each been in a prior marriage and of whom there were reports of continual conflict and occasional physical fighting; or (b) a lesbian couple which had

maintained a relationship and a household for several years and seemed to have a loving, peaceful relationship?

17. As a testimony to the perceived rejection and judgment felt by homosexual men and women in mainline churches, the Universal Fellowship of the Metropolitan Community Church was founded in 1968. This church openly welcomes and caters to the gay and lesbian community, contending that such persons want to be a part of a meaningful religious community. The Dallas Metropolitan Community Church has grown to one thousand members and is the largest MCC congregation of 235 churches worldwide.

Since this unique church is not welcome to assemble in most religious property, and its preachers are not recognized, fellow-shipped, or allowed to study in most seminaries and Bible colleges, the MCC may well be the most scorned and persecuted church since the first century.

How do you feel about this homosexual-based church? Do you think it has a moral right to exist, based on Jesus' statement "Anyone who comes to me I will in no wise cast out"? Or, are such homosexuals making a mockery of the Christian faith by trying to have their own church? Why not a church for murderers, another one for thieves, still another one for chronic liars, and another for adulterers?

18. Would you feel comfortable assigning a position of public service or participation in worship assemblies to a gay Christian who is not practicing homosexual activities? How would you feel about a gay Sunday School teacher? A gay preacher?

CHAPTER TEN

Animal Rights/
Environmental Ethics

On April 22, 1970, millions of young Americans from across the land joined together in conducting peaceful demonstrations, singing, listening to speeches, and expressing their concern over a special cause: the future of planet earth.

A generation of time has passed since that first Earth Day. Subsequent "Earth Days" have drawn much less fanfare, but the past quarter century has seen heightened concern and various pieces of legislation passed by the federal government to regulate toxic wastes, automotive emissions, and garbage disposal.

Still, many citizens contend that the nation faces an environmental crisis of potentially catastrophic proportions. Not only is our ecosystem in great danger, they contend, but human life as we know it is gravely threatened. Others dismiss these concerns as coming from uninformed alarmists and "environmental extremists."

The bottom line: there is much uncertainty about the nature and extent of threats to our planet posed by human lifestyle. There are so many unknown factors and forces which complicate any diagnosis of the present and prognostication for the earth's future. Nonetheless, according to Worldwatch's eleventh annual "State of the World" report on global conditions delivered in 1994, significant evidence has emerged indicating that the earth's biological limits have been reached. Signs cited in the "State of the World" report include a dramatic drop in grain production, a drop in fish harvests from oceans (with concomitant increase in seafood prices), the disappearance of much topsoil, vast deforestation and mismanagement of acreage, and an increase in water pollution.

Appropriately, ethical concern about our earth encompasses issues related to our attitude toward and treatment of animals. Non-human life composes such a vitally important part of the ecosystem. Not only do animals and insects of all species play their role in the earth's delicate balance of nature, but almost half of all American and European households have pets which are regarded as companions. Some people devote large amounts of time, attention, and financial resources to the care and feeding of these pets, often more than they give to their churches, to their neighbors, or to close relatives.

Several moral considerations arise: What moral responsibilities do we have toward non-human animals (hereafter, we will use "animals" in the sense of non-human animals) and the environment? Do animals have moral significance apart from their value to humans? And, if so, on what basis do animals have moral value? Do we have greater responsibility toward our pets than we do toward all other animals? Does the environment of billions of living organisms as well as masses of water and mineral resources possess moral significance? Do we have moral responsibilities toward the environment? Or do we have responsibilities only toward human beings because they only they bear God's unique image?

SEVEN MAJOR ENVIRONMENTAL CONCERNS

In the early '90s, concern about the environment was heightened to the point that almost any moderate to liberal public servant would claim to be an environmentalist. Major corporations announced the steps they were taking to protect the environment as, for example, in the announcement of major tuna processors that they would no longer sell tuna that was caught with dolphins. Other companies announced they would mass produce their products in recyclable containers. And after the widely touted and deeply deplored *Exxon Valdez* oil spill of eleven million gallons of crude oil on March 24, 1989, as well as the massive dumping of oil by Saddam Hussein in the Persian Gulf war, new concerns were raised about who is impacted most by ecological crises and whose responsibility it is to prevent a crisis and make reparation after one occurred.

Despite these expressions of concern, environmental problems continued to abound because of the ways the human family generates energy, manufactures products, transports people and cargo, and grows food. Though these problems continue to receive media attention, it is worthwhile to briefly cite them here:

1. Global warming. Atmospheric levels of carbon dioxide have increased significantly in the last century, primarily due to the burning of fossil fuels in transportation and manufacturing.

Carbon dioxide serves as a trap for infrared rays from the sun which otherwise would be reflected out into space, thus raising the surface temperature of the earth. The greenhouse effect is not all hazardous, of course, since a certain amount of heat must be captured in our atmosphere much like glass panes of a greenhouse capture heat.

In a highly plausible worst case scenario for the next two to three generations, scientists predict an increase in the earth's temperature from three to nine degrees — an increase which would melt polar ice caps, raise the sea level and flood coastal cities and villages, produce severe inland droughts and resultant food shortages, and threaten many species of plants and animals which are not able to adapt to a warmer climate. Other scientists doubt the likelihood of such a scenario but contend that the threat of global warming is real.

2. Ozone Depletion. An important component in the atmosphere above the earth, called stratosphere, is ozone. Ozone provides the crucially important service of shielding life on earth from the ultraviolet rays of the sun. Without this shield, humans would experience a significant increase in skin cancer and diseases of the immune system. We now know that the ozone layer has been depleted by chemicals released into the atmosphere during the last century. For example, chlorofluorocarbons (CFCs), once commonly used as a refrigerant and found in styrofoam products and aerosol sprays, are known to drift into the atmosphere and destroy ozone molecules. Since the connection between CFCs and ozone depletion was discovered, significant progress has been made to find suitable substitutes for the offending chemicals. Still, holes in the ozone layer have been spotted and appear to be growing.

3. Acid Rain. Certain oxides from burning fossil fuels — carbon dioxide, sulfur dioxide, and nitrogen oxide — are transformed into acids when released and become suspended in rain, snow, and fog. These pollutants can be carried thousands of miles by wind and upon descending again to the earth will damage streams and lakes and kill forests and other plant life by destroying roots and leaves. Acid rain also corrodes buildings and metal structures such as automobiles and bridges. Acidic soil also damages crops and ground water. The effects of acid rain may be far-reaching; however, further research is required before reaching specific conclusions.

4. Resource Depletion. Vast quantities of raw materials are extracted from Mother Earth in producing goods and services —

clothing, transportation, appliances, machinery, recreational facilities, homes and units in which to live and vacation and buildings in which to work.

Ours is a flow-through economy. Every functional item in our homes, office buildings, churches, and industries are reworked parts of creation. We extract parts of the natural environment and rework them into products and by-products which eventually become discards and waste. Oil, coal, and gas are burned to drive systems of transportation, machinery, and systems for heating and cooling. While some resources are renewable, such as cotton and wood, fossil fuels are not, of course, unlimited in supply. Clean water is used for cooking, recreation, manufacturing, and agricultural irrigation. Warnings have already been issued regarding the oil industry's technology to extract enough oil to meet an ever-increasing demand.

5. Trash and Garbage. Our society taps into creation's wealth and converts it into an endless array of products and by-products which are then used and either disposed of or recycled. Far too little is recycled — informed estimates indicate that only about ten percent of trash in our society is recycled.

In the United States more than seven million cars are junked every year; in New York City alone there are over 70,000 abandoned cars. Our citizens throw away 240 to 260 million tires, 40 billion metal cans, 26 billion bottles, and 65 billion bottle caps annually. This society throws away 16 billion disposable diapers and 2 billion disposable razors annually. All in all, Americans produce about four to six pounds of garbage per day, about double that produced by the typical Japanese, Swiss, German, or Swedish citizen. About 70% of the garbage Americans produce is compostable. Each year Americans bury enough steel to produce two million cars; enough paper to produce all our newspapers; enough wood to build one million homes.

The sanitary landfill is the most common solution to the problem of garbage and trash, but this system is not without serious problems: first, landfills are quickly filled because of vast amounts of nonbiodegradable materials such as plastic; and, second, landfills pose risks to surface and ground water. As for combustible waste, the chief alternative of incineration poses a hazard to clean air due to gases which are released during the process. Admittedly, there are no easy answers.

6. Deforestation and Species Extinction. Some environmentalists claim that approximately 90 percent of the species that ever existed on earth since life emerged many ages ago are now extinct, almost all from natural causes rather than human activity. The speed of extinction, however, has greatly accelerated due to the human family encroaching upon the natural habitats of both animals and plants. One estimate contends that, since 1850, 2.2 billion acres of natural lands have been converted to human uses. Names given for this conversion of natural ecosystems include deforestation (of forests), drainage or "reclamation" (of wetlands), irrigation (of arid and semi-arid ecosystems), and plowing (of grasslands and prairies).

The most extensive conversion under way is tropical deforestation, occurring at the rate of 25 million acres (an area the size of Indiana) every year. Over half the species of plants and animals currently on earth are located in (and only in) tropical rain forests. These unique species of plants and animals constitute important sources of food, energy, and medicine (such as antibiotics and cancer drugs) for the entire human family as well as providing a fundamental and irreplaceable source of the gene pool of earth. Given their role in photosynthesis, the loss of our forests means an increase in greenhouse gases and thus contributes to global warming.

The threat of extinction of animals is highly publicized in the cases of animals that people like to see in zoos or in *National Geographic*. The loss of thousands of other plant and animal species, many of which are still unidentified, should also concern us.

7. World Population. One catalyst contributes mightily to all other environmental challenges — human population. In 1900 there were approximately 1.6 billion human beings on earth; in 1991 there were 5.5 billion. Some prognosticate that world population will stabilize sometime during the twenty-first century at eight to fourteen billion people. Others contend that the earth cannot sustain such a high population. Regardless, an ever-increasing population makes ever-increasing demands for food, land, energy, and raw materials for goods and services and this demand diminishes natural resources and creates more waste.

THE JUDEO-CHRISTIAN TRADITION AND ANTHROPOCENTRISM

Beginning with the creation story of Genesis, the Judeo-

Christian tradition has affirmed that the environment and all that compose its wealth and beauty were placed here by the Creator for the purposes of human beings. According to Scripture, God commanded the first human family to "fill the earth and subdue it; and have dominion over the fish of the sea and over the birds of the air and over every living thing that moves upon the earth." Then, after the flood, the human family was instructed, "Every moving thing that lives shall be food for you; and as I gave you the green plants, I give you everything."

These biblical injunctions have been supported over the centuries in the western world by historic Christian theology. Christian doctrine holds that only human beings possess the *imago Dei*, the divine gift of ensoulment, and they thus occupy a superior position in the created order.

Aristotle, Locke, Kant, and Mill and most other traditional ethicists assumed that human beings were the exclusive focus of moral concern because they have an inherent worth that cannot be attributed to other natural creatures. Thus did the great French philosopher René Descartes (1596-1650) contend that nonhuman animals were non-feeling creatures of reflex and were no better than biological robots. Descartes argued that animals cannot reason or feel sensations since they possessed only a physical mind. Kant recommended that humans treat animals kindly, not out of any inherent worth of animals but because cruelty to animals might lead humans to develop cruelty to other humans.

Thus did anthropocentrism, the doctrine that humans are the center of all the universe, take root and develop for centuries. Dominion is a divine mandate. For God to share it with men and women, even delegating it to them, is a deep honor. To have the image of God is to be a ruler of the universe. All other nonhuman creatures, plants, and resources then are to be used for the purposes and betterment of humankind. And all other of the earth's vast resources must find their worth only in relationship to human beings.

In traditional western views, therefore, human beings owe the animals and physical environment nothing. Humans may have moral obligations concerning animals and environment, however, but ultimately those are obligations to other humans. We ought not to destroy someone's prize thoroughbred horse for the same reason that we ought not to destroy another person's highly-charged stock car. Both the horse and the stock car can win prize money for their owners and sponsors and both must be respected as someone's property. We do not poison a neighbor's dog whose bark annoys us for the same reason we do not destroy the neighbor car which has a loud muffler, because humans have a moral obligation to respect others' property.

Contemporary thought and practice are not as extreme as these illustrations might suggest, of course. Descartes' view of animals as non-feeling creatures of reflex has long since been widely repudiated by better understanding of animal feelings and behavior. No one would contend that animals cannot suffer and most of us would be sympathetic to organized efforts which promote humane treatment and punish cruelty to animals. How far concern about humane treatment should extend ranges from opinions held over hunting and trapping animals to obvious cases of mistreatment of work or sport animals or pets and then to less apparent but widely accepted practices of animal experimentation and factory farming. There are enough issues and practices regarding animals to keep citizens debating almost endlessly.

BIOCENTRIC ETHICS AND "DEEP ECOLOGY"

Do we really owe the environment and animals nothing? A life-centered ethic, called biocentric ethics or "deep ecology," makes a radical break with traditional western views by affirming the intrinsic moral worth of all living things, including nonsentient animals and plants.

Many contemporary Christian ethicists now focus on the moral value and integrity of God's creation as a whole and their perspective is drawn from Holy Scripture. "Integrity" implies unity or integration. "Integrity" also implies basic identity, inner consistency, a sense of overall connectedness, and divinely-bestowed dignity.

In a general way, the Bible hints at the role nature plays in the divine scheme of salvation. The narration of creation in Genesis, the use of natural imagery in the wisdom literature of the Old Testament, Jesus' parables that are drawn from simple observations of nature at work, the Apostle Paul's declaration that all creation is in labor for redemption, and the picture in Revelation of the old natural system (old bodies; old earth) being transformed or replaced by a new heaven and new earth all suggest that the natural world is valued as "very good" by the Creator and that it serves divine purposes.

Several Scriptures focus on the goodness of the whole creation. As noted, God declared his creation to be good. This goodness is not relative to human beings; contrariwise, the creation is good quite exclusive of human beings within it. The commandment to be fruitful and multiply is given first to the creatures of the sea and the air.

God's commandment to Noah to build a spacious ark was intended to provide shelter and sanctuary for the preservation of the rich diversity of species. When the ark landed, God orders Noah to bring forth the sheltered animals so that they may breed abundantly upon the earth (Gen. 8:17). The covenant that God makes with Noah, pledging that no such disaster will again be inflicted upon the earth is also made with all living creatures (Gen. 9:10, 12, 15-17). The Psalmist spoke and sung frequently of how the whole created order praised Yahweh and declared his handiwork.

Jesus seemed to be at peace with nature, although on occasion he made it clear that he was Lord of all nature so that "the wind and sea obey his voice." He considered long periods in the wilderness alone to be conducive to spiritual discipline and commitment to his mission. The Jewish paschal lamb gave Jesus and his closest disciples sustenance, even as it became a symbol of his own atoning death. Both fish and loaves were multiplied to feed the hungry throngs who gathered to hear his message. Jesus taught that a human life is "of more value than many sparrows" (Matt. 10:31), but this self-evident truth should never lead anyone to conclude that sparrows have no value. Indeed, the Master taught his Heavenly Father cares for the birds of the heaven and the lilies of the field (Matt. 6:25-30).

Albert Schweitzer (1875-1965) highlighted this biocentric ethic with his phrase "reverence for life." "I am life which wills to love," he contended, "in the midst of life which wills to live." Schweitzer concluded that if a human being finds meaning and goodness in acting on the will to live, then consistency requires that person to render a similar affirmation for *all* living things. Life has intrinsic value, quite beyond and exclusive of its value to any other living thing. Life of any kind is sacred. To Schweitzer this meant no crushing of insects, stomping on grass, plucking flowers, or pulling leaves from a tree.

Most ethicists would reject Schweitzer's refusal to rank the value of the many living things in our world. Common sense informs us that different life forms have different degrees of value. A family enjoying a summer cookout on its patio might be friendly toward someone's pet dog or cat invading family space or it might gently encourage the dog or cat to return to its own home; the same family would think nothing of swiftly and mercilessly swatting flies or mosquitoes which appeared uninvited at the family dinner table.

THE MORAL WORTH OF ANIMALS

On what basis do we attribute moral worth to animals? And should all animals be considered equal?

The questions are important. The attitude of most classical philosophers, as pointed out already, was that animals, including even higher mammals, have no intrinsic moral worth of any kind, and that their value emanates from human estimates of worth to themselves or other humans. This extremist attitude is surely wrong when we consider the following realities:

1. Many animals do experience emotional states and have needs and desires somewhat similar to those of humans. As conscious creatures, they can experience pleasure and delight. They provide nurture and sustenance for their young and protect them against predators or other forces of nature of which they are aware. It would be improper to attribute human-like, complex mental states even to higher mammals, but then neither do we attribute such mental faculties even to human infants or severely retarded adults.

2. Some animals are capable of providing valuable companionship to human beings. A good pet can interact lovingly and sensitively with human families. A pet may provide meaningful companionship for those aged people who are lonely or for people with physical limitations; in each case a bond can be established between human and pet on the basis of caring. Arguably, a pet may provide an appropriate outlet for a woman or man's desire to love a "significant other."

3. Some animals are capable of providing service, security, or recreation and entertainment for humans. A leader dog can provide great assistance to legally blind persons. A shepherd dog may assist a farmer in keeping a flock together. Since the beginning of time, the plowing of fields, carrying of burdens, and the pulling of wagons, to cite only three examples, have been performed by work animals. A dog's bark may have deterred many a home burglar. And who hasn't enjoyed spending some time horseback riding?

4. Animals can suffer. Anyone who has witnessed an injured animal has no doubt that they can. The thought of a loved pet suffering has haunted many people, adult and child alike. Many animals can instinctively anticipate and have fear about potential suffering and death when they find themselves in a dangerous situation. Animals can also anticipate dangers to their offspring and will plaintively cry out in warning to their young in the presence of a predator.

5. Higher mammals can develop their own personality uniqueness. They can respond to human communication. They can also develop traits that we value in humans, such as predictability, dependability, and loyalty. This provides a rationale for providing legal protection for dolphins, whales, chimpanzees, and gorillas.

It seems logical, therefore, to ascribe some moral worth to animals without the need to grant them the full moral status we ascribe to human beings. Everything in Christian theology and common sense informs us that a human life takes priority over nonhuman life and that animals do not deserve the rights of human beings. As a corollary, it would seem, not all animals have equal moral worth. The moral worth of animals would logically seem to reside in their capacity to feel pleasure and pain, to act meaningfully and purposefully rather than randomly and aimlessly (admittedly difficult for human observers to judge), and to interact socially with one another and with humans.

KEY TERMS

Acid precipitation — The deposition of wet acidic solutions or dry acidic particles from the air; commonly known as acid rain but also includes acid fog, snow, etc.

Ahimsa — The Buddhist moral principle of nonharming: whenever avoidable, humans should not harm any living creature.

Anthropocentrism — The belief that humans hold a special place in nature; being centered primarily on humans and human affairs.

Anthropomorphism — To think or speak of things that are not human (especially plants and nonhuman animals) in terms of human or personal characteristics; humanization.

Biocentric preservation — A philosophy of preserving nature for its own sake.

Biotic Community — The community of all living organisms; the community of life.

Deep ecology — An integrated combination of beliefs, lifestyle, an activism based on voluntary simplicity, decentralization, personal freedom, the sacredness of nature, and direct action in environmental protection; herein, human beings function as one species among others, thus contributing to the richness of the whole.

Ecojustice — Justice in the social order and integrity in the natural order.

Environmental ethics — A search for moral values and ethical principles in human relations with the natural world.

Environmentalism — A social movement concerned with the health of the entire environment, both natural and built by humans.

Extinction — The irrevocable elimination of species; can be a normal process of the natural world as species out-compete or kill off others or as environmental conditions change.

Fossil fuels — Fuels derived from the residues of plants and animals changed by heat and pressure deep below the earth's surface.

Gandhian sufficiency — A view that the world has "enough for everyone's need, but not enough for anyone's greed."

Habitat — Describes the place or set of environmental conditions in which an organism lives.

Human ecology — The study of the interactions of humans with the environment.

Instrumental value — Value or worth of objects that satisfy the needs and wants of moral agents. Objects that can be used as a means to some desirable end.

"Integrity of Creation" — The special unity and interrelatedness of all of God's creation that implies inner consistency and dignity; human beings may view nature as a partner deserving respect and whose integrity they must not violate.

Imago Dei — The theological doctrine that humans, and humans alone, are created in the image of God.

"Lifeboat ethic" — A harsh ethic or attitude toward poor nations of the world based on the metaphor of a lifeboat in an ocean of drowning people. Since the lifeboat has limited capacity, occupants of the lifeboat only put themselves and everyone else in peril when they attempt to rescue people for whom they have no room in the lifeboat and who will have no compassion for a guilt-ridden passenger who relinquishes his secure seat to perish so that a needy person might live.

Majority world — The poorest 80% of humanity which consumes less than half of the world's resources.

Malthusian growth — A population explosion followed by a population crash; also called irruptive growth.

Natural history — The study of where and how organisms carry out their life cycles.

Ozone — A highly reactive molecule containing three oxygen atoms; a dangerous pollutant in ambient air. In the stratosphere, however, ozone forms an ultraviolet absorbing shield that protects us from mutagenic radiation.

Pantheism — The doctrine that equates God with the forces and laws of the universe; the pantheist contends that the divine is in everything.

Population — A group of individuals of the same species occupying a given area.

Recycling — Reprocessing of discarded materials into new, useful products; not the same as reuse of materials for their original purpose, but the terms are often used interchangeably.

"Reverence For Life" — The principle of the sanctity of all life drawn from the teaching and lifestyle of Albert Schweitzer; all living things have intrinsic value and should be humans' object of moral concern; the killing of any living thing is permissible only when "unavoidable" or "necessary."

Sentience — Responsive to or consciousness of sense impressions; awareness; sensitivity in perception or feeling.

Species — A population of morphologically similar organisms that can reproduce sexually among themselves but that cannot produce fertile offspring when mated with other organisms.

Speciesism — "a prejudice or attitude of bias toward the interests of members of one's own species and against those of members of other species" (Peter Singer).

Stewardship — Trusteeship; guardianship. As used by ecologists, stewardship means to consider nature an endowment that human beings ought to promote, safeguard, preserve, and help to flourish for the next generation.

Stress — Physical, chemical, or emotional factors that place a strain on an animal. Plants also experience physiological stress under adverse environmental conditions.

Wildlife — Plants, animals, and microbes that live independently of humans; plants, animals, and microbes that are not domesticated.

Zero population growth (ZPG) — The number of births at which people are just replacing themselves; also called the replacement level of fertility.

KEY SCRIPTURES

Genesis 1:26-28, 31; Leviticus 25:1-2; 20:14, 32, 35; Psalm 8:6; Psalm 19:1; Psalm 24:1; Psalm 148; Isaiah 5:8; Jeremiah 2:7; Matthew 6:25-30; Romans 8:9-25; Ephesians 4:6; Revelation 4:11

KEY ISSUES/ARGUMENTS
Do Christians have moral responsibility toward animals and the universe? YES:

1. Humans hold no special place in nature and nature does not exist just for human purposes.

"Take away your biblical theology for a moment and then ask yourself: 'What's so special about human beings anyway?' It's pure vanity for humans to think that they are situated atop the pyramid of all earthly life, that they have the right to treat all over life exactly as they want. Nature was around long before men and women made the scene, with its beauty and majesty. And nature does not need the presence of human beings to exist in that beauty and majesty. We're just part of the plan, not the master of that plan. And we have no right to interfere with that plan."

2. There is an overall connectedness of all living things in the earth's single ecosystem.

"Everyone's who has ever studied biology has heard of the 'chain of life' principle. The way things have evolved over long periods of time is that certain living things have become interdependent with other living things. We are all part of a life community as large as the earth itself. The first principle of any community is cooperation. Another principle of community is respect. These principles apply to the biotic community of which human beings are such a vital part. It's time for all of us to cooperate with the laws of nature and to show respect for the other members of this vast community."

3. All creatures and other living things have intrinsic value.

"All living things have value in and for themselves. It's easy to read the story of creation and to learn of the special status of Adam and Eve and then to forget of the special tending and nurturing responsibilities that God gave this pair. And if somehow Adam and Eve were to disappear from the scene, the natural world would still have retained its value and beauty. This world was not designed by some mere human. God made it all and God 'don't make no junk.' Anything that God created has intrinsic value. Let's treat it as such."

4. Trivial human interests are not as important as important interests of nature and animals.

"Given the premise that all living things in nature have intrinsic value, how can humans justify so much of their lifestyle? Take eating meat, for example. Sure, meat provides protein but so do beans and other vegetables. A vegetarian can be just as healthy as a beef-eater. Therefore, meat-eating is trivial when compared to the cost of meat production and the pain of factory farming of animal food. The wearing of animal furs provides a more obvious example of trivial human interests which weigh so little in comparison with the greed and cruelty of people in the furrier industry. As for using animals in research, surely there are alternative ways of discovering what society needs to know without torturing innocent animals."

5. Human good and human pain are not the only good and pain in the universe.

"We hear a lot about what's good for humans. But what about what's good for a lake or stream or forest or a species? Again, we are putting ourselves at the center of the universe. We all know that pain is bad. Nobody likes to suffer. Well, an animal's pain can hurt just as much as a man or woman's pain. Sure, an animal can't put its pain into theological or philosophical perspective, but the pain is just as bad regardless. Our moral responsibility is to admit that all pain is equally bad and then work to treat all animals, human and non-human alike, with kindness and compassion."

6. Humans should give something back to nature.

"People have been taking from nature for many generations without giving anything back. They have polluted air and water, burned forests to make crop land or pasture, cleared woods to build more houses, and turned mountain majesties into crowded tourist resorts. Anyone can cut down a giant redwood tree in a few minutes time to make picnic tables and benches and patio furniture, but it takes many generations of growth to replace that tree. We certainly can't replace all that we have selfishly taken, but we can slow down the senseless exploitation and spoilage of land and sea and then encourage the process of reclamation."

7. Humans should give something to future generations.

"Surely we don't plan to be the last generation to live on the face of this earth. Don't we expect a decent life for our children. Presently existing men and women have a moral duty to make some sacrifices in order to protect the rights, especially the right to enjoy the natural beauty and resources of the earth, of the people who will come after them. A little sacrifice will be needed to prevent our bequeathing to future generations a planet that is no longer capable of sustaining a quality human life."

Do Christians have moral responsibility toward animals and the universe? NO:

1. Scripture charges humans with the mandate to subdue and have dominion over the earth.

"Beginning with the Genesis account of creation, Judeo-Christian thought has instructed us that all things in the environment were placed here for the purpose of humans. To 'subdue' and 'have dominion' means to exercise control. God made human beings for his own pleasure. God made animals and plants and flowers for the pleasure of humans. To overturn this notion is to overturn centuries of Christian thought."

2. Scripture has uniformly supported the use of animals for humans' food and other needs.

"Both Scripture and common sense tell you that human beings have the right to eat beef, or pork, or chicken, or fish though they certainly do not have the duty to do so. One is free to be a vegetarian if he/she chooses not to participate in a wide-scale system of killing. While the ancient Jews had dietary laws which distinguished clean and unclean animals, clearly God wanted his people to know that he had created and placed animals on earth for human sustenance. In Bible times there is reference made to all kinds of meat-eating with the possible exception of pork."

3. People count more than trees and bugs.

"Sure, we need to protect wilderness and wildlife, but the reason we do is because this is our environment. It is our quality of life that is being protected. Our survival may be at stake. Is it important whether a redwood tree survives? A plant, or tree, or flower has no interest in its own survival. People are what counts. You and me. Because people can experience self-awareness and intelligent reasoning and possess an eternal soul, their interests must come first and foremost."

4. From a legal and a moral point of view, speciesism is ridiculous.

"All this talk about animal rights, animal liberation, and speciesism is a slap in the face to people who have been victimized by real prejudice and discrimination. How can you compare raising animals for laboratory research to people who could not vote because of the color of their skin? How can you compare raising beef cattle for market to breeding humans for a slave market? Farm animals can't be robbed of their dignity. Humans can know humiliation; animals can be mistreated but the impact on their emotions cannot be compared with human emotions after humiliation.

"The law of Moses nowhere equated the life and value of an animal, even a beast of burden, with the life of another human being. Consider that God allowed and even commanded animal sacrifice in religious devotion. Only in the case of Abraham's test of faith did God ever command one human to sacrifice another human."

5. Equal treatment of species would bring disastrous consequences.

"Suppose, for the sake of argument, that we treated other animals as equals to ourselves. Think of the impact on the economy. What would happen to farmers, ranchers, butchers, fishermen, meat-processors and the millions of others whose jobs would disappear?"

6. Dialogue about animal rights and environmental ethics is elitist.

"Only in societies as affluent as America or nations in western Europe can people afford to talk about environment and animal rights. Most cultures on the globe do not have that luxury; their survival needs are so overbearing. Furthermore, the 'small' sacrifices that some environmentalists call for may not be so 'small' for communities which are based almost entirely on a certain industry such as logging, mining, fishing, or manufacturing."

7. There is no real threat humans make to the survival of the ecosystem.

"There are times in which we are able to see how small we humans really are and how great and large is our God's world. In the aftermath of the Exxon Valdez oil spill, every reference to the environment seemed to be prefaced with the adjective 'fragile.' Nothing is further from the truth — the environment is nearly indestructible. It has survived ice ages, collision of comets and meteors and it can survive anything that you and me can do to it.

"The ecosystem is forever in a state of flux. To Mother Nature, all our concern with endangered species must seem like a shallow sentimentality since such a large number of entire species have now become extinct. Ultimately, there's very little that humans by themselves can do to alter the fundamental character of the ecosystem. We just need to take care of our own little part of God's big world and not worry about what everyone else is doing."

8. The current generation does not owe anything special to succeeding generations.

"What's all this talk about future generations? Doesn't the Bible teach us that no one knows how long time will last, that Jesus is coming soon? We are just responsible for the 'here and now.'

"Presently existing people actually do exist. Their needs are real. On the other hand, future people on earth are only a possibility; they may exist. It may seem highly probable that people will be around a century from now, but, given all the scenarios of mass disease or famine and nuclear war, no one can be certain. Certainly the interests of other people must count for something, but not nearly as much as the interests of living generations.

"Suppose this generation were to deplete all of the oil and coal embedded in the earth. Ultimately, all fossil fuels will be used. Is that reason for humans to conserve? Only the human intelligence is forever renewable and surely by the time all fossil fuels have been almost depleted that human intelligence will have discovered or invented another means to provide energy and fuel. Let's not worry about future generations or feel curtailed by their potential needs."

SELECTED QUOTATIONS

So God created man in his own image, in the image of God he created him; male and female he created them. God blessed them and said to them, "Be fruitful and increase in number; fill the earth and subdue it. Rule over the fish of the sea and the birds of the air and over every living creature that moves on the ground."

—Genesis 1:27-28

Human demands are approaching the limits of oceanic fisheries to supply fish, of rangelands to support livestock and, in many countries, of the hydrological cycle to produce fresh water. . . . We have surpassed the planet's carrying capacity.

—Worldwatch "State of the World"

Should a Christian love nature? Most have not over the last two thousand years and many today still don't. In some circles, loving nature is "pagan" or what Goddess worshippers do. Of course, Christians should respect nature, use it carefully, and even protect it, but isn't loving it a bit extreme? Should we love nature? My answer is a resounding Yes. Christians should because, quite simply, God is with us here in and on our earth. That is what the incarnation claims. God does not despise physical reality, but loves it, has become one with it. The Christian tradition is full of body language: the Word made flesh, the bread and wine that become the body and blood, the body of the church. Physical reality, earthly reality, is the place where we find the presence of God — that is what an incarnational theology tells us.

—Sallie McFague

"Do not take advantage of each other," warns the Law. "The land must not be sold permanently, because the land is mine and you are but sojourners. . .the land must be returned to the poor and the meek."

—Leviticus 25:23, 28

The churches are the sleeping giants in the environmental movement, an army who is taught to love and care for their neighbor. They just need to understand that the sickest neighbor now is Mother Earth. Whether we are Christians, Muslims, Jews, Hindus, we have to learn to be less wasteful and live more gently than we do. The Bible teaches the concept of the Sabbath. The Sabbath should be every day. We should keep the Earth holy. It's in our power to destroy the Earth but not to recreate it.

—Mack Prichard

Environmentalism is a conservative ethic, not a liberal ethic. I have fairly consistently taken the posture that, as a conservative, I have something to say about environmental conservation. There is also an analogy with fiscal issues. When you exploit the environment, you are simply building up debt that is passed on to the next generation. If you want to look at it in terms of cost efficiency, it is much cheaper to protect the environment from harm than it is to retroactively reclaim it from exploitation.

—Paul Henry

Nature carries the sacrality of divinity itself. Ancient peoples often saw this more clearly than modern peoples have. Nature is the oldest face of God, and in any healthy culture nature remains venerable. The necessity of having to hurt plants and animals in order to survive so preoccupied ancient peoples that they developed many rituals of petition and appeasement. The Christian can say that all those rituals struggled to express a conviction that human beings do not have the right to use natural materials wantonly. Certainly, Christianity has accorded human beings a special dignity and given them the right to subordinate the fates of inanimate, plant, and animal creation to their own. But this subordination (and so desacralization) of nature has stood in tension with intuitions decrying the destruction of nature. Indeed, our current ecological crisis has made it clear that the "dominative" reading of Genesis 1:28, according to which human beings have the charge to "subdue" the earth, has been fraught with lethal consequences.

—Denise L. Carmody and John T. Carmody

The edifice of civilization has become astonishingly complex, but as it grows ever more elaborate, we feel increasingly distant from our roots in the earth. In one sense, civilization itself has been on a journey from its foundations in the world of nature to an ever more contrived, controlled, and manufactured world of our own imitative and sometimes arrogant design. And in my view, the price has been high. At some point during this journey we lost our feeling of connectedness to the rest of nature. We now dare to wonder: Are we so unique and powerful as to be essentially separate from the earth?

—Al Gore, Jr.

How can I rest beneath a tree
If it may soon be suing me?
Or enjoy the playful porpoise

While it's seeking habeas corpus?

—John Naff

All of nature is a gift-exchange, a potluck banquet, and there is no death that is not somebody's food, no life that is not somebody's death. Is this a flaw in the universe? A sign of the sullied condition of being? 'Nature red in tooth and claw'? Some people read it this way, leading to a disgust with self, with humanity, and with life itself. They are on the wrong fork of the path.

—Gary Snyder

Our demographic future is in our hands. Several routes could lead to a stationary population, including one-child families and moderate, continuous immigration; or two-child families and no immigration. If these models seem unappealing, we can go on with unchanging policies and end up with 550 million Americans, primarily in 20 urban areas in seven or eight states, in 2070 — and a billion Americans 70 years after that. In short, demographic reality will not permit us to evade hard choices.

—Meredith Burke

In the simplest terms the animal rights position I uphold maintains that such diverse practices as the use of animals in science, sport and recreational hunting, the trapping of fur-bearing animals for vanity products, and commercial animal agriculture are categorically wrong — because these practices systematically violate the rights of the animals involved. Morally, these practices should be abolished. That is the goal of the social struggle for social struggle for animal rights. The goal of our moral and economic ties to these injustices — for example, by not wearing the dead skins of animals and by not eating their decaying corpses.

—Tom Regan

May creatures all abound
in weal and peace; may all
be blessed with peace always;
all creatures weak or strong,
all creatures great and small;

* * *

— may all be blessed with peace!
[L]et all-embracing thoughts
for all that lives be thine,
— an all-embracing love
for all the universe

in all its heights and depths
and breath, unstinting love,
unmarred by hate within,
not rousing enmity.

—Buddhist hymn

To see the difference between the issues of inflicting pain and taking life, consider how we would choose within our own species. If we had to choose to save the life of a normal human or a mentally defective human, we would probably choose to save the life of the normal human; but if we had to choose between preventing pain in the normal human or the mental defective — imagine that both have received painful but superficial injuries, and we only have enough painkiller for one of them — it is not nearly so clear how we ought to choose. The same is true when we consider other species. The evil of pain is, in itself, unaffected by the other characteristics of the being that feels the pain; the value of life is affected by these other characteristics.

—Peter Singer

Dominion has been badly, even perversely, expressed in the degradation and destruction of those over whom it is exercised. . . . When whites were forced to acknowledge that blacks shared all the relevant human characteristics, they had to back down on their justification of slavery. When males are forced to acknowledge that females have all the relevant human characteristics for participation in public life, they have to back down on their justification for denying women equal political and legal rights. When humans are compelled to acknowledge that other animals share the characteristics relevant to the right to life, humans will have to back down on their arrogant assumption that they, and only they, have the right to live and hence that they have the right to kill other animals.

—John Cobb

All creatures of our God and King,
Lift up your voice and with us sing,
Alleluia! Alleluia!
Thou burning sun with golden beam,
Thou silver moon with softer gleam!
O praise Him, O praise Him!
Alleluia! Alleluia! Alleluia!

Thou flowing water, pure and clear,
Make music for thy Lord to hear,
Alleluia! Alleluia!

Thou fire so masterful and bright,
Thou givest man both warmth and light!
O praise Him, O praise Him!
Alleluia! Alleluia! Alleluia!

Let all things their Creator bless,
And worship him in humbleness,
O praise him! Alleluia!
O praise the Father, praise the Son,
And praise the Spirit, Three in One!
O praise Him, O praise Him!
Alleluia! Alleluia! Alleluia!

—Francis of Assisi

An ethic for the liberation of life is a call to Christian action. In particular, how animals are treated is not "someone else's worry," it is a matter of individual and collective responsibility. Christians are called to act respectfully towards "these, the least of our brothers and sisters." This is not a simple question of kindness however laudable that virtue is. It is an issue of strict justice. In all our dealings with animals, whether direct or indirect, an ethic for the liberation of life requires that we render unto animals what they are due, as creatures with an independent integrity and value. Precisely because they cannot speak for themselves or act purposively to free themselves from the shackles of their enslavement, the Christian duty to speak and act for them is the greater, not the lesser.

—World Council of Churches, 1988

The loss of mystery and awe about nature and the sense that we alone in all of creation have subjective feelings, these have contributed to the mind-set that accepts the destruction of the environment as a necessary evil. Science has brought on a loss of emotional affinity, and that has caused trouble.

Only people who do not consider the feelings of animals can kill them for fun. Only those who sense nothing "holy" about the forests and the plants can destroy them with little concern. Only those who do not sense the stars and galaxies declaring the glory of God can be indifferent to the pollution that hides them from view.

A world without God is not viewed with a sense of awe. A universe in which his presence is not felt is doomed to abuse.

—David J. Gyertson

In the relations of humans with the animals, with the flowers, with the objects of creation, there is a whole great ethic scarcely

seen as yet, but which will eventually break through into the light
and be the corollary and the complement to human ethics.

—Victor Hugo

The answer then to the question, Is the right to a livable environment a human right? is yes. Each person has this right *qua* being
human and because a livable environment is essential for one to
fulfill his human capacities. And given the danger to our environment today and hence the danger to the very possibility of human
existence, access to a livable environment must be conceived as a
right which imposes upon everyone a correlative moral obligation
to respect.

—William T. Blackstone

"The earth is the Lord's, and everything in it, the world, and all
who live in it; for he founded it upon the seas and established it
upon the waters."

—Psalm 24:1-2

Whoever coined the phrase "save the planet" is a public-relations genius. It conveys the sense of impending catastrophe and
high purpose that has wrapped environmentalism in an aura of
moral urgency. It also typifies environmentalism's rhetorical
excesses, which, in any other context, would be seen as wild exaggeration or simple dishonesty. . . . The rhetorical overkill is not just
innocent excess. It clouds our understanding. . . . The worst sin of
environmental excess is its bias against economic growth.

—Robert J. Samuelson

Whatever befalls the earth befalls the children of the earth. We
are a part of the earth and the earth is a part of us. For we did not
weave the web of life. We are merely a strand in it. Whatever we do
to the web, we do to ourselves.

—Chief Seattle, Native American, 19th Century

Exploitation of other human beings has always evoked a
prophetic criticism. The prophetic voice raised against the exploitation of what is not human has been a much weaker voice . Today
we are looking for a way to convert from our death-dealing dominion, from being Earth degraders to earth-keepers.

—Mary Evelyn Jegen

If our governing ethic were 'the Earth is the Lord's and all that
it contains," if we resolved to bless and keep the creation as the
Creator blesses and keeps us, if we would affirm through our
actions the long-standing belief that avarice and greed are vices,
then this crisis would not be upon us.

Mother Earth cannot heal herself alone. She needs our help. We two-leggeds must all come together and form a commonality of realization, a realization of potentially fatal calamities. Most of our remedies will be to cease, or drastically curtail, what we have been doing. Rising temperatures, vanishing rain forests, overpopulation, pollution of waters, and acid rain can be, and will have to be, addressed by abrupt remedies.

—Ed McGaa, Eagle Man

Every country can be said to have three forms of wealth: material, cultural and biological. The first two we understand very well, because they are the substance of our everyday lives. Biological wealth is taken much less seriously. This is a serious strategic error, one that will be increasingly regretted as time passes.

—E. O. Wilson

DISCUSSION QUESTIONS AND BRIEF CASE STUDIES

1. The Bible does not treat the environment or animals' rights as a special "issue" to be treated by God's people. Is our personal treatment of the earth's environment, including all living plants and animals, a matter of Christian concern and ethics or should we conclude that Christians can live as disciples in any physical environment (perhaps even on the surface of the moon) and treat animals however they like?

2. The Creation is essentially a mystery. Do you agree? What personal evidence could you provide for the existence of such a mystery?

3. Does the biblical doctrine of the Sabbath (Gen. 2:3; Exod. 20:8-11) have any relevance for a theology of the environment? Is "keeping the Sabbath holy" simply a call to public worship or can the concept have much deeper meaning about how we relate to our God, to ourselves, to our neighbors, and to the world about us?

4. What are some concrete ways that the church as the "now" body of Christ can get involved in environmental concerns? Do you agree with the following assertion by popular evangelical speaker and author Anthony Campolo: "Spirituality and creation-care are tied together. To be properly committed to one should lead us inevitably to commitment to the other. If there is anything that becomes clear as you read the writings of those Christians who have stood historically as models of spiritual maturity, it is that along with their deepening awareness of God came a growing sensitivity to nature and a profound sorrow about its suffering"?

5. David was inspired and drawn closer to God by experiencing nature. Can one draw close to God in nature apart from involvement in a Christian community? Should Christians love nature? Did not the pagan worship of nature lead the Gentiles away from God into idolatry? Where does one draw the line between a healthy love and respect for nature and the worship of nature?

6. Do you agree with Schweitzer's "reverence for life" principle? Do you agree with him that all living things have a "will to live"? If so, do the following organisms have a "will to live" in exactly the same moral sense: adult humans, infant humans, dogs, cats, horses, cows, rabbits, squirrels, gnats, amoebas, trees, flowers, weeds? How does one make moral distinctions?

7. Do you feel that it is always easy to adjust to a crisis? Consider words of Richard Cartwright Austin in an interview: "We have to

make this shift in thinking because while the media alarm us regularly with crises, we adjust to crises. We can't live in terror and fear indefinitely so we adjust to the most awful things — hydrogen bombs hanging over our heads, the greenhouse effect. We will adjust to anything, usually to our loss. Crisis gets our attention, but only love and engagement will hold our attention and commitment."

Do you agree that the human family "will adjust to anything"? Will the human family, little by little, destroy an environment which is conducive to easy, healthy living?

8. Is there an irony in the fact that "Christian nations" of the western world have been among the most capitalist, consumptionist, and wasteful cultures in the world? Do not Christians make some of the best consumers or is such a question unkind and unfair?

9. Paul Ehrlich contends that much of the popular concern in the United States about our environment is commendable, but that the publicized "Earth Days" tend to focus on symptoms more than on the cause of the environment's basic disease: the deterioration of the life-support systems of the planet and the consequent lowering of its "carrying capacity." The popularity of many publications, such as *50 Things You Can Do to Save the Earth*, encapsulates this misplaced emphasis. While the suggestions in these books are useful, such as how to reduce junk mail or conserving energy in one's home, almost all deal with symptoms. Society could follow all of those suggestions carefully and "earth would still go down the drain."

What is the earth's major problem — the problem which must be addressed as the simplest and most effective thing anyone can do to save the earth? Answer (according to Ehrlich and many other environmentalists): Overpopulation and continuous unchecked population growth. Earth does not have long-term ability to endlessly support people.

The human family has indeed fulfilled the biblical mandate to replenish and subdue the earth. Should Christians consider population control to be a moral concern? Should a Christian couple feel any sense of moral judgment if they should choose to have five or six of their own children? And how do you feel about the televangelists who have urged Christian couples to raise as many children as they can possibly afford in order that Christians can regain some numerical and voting strength to counter secular, non-Christian influences in the world?

10. What do you think about the "Lifeboat Ethic" which contends that the rich nations of the world should not send food or other aid to the poor nations during a time of famine or other crisis? Does sending food and medicine simply enable these nations to continue to proliferate in population, thus increasing the burden in the lifeboat for the next generation? Isn't the "lifeboat ethic" a cold and callous perversion of a Christian ethic that calls for compassion and mercy?

11. Situation: You work and travel with Robert. At times you share a room with him when your work takes the two of you on the road. You are bothered by some of Robert's habits. You note that he wastes electricity when he leaves lights or appliances turned on while away from his room or office for hours. In the motel Robert turns on the water full force in order to occasionally dampen his comb while slowly and meticulously combing his hair. Robert lets the hot water run continuously while shaving. On several occasions Robert turned on the hot water in a shower to produce steam for a motel room that was not heating quickly enough. You have seen Robert waste gasoline. In restaurants he orders food that he hardly touches.

Robert's small habits trouble you. You have confronted him with his little habits of waste, but his reply was simply that such actions are so insignificant that any changes he might make toward conservation would have no measurable impact on environmental problems. "Don't worry about it!" he demands. How should you feel now? Should you just not worry about it as Robert requests?

12. How does our attitude toward pets differ from our attitude toward animals in general? For example, do you find it ironic that most people have no trouble eating the flesh of cattle and fowl, but would find the thought of killing and grilling the meat of their pet to be as abhorrent as eating human flesh?

13. What are some values of pets to human beings? Have you had pets? In what ways did you value them?

14. What does the Judeo-Christian tradition teach us about the purpose of animals on earth? (Begin with the creation story of Genesis; see also Matt. 10:31.)

15. How is God depicted in his attitude toward animals of the earth? What can be derived about animals from the story of Noah and the Ark?

16. Do you feel that animals have moral significance regardless of any human's attachment or non-attachment to them?

17. Should human beings attempt to eliminate the suffering of animals? Why should animal suffering really matter? Consider that nature itself makes animals suffer, and in nature animals kill animals, often inflicting great pain. Certainly one would not want to torture an animal that is found along the road when it threatens no human interest, but why all the concern about animal suffering in animal testing and animal farming? Does it really matter?

18. Is there any moral wrong in humans torturing or unnecessarily killing an animal? What about those who like to hunt and kill for trophy rare beasts in less populated regions of the world? How do you feel about entrepreneurs who maintain a wildlife preserve or sanctuary where exotic animals can be easily killed for sport?

19. There are approximately 60 million dogs and 60 million cats in the United States and the population is growing. Every hour, on average, more than 2,000 dogs and 3,500 cats are born. Among humans, 415 babies are born every hour. Each year animal shelters take in as many as 25 million dogs and cats. Some two million are later claimed by their owners; half or more of the remaining animals are killed. Do you think that human beings are responsible for the woes produced by overpopulation of animals, especially dogs and cats?

20. Is it morally right to eat animal food? On what do you base your answer? Consider that it is possible to live a healthy and normal life as a vegetarian. Consider also that contemporary mass production of meat does involve considerable suffering for animals. One well-publicized example is the way calves are treated, taken from their mother at a very young age and kept off their feet in cramped stalls and fed only liquid, in order to produce veal. Is this humane treatment?

21. The Food and Drug Administration requires that many new substances be tested on animals before they are marketed for human consumption. New cosmetics, for example, must be tested for possible eye or skin damage on humans; some of these cosmetics have been forced into the eyes of non-anesthetized rabbits to measure the reaction. Given that some products must be tested because they relate to human health issues, should animals suffer intensely so that a new kind of lipstick or mouthwash or floor polish can be put on the market?

22. And how about even using animals for testing in human health issues? Can one species morally use other species to solve their own health problems? If tens of millions of people elect to

smoke and expose themselves to the risks of cancer and heart disease, do humans have the moral right to subject animals that would never smoke to those same cancers and heart diseases?

23. Many pet owners spend more on their pets than they spend on pressing social problems such as world hunger. True enough, money spent on cat and dog food would help save human lives. Are there any moral limits to what should be spent on pets or is the whole issue a petty and insignificant one?

24. Is there anything inconsistent about having a caring relationship with one animal and being willing to slaughter for profit other animals of the same species? Ethics professor Mike W. Martin reminds us of how commonly farmers become emotionally attached to one member of a species whose other members they are willing to eat. He then reminds us of the Old Testament story of the prophet Nathan, whose only reported assignment was a visit to the king. Nathan told King David of a poor farmer who had developed a caring relationship with a domesticated lamb. This lamb was like a human child to the poor farmer, living in his house and eating at his table.

Could a person care for a calf or a lamb until it dies of old age, all the while eating beef and mutton? Would this be morally inconsistent?

25. Farmer Jones often finds cats and kittens, at times even puppies, dropped off on the road in front of his farm house. He has no interest in these animals or in feeding them. The bigger dogs he will shoot with a shotgun. The kittens he will toss into his pond. Is Farmer Jones acting morally? What would you say to Mr. Jones?

26. What is anthropomorphizing of animals? Is there any harm in treating pets as if they were human? Is there anything morally offensive in the cartoons of Gary Larson's "Far Side" which attributes human names and human emotions to a wide variety of mammals and insects?

27. The construction and maintenance of zoos for human pleasure and education is widely assumed to be worthwhile. Visits to zoos are almost universally considered to be positive experiences, at least in principle. Visits to zoos expand people's awareness and appreciation of their natural world. On the other hand, zoos depend on the capture and confinement of animals whose natural habitat is in the wilderness. Tigers, lions, elephants, llamas, monkeys, baboons, exotic birds, and on and on we could go, must

lose their freedom to serve human commercial interests. The tiger or lion that paces around in its cage, simply awaiting to be ushered ceremoniously into the circus ring, is another example of animal frustration.

Do you think that zoos and circuses unnecessarily exploit wild animals? Is such exploitation a moral concern? Do the positive goods of education and entertainment from a human perspective outweigh any concern about animal rights?

28. Case study: The opossum and her seven babies made the mistake of crossing in front of Steven Garity's car. They were squished. Garity made the mistake of being in front of a police car. He was seen to suddenly change lanes and hit the mother opossum and the youngsters clinging to her. He was accused of intentionally running down the opossums and charged with cruelty to animals. A judge dismissed the case and declared Tumwater's [Washington state] animal-cruelty ordinance too vague.

Are opossums such pests that you can't be cruel enough to them? Or do they deserve as much respect as any other living creature?

The above incident occurred on March 31, 1994. "They're pests," the driver said. "All they do is eat dog food and cat food and be a pest. They just hiss at you." Garity's convictions must have been strongly held — he had to suddenly change lanes to hit the mother opossum and her offspring.

Do you think the homely opossum — a beady-eyed, naked-tailed marsupial that looks as if nature built it from spare parts — deserves human concern and protection?

29. What does this generation owe future generations? Does the current generation have a moral duty to make some sacrifices in order to protect the rights and liberties of the people who will probably come after them? If the current generation uses all or most of the natural resources, especially fossil fuels, have we deprived another generation of its right to life? Why does it really matter if the present generation uses up all the world's resources or poisons the rest of the planet beyond the borders of the continental U. S.?

30. Is it possible that parents seeking to please their young children can give them pets that they are not emotionally or temperamentally ready for? Erma Bombeck tells a personal story of when she was ten years old, missing her father who had died a year earlier, and her mother purchasing her a small rabbit for Easter.

"The first few weeks, the rodent-like animal and I were attached like Velcro. The rabbit's feet never touched the ground. Life was just one big salad," Erma states. "In the weeks to follow, the rabbit became less charismatic (or maybe he never was), and my mom would say, 'Have you fed your rabbit today?' and I would say, 'No, but he's getting too big anyway.' . . . A few months later I found the rabbit huddled under the porch steps. He died a few hours later . . . of neglect."

"I'm not telling you this because I'm proud of it," Erma concludes, "but because children are sometimes not ready for the responsibility of an animal even though they think they are. It doesn't matter if it's a chicken, a parakeet, a hamster or a lizard; they have an interest span of possibly a day and a half."

Do you agree with Bombeck's point? Does a non-traditional pet which is only partially cared for provide an important example of abuse to animals? Bombeck remembered this story from her childhood. What might that suggest about the impact of neglecting a pet and the pet's suffering or death on the child responsible for the neglect?

CHAPTER ELEVEN

Community: Political Involvement, Citizenship, and Lifestyle

One of the most familiar stories in our Christian heritage is the conversion saga of Saul of Tarsus. While the highly placed Jewish official traveled the Damascus highway, preparing to persecute even more new disciples of Jesus, he was blinded and laid low by a heavenly light and a startling voice. From this seeming catastrophe, Saul comes to see reality more clearly. He experienced the living Lord, transferred his allegiance and loyalty to Him, and became an apostle of good news and peace.

Occasionally, events in our nation impact our collective consciousness so dramatically that we feel blinded and laid low. Our only realistic option is to consider what truths they reveal. Surely, the April 19, 1995, bombing of the Alfred P. Murrah Federal Building in Oklahoma City which claimed the lives of 168 people, including several children, was one of these events. Our eyes were opened to the fact that within our midst are fellow citizens and neighbors whose paranoia, hatred, and lunacy, combined with technology to build terrible weapons, present a menacing threat to the safety and security of everyone else.

The May 1992 verdict in the Rodney King trial and subsequent riots and destruction in Los Angeles — totaling more than fifty fatalities and nearly a billion dollars in cost — also opened our eyes to some profoundly sad realities that some citizens have conveniently tried to ignore. One might wonder how differently we might have received a message about our cities and our fragile social fabric if those 81 seconds of videotape had not been recorded by a chance bystander.

Is there an alarming disintegration of the concept of community in our land? Is our nation experiencing what distinguished historian Arthur M. Schlesinger, Jr., called "the disuniting of America"?

As we conclude our study of ethics and survey of controversial moral issues, several questions seem appropriate: What is community? How is national community built? Can Christians who take citizenship seriously act constructively to build and maintain community? Should Christians become social and political activists?

Community is one of those popular buzzwords with a wide range of connotations, all positive. For some, any racial or ethnic group living in loose proximity is a community. For others, an aggregation of occupied residences, pinpointed at the same region on a map, may be called a community. Many would contend that any nation of people may be called a community. Little wonder that "community" has lost its rich meaning with such varied common use.

At the outset, the Christian thinker begins with one profoundly important insight: a community is not created by geography, heritage, law, accident of birth or economic interdependence. All of these may be dynamics which serve to enable a community's viability but they alone are insufficient to produce genuine community.

"Community" is rooted in "commonalities" or "commonness." A common life — life that is shared at the deepest levels of human existence — does not develop by accident, but is created by the will of women and men resolute in desiring and maintaining a genuine human community.

Several major elements exist within a meaningful community: (1) commitment to core beliefs, values, and ideas such as freedom, liberty, equality, and justice; (2) an awareness of duty owed by one person to another and, in our religious communities at least, an awareness of duty to God; (3) deep concern about the "common good" or "public welfare" which leads people to guard and protect zealously the core beliefs, values, and ideals. The development of the richest sense of community emerges from sharing together the deepest experiences of human existence as well as a hope for a glorious future.

Historically, our nation has identified itself as a special community of many peoples, many nationalities, many races, many cultures. We have opened doors to the poor and politically oppressed, those "huddled masses longing to breathe free." Such self-identity provides a mix of both reality and myth, but it is authentic enough for us to consider the foundation and cohesive forces for such a unique political community.

The foundation for American community has been called by different names, such as "Americanism," "the American way of life," and, more recently, "American civil religion." The great value of American civil religion has been its promotion of a keen sense of corporate identity and common good. No nation on earth owes its sense of community more explicitly to fidelity to an idea. Our country was born "dedicated to a proposition."

Historically, what has provided cohesion to the various social and political groups of Americans has been a dedication to certain "self-evident" moral propositions. America's uniqueness has been its common purpose and commitment to a constellation of moral values and ideals. As one glances casually at news developments and crime reports or takes in our society's entertainment offerings in the fields of motion pictures, television, and pop music, however, three serious questions emerge: Is our society jettisoning its common core ideals and values? Is our lifestyle selfish and extravagant? Is our community spirit almost vanquished? The most we can do here is simply point the direction toward an answer.

A LOSS OF COMMON CORE IDEALS AND VALUES?

Modern technology and engineering, providing ease of communication and mobility, may be accelerating this threat to community. The quest for better salaries and upper mobility has led Americans to change careers and either dissolve marriages or move families from one locality to another. The placing and maintaining of roots in one local community, with devotion to community churches, schools, and civic enrichment, is a threatened tradition. Americans are dwelling among strangers, in apartments, condominiums, and suburban subdivisions where, even after several years, they may not remember the name of the person next door even if they have met him or her. In the same inner city neighborhood, some decent citizens, especially among the elderly, have become virtual prisoners in their own homes, afraid to venture out into sidewalks and streets where the law of the jungle seems to prevail in both night and day. Even in suburbs, prosperous citizens may arrive home at the end of the day and never have to put a foot onto the turf of an open yard as they drive into the attached garage with an automatic door enclosing them in privacy for the remainder of the day.

We may pine for a simpler past — a time in which Americans lived mostly in rural and small town communities and enjoyed leisurely porch repartee or backyard block barbecues. Or a time when the few local churches were a social center as well as worship center and all the denominational preachers delivered the same basic messages about the meaning of life, suffering, and death.

What a paradox! While our society is mobile, urbanized, and culturally diverse, and while the quest for an M.B.A. is like a crusade for the Holy Grail, most of our national myths and values are rooted in the rural past. We work in cities, live in suburbs, and dream of the countryside and rugged west. Our myths include wagon trains pushing west, courageous homesteaders conquering the plains, presidents born in log cabins, lonesome cowboys, plantation belles, and happy family life in the prosperous 50s.

That past, to a whatever degree it was real, is irretrievable. We can no longer expect our public schools to provide public Bible reading and oral prayer. With the dramatic increase in unwed motherhood and a fifty percent failure rate of first marriages, we can no longer expect the nuclear family of two parents and children under one roof to be the norm — the concept of family must be re-defined. Outside of our homes and churches, we can no longer assume a consensus about integrity in business, the sanctity of God's name, extramarital and deviant sex, drug use, and the nature of ethics. Nor can we, short of a grand reversal, assume that our homes and churches will be our youth's primary mentors about lifestyle and morals.

While the loss of community is viewed as positive by those who seek to live lives of quiet anonymity and be free from the responsibilities of neighborliness and the judgments of fundamentalist fanatics, in general the disintegration of community is unhealthy. The breakdown of community means disconnectedness, alienation, and anomie. With the loss of moral authority comes confusion, suspicion, distrust, and eventually, chaos and perhaps anarchy. With the loss of community is the loss of the uncontested right to apply moral standards to civil liberties or political issues. Consider, for example, that concerns such as pornography or abortion are viewed not so much as fundamental moral issues as they are public policy issues to be dealt with in courts of law and legislative bodies and decided by slim majorities.

As community spirit weakens, the American melting pot becomes a boiling cauldron of warring factions, each claiming its entitlements, each suspicious of the other, each making non-negotiable demands, each writing its own tribal code of rules and laws.

A SELFISH AND EXTRAVAGANT LIFESTYLE?

There is some cold, hard data that American Christians may not enjoy hearing, facts which may disturb some cozy nests of ease and luxury. First and foremost is the wide disparity between United States wealth and the dire poverty of many other parts of the world, especially in what social scientists have called "third world" or "underdeveloped" nations. American citizens constitute six percent of the world's population but consume thirty percent of the world's energy.

The United States is the world's third largest nation in population, now numbering more than a quarter-billion people, but the average American consumes more of the earth's resources than an average citizen of any of the other "big ten" nations with more than 100 million people: China, India, the aggregate of old Soviet Union republics, Indonesia, Brazil, Japan, Nigeria, Bangladesh, and Pakistan. The average citizen in the U. S. consumes fifty times the amount of energy consumed by a citizen in India.

Given our hopes and desire to think of the United States as a "Christian nation," should the vast difference in economic and leisure lifestyle become a moral concern? Does it matter that such a small percentage of the world's population controls a disproportionate amount of the world's wealth?

Consider the automobile, a commonplace machine in developed nations but a burden on the environment in several ways. The depletion of oil reserves, the pollution of air, the manufacturing of steel, the massive amounts of money and energy used to build an infrastructure (roads, bridges, etc.) to maintain and support private automobile transportation create incalculable costs. More than 150 million automobiles (a general estimate) are registered in the United States. Does it matter that this total is ten times greater than the number of cars in Brazil, 135 times greater than the number in India, and more than a thousand times the number in Kenya? In recent generations the one "family car" was a commodity to be shared by the entire family unit and reserved by any family member who sought private use. In most American families today, to have earned a driver's license and not own one's personal car is tantamount to near shame and embarrassment.

Americans do not enjoy criticism of their consumerist ethic. After all, most older adults, especially those who survived the Great Depression or other hard times, have generously wanted life to be easier and more rewarding for their children than what they experienced. Furthermore, the dynamics of consumerism are driven by the creativity of Madison Avenue, that famous New York street which has become a figurative allusion for the entire megabusiness of advertising.

Are there any enduring values that guide consumer choices about products and services? To view the color ads on television or in the print media presents consumers with a celebration of wealth, power, glamor, comfort, luxury, prestige, status, efficiency, and, most of all, sex appeal. Advertising decrees that we purchase all consumer goods and personal services which guarantee these values. How many messages about sex and status can the average Christian man or woman, living in the U. S. and watching television for five to six hours a day, see or hear over an extended period of time? And will such a barrage of messages wield any negative impact on that person's spiritual life?

A DEFEATED COMMUNITY SPIRIT?

The tone of our reflections on previous questions may have seem filled with total gloom. As it turns out, amidst the angry voices on talk shows and the seemingly endless reports on violent crime on the late news, people still care about each other more than cynics give them credit for. The communal spirit survives, especially among the young.

Voluntary service and giving to community efforts occur on a massive scale in the United States. Community volunteerism is definitely not the exclusive pattern of a few wealthy foundations and rich people. In fact, wealthy citizens and foundations account for only ten percent of private donations. The majority of donations come from middle class families. According to one survey, at least forty percent of first-year college students are involved in at least some kind of voluntary activity. Each spring, for example, thousands of university students in the Midwest and Southeast opt to forego the alluring beaches of Florida or mom's home cooking and spend their break from books constructing houses or providing other community service for less privileged. Local businesses are involved in community service at unprecedented levels. Intergenerational volunteerism is rapidly increasing.

There are approximately two million nonprofit organizations in the United States — one for every 125 Americans. The number of local community foundations has doubled since 1987. Americans continue to be big "joiners." We find much satisfaction from our communities and affiliations. True enough, some of these groups pursue unworthy ends or narrow goals and still others may exploit ignorance or prejudice. The vast majority of community organizations enrich the communal spirit by identity with a place of residence, shared traditions and culture, or a common cause on behalf of their own membership or others within the community at large.

KEY TERMS

Altruism — Unselfish regard for or devotion to the welfare of others. The essential characteristic of altruism is consideration of others, demonstrated in friendly understanding of their needs and providing selfless service for meeting those needs.

American civil religion — An organic structure of ideas, beliefs, values and even myths concerning our nation that is common to the diverse peoples of America; our national self-understanding of our history, our contemporary situation, and our future as a nation.

Charity — Benevolent good will, generosity, or helpfulness toward humanity, especially for those in need or suffering. The term is now replaced by "philanthropy" and "voluntary service" because of its vagueness (in King James Version usage it refers to love) and even negative connotation (in the sense of condescending gifts that suggest pity rather than compassion).

Community service — Paid or unpaid service to the community at large; may also be implemented as a way of repaying student loans or satisfying a court sentence.

Generosity — Liberality in spirit or act; the basic human concern to share the good things of life with those we love or care about.

"Global village" — The worldwide community of which all humans are connected by vital mutual interests to all other human beings.

Intergenerational Volunteerism — Community service in which the young help the old and the old help the young.

Justice — Giving to every person his/her due; granting equal access to the sources of human fulfillment within a community.

Justice is concerned with the rights of all people, while love is concerned with the needs of all people and going beyond what they are due.

Philanthropy — Good will to fellow citizens; acts to promote the general welfare of a community. Philanthropy connotes major gifts or actions offered by rich donors, but properly includes all giving for community or public purposes.

Supererogation — The morally good act of performing or giving more than is required by duties to others or by human need; its omission is neither wrong nor deserving of sanction.

KEY SCRIPTURES

Matthew 25:31-46; Mark 12:41-44; Luke 10:29-37; Romans 12:17-21; 13:1-7; James 2:15-16; I John 3:17-18.

ARGUMENTS AGAINST SOCIAL AND POLITICAL ACTIVISM

1. People who are subjects within the kingdom of God have renounced all loyalty to the kingdoms of this world.

"There are two kingdoms, the kingdom of humanity and the kingdom of God, and each person must decide which he/she will support. Loyalty cannot be divided or equivocal. If one is loyal to God, he is a citizen in an apolitical, anational kingdom which knows no territorial boundaries or political ideals, but consists of men of every language and nation [Rev. 7:9]. Such a citizen does not fear any carnal enemy or even death itself [cf. Matt. 10:28], but lives in peace and union with fellow citizens as they engage in a far more important battle, one not with flesh and blood but with the principalities and powers of the air who are at war with the Almighty [Eph. 6:12].

"So much of the present world is evil and we must refrain from contact with it as much as possible. Nor can Christians defend worldly systems by fighting for them. Jesus instructed Pilate, "My kingdom does not belong to this world' [John 18:36], and the apostle Paul warned the Philippians against enemies of the cross whose 'mind is on earthly things. But our citizenship is in heaven. And we eagerly await a Savior from there, the Lord Jesus Christ' [Phil. 3:19-

20]. Of course, Christians must pay taxes and obey laws to maintain civil order and provide legitimate services, but the main purpose of civil government is for non-Christians to govern themselves."

2. The Christian's chief responsibility is to save souls.

"Doesn't the Bible tell us that 'he that winneth souls is wise'? The salvation of the world does not hinge on who is elected to any given political office; an election that seems important to us now will eventually look trivial when compared with the truly crucial issues of human existence. The Great Commission that Jesus gave his disciples just prior to his ascension is totally irrelevant to political activity; it commissioned them only to proclaim the gospel. Political involvement, then, can only distract disciples from their major teaching responsibility and from concern for their own spiritual condition.

"Granted that political activity can at times be profitable, the faithful Christian simply does not have time for it. As long as one lost soul in the world has not heard the gospel, the Christian is responsible for giving that person a message of hope."

3. Political and social activism do not strike at the core of the sinner's problem.

"The political and social activist will only offer a temporary solution to a permanent problem. Of course, we should be benevolent to those in need. We should always minister to the physical and emotional needs of people in our world. However, our primary task is preaching the gospel.

"People in sin do not need food, money, open housing, welfare, or more political empowerment nearly as much as they need something that will touch their hearts and souls. You can't take people out of the slums until you take the slums out of people. The essential thrust of the gospel is spiritual, not social, and the gospel relates to eternal salvation, not social and political reform."

4. Ordinary Christians and church leaders have no more special expertise to speak on political and social issues than do leaders from other segments of society.

"Why should we think that Christians have any special expertise about political, social, or even legal issues unless they have chosen to enter those fields professionally? Sometimes Christians have advocated policies which looked good originally, but that in administration and practice turned out to be a bureaucratic nightmare. Christians have something to offer society that is qualitatively different from the handouts and opportunities of bureaucracies and humanitarian groups.

"Consider how intractable most political and social problems are! There is very little that even politicians and social workers can do to solve them, much less what Christian lay people can do. How much of the misery and unhappiness that afflict most people you know is attributable to the shortcomings of public policy or social reform? Do you think there is any less racism in our culture now than there was in the 50s and 60s before the Civil Rights Act, the Voting Rights Act, and Affirmative Action? All the political and social reform, all the do-good legislation and humanitarianism, can do comparatively little to improve the plight of an unhappy man or woman who does not know the Savior."

5. Politics is so tainted with compromise, corruption, and unprincipled behavior that it is dirty.

"Nearly everybody would agree — politics is dirty. Anybody who would not agree with that statement has a head buried in the sand so as not to read about the scandals, beginning with Watergate and all the other "gates," cut-throat deals, perjuries, ballot box stuffing, pork barreling, influence peddling, and all the other dirty activities in which politicians have been caught.

"By contrast, the Christian life is one of no compromise. Nor does it seek the comfortable neutrality or fence straddling that are so inherent in American political life. "He who is not with me is against me, and he who does not gather with me scatters," Jesus declared [Matt. 12:30]. Nothing vital to Christian life and doctrine can be compromised or altered. Bargaining, back-room scheming, high-handed power plays, and the like are the very antithesis of the Christian lifestyle. The Christian must avoid the very appearance of evil in all his relations with others."

6. Political activism and social reform have so little impact upon the course of events and upon history in general that neither is worth the trouble.

"It's so easy to feel that there is nothing the nation can gain by having my vote. There is such a remote and distant connection between social and political activism and the major changes that affect our society. The war in Vietnam, for example, was not started by a popular vote and despite major protest throughout the nation the war continued for several more years. It's so easy to agree with the philosophy of the little old lady who, when asked whom she intended to vote for, declared: 'I never vote. It only encourages 'em.'"

ARGUMENTS FOR CHRISTIAN SOCIAL AND POLITICAL ACTIVISM

1. Complete Christian neutrality and non-participation in the system are impossible.

"Every Christian is a citizen of his/her nation. Every Christian and every Christian church is involved in political society and its problems. There are no exceptions. Whether we choose to become actively involved in society's problems, or even vote, we enjoy the rights granted and guaranteed by the state; we may appreciate their value or take them for granted, but we need them all the same.

"Christians who attempt to avoid involvement in all political and social processes are making two statements: first, that Christianity is irrelevant to social problems except to the extent they can be solved through individual regeneration; and second, that the status quo on any given issue should prevail. Those who say, 'We can't take a stand on this issue' have already taken a stand *for* the current system."

2. Political democracy makes a big difference.

"In biblical times the only form of government that people knew was totalitarianism or dictatorship. No wonder that people did not talk about having a voice in government. Democracy is a relatively recent development of more enlightened political thought and concern about people's rights. Involvement was unnecessary in the New Testament world, but, if there were no citizen participation and social activism in a democracy, the whole political and social structure would crumble. It is imperative that persons of the highest moral caliber be elected to public offices.

"The 'powers that be' in America today are the laws of the land, beginning with the Constitution, and since our laws and institutions are based on participation by the people, Christians must participate if the system is to be preserved and the Constitution is not to be subverted. The way we 'honor the king' today is by being involved in our world and making certain that no more is rendered to Caesar than should be."

3. Individual piety alone may not be enough to produce a better world and restrain the forces of evil.

"To hear some people talk, all we need to do is send out more missionaries and evangelists to convert the world to Christ. Even if that could be successfully accomplished, does this mean that deep levels of poverty and ignorance and high unemployment in certain areas of the nation would be eliminated? We are not discounting the value and power of collective individual piety, but is it enough? We all live in the real world. People do need Jesus more than they need anything else. But most sin and failure are related to both individual and social factors. Evangelism is more than simply getting the message out. We must not be so heavenly-minded that we are of no earthly-value."

4. Some biblical personalities were active in social and political life.

"There were plenty of Spirit-filled characters in Bible times who were active in changing the society in which they lived. In olden times, men of God negotiated with ungodly governments. Others served in governments who were opposed to God's people. Joseph's integrity and faithfulness led to his climbing the political ladder in ancient Egypt until he was one of the top administrators and bureaucrats of the land. Mordecai was a Jew in exile who helped remove the specter of genocide his people faced under King Ahasuerus. Daniel's stern self-discipline led to his selection for political service. Jesus commended the faith of one Roman official [Matt. 8:10] and a Roman centurion became the first Gentile convert to Christianity. All of this shows that political and social action can be a viable means of effecting the will of God on earth."

5. Compromise is not necessarily evil.

"Politics is all compromise and no principle? Think again. Why is there such prejudice against compromise? Compromise is necessary to the smooth running of the political and community machinery. It is also the key to reducing conflicts of opinion in business, church, and home. Without compromise there would be no lasting peace. Sure, there might be some issues you'd never compromise on, but they should be few in number. In the real world, sometimes a half loaf is better than no loaf at all."

6. Christians must see their world, and also their role and mission in it, as essentially one world and one mission.

"It's all too convenient to segment the world into airtight compartments of the political, the social, the economic, the religious, the personal, and so forth. This 'hardening of the categories' enables some people to be concerned about 'religious' issues and apathetic about all 'this-worldly' matters.

"How can anyone make such distinctions? A man or woman is not some kind of spiritual-sacred amphibian who is 'religious' when praying or attending worship and then 'secular' when he/she donates blood, contributes to a scholarship fund, or tutors children in the inner city who need assistance with their homework. Jesus himself offered compassion and aid to people at all levels of human need without explaining whether he was performing spiritual service or community service. He directed his disciples both explicitly and implicitly to concern themselves with the quality of family life, hunger, sickness, relieving the oppressed, comforting the distressed, the demands of justice, and loneliness. These are still controversial issues today for they are part and parcel of the human condition. If we are truly his disciples today, how can we ignore such issues?"

7. A major dimension of our nation's strength has been created by the good-willed, public-spirited volunteerism, and there are plenty of opportunities for all citizens to serve.

"If the Oklahoma City explosion exposed America's darkest side, it also lit its brightest candle — hundreds of fellow citizens of different race and religions set aside their anger and their grief to join hands in common cause. The majority of people care for each other and they prove it by political and social activism.

"There are literally hundreds of ways and organizations through which to be involved: STRIVE; HOPE; Jobs for Youth; Delancey Street; Alternatives for Girls; National Retiree Volunteer Coalition; Habitat for Humanity; One Church — One Addict; I Have a Future; Mad Dads; MADD; Parents as Teachers; Robin Hood Foundation; Room in the Inn; Greenpeace; and STAR Program, just to name a few. All of these organizations care about helping people. There are even organizations which care for animals. Each organization recognizes a need and invents innovative ways to meet it. Remember that Jesus taught that whoever gives a cup of cold water in his name shall be blessed."

SELECTED QUOTATIONS

Righteousness exalts a nation, but sin is a disgrace to any people.

—Prov. 14:34

Why do Americans feel so bad when they've got it so good? [A survey of several prominent leaders concluded:] "Varied as the answers are, there is a fairly common thread. It isn't the national debt or the unemployment rate or the current recession that bothers the nation's thinkers. It is not an economic mess that they see. It's a moral mess."

—*Forbes* magazine

We are to love our fellows, to love all people, in fact, as neighbors. All people bear the image of God.

—Francis Schaeffer

While the Church remained a small minority body within the empire, even though suspected and often persecuted by the government, its members were exhorted to be cooperative, law-abiding citizens. . . . If we are to follow the same principle today, this will mean that as Christians we must cooperate especially closely with fellow Christians in the sharing of all the values we associate with Christ. At the same time, as we seek the production of values to which Christ calls us — such as economic justice or world peace — we are to cooperate with all who will work with us toward those ends. In fact the boundaries of the body of Christ are now ill-defined. Many people professedly in the Church know little of historic Christian faith and are little concerned about many of its values. On the other hand, both from centuries of Christian teaching, and also influenced by other sources, many people outside the churches labor diligently for some of the goals approved by the most sensitive Christian conscience. We have every reason to cooperate with them for the purpose of seeking to achieve those goals.

—L. Harold DeWolf

Pray for the people who are taking the heat in the arena of public debate. The world of the Christian activist can be a very lonely place. War is always tough on those who are called to fight it.

—James Dobson

What holds the United States together is not, as it is with other nations, geographic proximity, ethnic loyalty, dynastic loyalty, religious conformity, but the common purpose, however inadequately conceived and ineffectively put into practice, of living up to certain moral propositions, which can be defined as equality in freedom. Put into question the viability of this purpose and you have put in jeopardy the very existence of America as a distinct social and political entity.

—Hans J. Morgenthau

Modern science has made the world a neighborhood. It will take Christ to make the world a brotherhood. . . . We must learn to live together as brothers or we will perish together as fools.

—Martin Luther King, Jr.

Almost without exception, the documents that eventually became the New Testament and most of the other surviving documents from the same period of Christianity's beginnings are concerned with the way converts to the movement ought to behave. These documents are addressed not to individuals but to communities, and they have among their primary aims the maintenance and growth of those communities. In these documents we can see, though not always very clearly, the very formation of a Christian moral order, of a set of Christian moral practices. My thesis is that we cannot begin to understand that process of moral formation until we see that it is inextricable from the process by which distinctive communities were taking shape. Making morals means making community.

—Wayne A. Meeks

If we are going to use the word [community] meaningfully, we must restrict it to a group of individuals who have learned how to communicate honestly with each other, whose relationships go deeper than their masks of composure, and who have developed some significant commitment to "rejoice together, mourn together," and to "delight in each other, make other's conditions our own."

In genuine community there are no sides. It is not always easy, but by the time they reach community the members have learned how to give up cliques and factions. They have learned how to listen to each other and how not to reject each other. . . . Just because it is a safe place does not mean community is a place without conflict. It is, however, a place where conflict can be resolved without physical or emotional bloodshed and with wisdom as well as grace.

—M. Scott Peck

The Christian life is lived within the Christian community. Despite the superficial talk about a "personal" religion among those who have become disaffected with the Church, there is no such thing as a purely personal Christianity. It has been so from the beginning.

—George F. Thomas

Like the earth we live on, self-contained and self-sustaining, we too would be without warmth or productivity separate from our systems of mutual support. In order to keep its proper place in the solar system, the earth responds to the gravitational pull of the sun and rotates around it. Without the sun the earth would be cold and dark and uninhabited. In fact, the interdependent attraction of gravity holds all the heavenly bodies in their proper places and keeps the universe working together without calamity.

When we have matured, and like the earth are self-contained and self-sustaining, we then realize the interdependent nature of life. We need others. We too require a solar system. Our productivity depends on an appropriate response to those in our system. Our emotional and intellectual maturity allow us to support others and to accept support from others. We are ready to live at peace with ourselves and people around us. Like the planets in the solar system, communities exist because of mutuality. A community may be a collection of people, but a collection of people may not be a community. Communities emerge from communal concerns and common needs.

— Douglas Davis

It is true that our political and social problems are monumental and need solution, but it may very well be at their root is a deep spiritual crisis which makes any cleaning up operations frustrating illusions. The truth is we have lost touch with the depth of being and hence have become alienated from our environment as a whole. The man who is divorced from his own unconscious can hardly be reconciled with his brother. Our society, like Humpty Dumpty, cannot be put together by all the king's horses and men, no matter how well financed they be. In fact, they may only make matters worse.

—Jay G. Williams

I am persuaded that we conservative Christians should not hesitate to associate with any and all our sisters and brothers in Christ, however liberal, charismatic, fundamentalist, etc., they may be. That is the only way we can truly be God's community on earth.

We are going to have our differences. That is a given. It is our choice as to whether we allow differences to keep us from associating with each other. If He whom we profess to follow associated with unclean lepers, despised tax collectors, and rejected prostitutes, how much more should we reach out to those who worship the same God as ourselves, of whatever name. Can we not do things with those in other churches without approving of everything they may believe and practice?

—Leroy Garrett

If we don't accept Jesus in one another, we will not be able to give Him to others.

—Mother Teresa

DISCUSSION QUESTIONS AND BRIEF CASE STUDIES

1. What is "community"? What characteristics must be present to maintain a "moral community"?

2. Do you think the United States is a community in its truest sense? What are the elements that hold the United States together?

3. We have always boasted that cultural diversity was our special strength because each race and ethnic group brings its unique special experiences and insights to the mainstream of society. In recent years, however, do you think that cultural diversity has threatened some core values? Have fanaticism and intolerance produced fragmentation? If so, is it possible to sustain a sense of national community and maintain a foundation of common values? What are the forces and the factors which lead to a diminishing of the concept of community? Do you believe there is a breakdown of consensus on important issues in the United States?

4. What are forces which can strengthen the sense of community within a nation of diverse, multicultural groups?

5. Do you believe that television has done as much to diminish the concept of community as any other non-human factor? Consider that television served to bring the nation together in the 50s when it seemed all the nation was watching Milton Berle, "I Love Lucy," "Life of Riley," and Ozzie and Harriet, the latter an Eisenhower-era prototype for American marriages.

Now, however, today's cable television has produced the opposite effect by fragmenting an audience of millions. Indeed, members of almost any identifiable subgroup — black, Jewish, rock fan, sports fanatic, political junkie, show-biz follower, trash TV devotee, romance and soap opera lover, news buff, porn consumer, fundamentalist — may retire to the privacy of their own rooms and be massaged by their own specialized magazines, advertisements, and cable television and radio stations. The choices are staggering. Do you believe that these choices are the seeds of isolation, perhaps even of alienation?

6. One controversial new book, *Alien Nation* by Peter Brimelow, warns that current U. S. immigration policies are a recipe for disaster. Brimelow is concerned about the survival of the English-speaking heritage in this country. The Immigration Act of 1965 eliminated the pro-European bias in previous U. S. policy, but led, quite unexpectedly, to much higher levels of immigration, virtually all of it from Latin America, the Caribbean, and Asia.

Toward eighty percent of all "new immigrants" are persons of color. Illegal immigration totals at least 500,000 per year. Does it matter that by the year 2050, if current immigration trends continue, the United States will no longer be a white-majority country? Does it matter that English would be only a second language for more and more millions of Americans? What will being an American mean in the age of multiculturalism? Can the "melting pot" concept still work or is our nation moving toward intense racial and ethnic polarization? Do you think it is racist and/or ethnocentric even to raise these questions?

7. In your opinion, how strong is the case for Christian detachment and non-involvement in political and social affairs? Consider the practical arguments that non-involved Christians make.

8. Is it possible for Christians to be politically non-involved and separated from the world in the purest sense?

9. Who are the "powers that be" in the United States today and would Scripture command us to pray for them?

10. "Most sin and human failure are rooted in both individual and social factors." Do you agree?

11. "Do not love the world or the things in the world" (1 John 2:15, 16). What does this mean? Is it helpful to employ the stock comment that the church is "in the world, but not of the world"? How does the church maintain that delicate balance?

12. Is it important for Christians to vote? If so, what other kinds of Christian activism would you advocate? Should Christians organize "as Christians" and endorse candidates or announce official positions? Should Christians publicly commend or criticize public officials?

13. Should Christians be liberal or conservative in their political leanings?

14. If Jesus were living today in the United States, would he be a Republican or Democrat? If neither, then why not? Would Jesus vote? (Obviously, these are loaded questions for which we do not have definitive answers.)

15. How may Christians prepare to make wise political choices?

16. Morals and family values were injected into the 1992 presidential campaign, as they have been in other campaigns. Charges of marital infidelity have been leveled at various presidential aspirants. Are strength of family life and marital fidelity relevant concerns in considering a candidate's fitness for office?

17. Does abortion belong in a political campaign and party platform?

18. Is there any one issue on which you would not compromise and which would determine how you vote regardless of other issues?

19. Can anyone who is a political or social activist ever completely transcend self-interest?

20. Should a Christian tolerate or allow to be legalized behavior or communication that he/she finds offensive (e.g., homosexual behavior or sale of pornographic materials)?

21. "Righteousness exalts a nation, but sin is a reproach to any people." Can the state punish sin?

22. If a nation should live by divine principles, what are some divine principles which should be honored in this nation?

23. A case study offered by Jesus in a parable:

A lone man traveling a highway is beset by personal disaster — the unfortunate, unnamed traveler is assailed and mugged (an incident all too common in our large inner cities). Then comes the dreary passage of conventional citizens, each with a sufficient sense of ordinary responsibilities which for them precluded personal involvement. How mistaken we would be to perceive the priest and the Levite as evil men. They were no worse than other citizens equally ensconced in ordinary career life, personal responsibilities, societal stereotypes, and unimaginative, stifling legalism. Developing a rationalization for reneging on immediate involvement for the beleaguered traveler was surely no difficult task. Their service in the temple or synagogue was, after all, the greater good to which they, with certain regret, were summoned.

Another traveler arrives on the scene of the crime. He perceives the victim compassionately. He stops. Perhaps with absolutely no thought about the historically entrenched animosity between Samaritans and Jews, this anonymous Samaritan perceives a duty and unselfishly performs it. Two men on one road. Two cultures. Two races. Two religious heritages. Amazingly, in the very act of compassion, a moment of crisis is shared. A ministry is rendered. A community is born. This Samaritan and this Jew are no longer strangers. There is a human society.

We begin with the question Jesus asked:

(a) Of the three men who passed along that highway, which one was a true neighbor to the one who had been assailed and robbed?

(b) If the priest and Levite were en route to fulfilling their religious and ceremonial responsibilities, would not religious ritual and ceremony serve as important cohesive forces in a community? How does one resolve conflicting duties?

(c) Does doing the "right thing" or the "sensible thing" ever prevent us from doing the "Christlike thing"? How and in what situations? Is it fair to think that most people serve others only in ways that are convenient and risk-free?

(d) Would the threat of a possible lawsuit deter you from stopping to render first-aid to someone injured along the road? Had you rather face a jury because you stopped to help and did the best you could or face your conscience because you turned and went away?

(e) Provide a moral rating of the characters in the story from best to worst and be ready to tell why you rated them as you did: (1) traveler; (2) criminals; (3) priest; (4) Levite; (5) Samaritan; (6) innkeeper.

(f) Can you retell this ancient story in terms of your own contemporary culture and community?

24. Is there anything morally wrong with a Christian who says, "I give approximately ten percent of what I earn to the church. I think that's pretty generous. I don't intend to make any other contributions to any other organization or to any individual. The church is fulfilling one grand mission of preaching to the lost, so I don't intend to do any voluntary service for others in my community"?

25. Is it better to give one or two major philanthropic gifts of sizable sum or to make numerous smaller contributions which make at least token support for worthy causes? Is there any advantage to either style?

26. An incident happened in the life of Jesus and his disciples which evoked an insightful observation. Jesus was once observing contributions of his people into the temple treasury, especially how wealthy people cast in a large contribution. A poor widow made a contribution of two small coins, yet the contribution enabled Jesus to make a point to his disciples. "This poor woman has made a greater contribution into the treasury than did the wealthy citizens."

On what basis did Jesus found his evaluation? Is generosity a matter of *quantity* of gift or *quality* of gift? How could one measure the quality of someone else's gift?

27. Is there any moral difference between the act of regular donation of blood and the act of selling blood to a commercial

blood bank? Is there anything wrong with selling blood or human organs? After all, there are people who allow their own hair to grow to a certain length for it to be cut, sold for profit and woven into a hairpiece.

28. Do you believe it is appropriate for Christians to become involved and active in social and political reform? Assuming that you do, at least at some level (or likely you would not have acquired this volume), what answers would you give to people who will not get involved and offer the following assertions:

(a) "All politicians are crooks. Some are just worse than others."

(b) "Why should Christians even vote when they cannot possibly know which candidates are sincere and what they will do once in office?"

(c) "Politics is all compromise and no principle."

(d) "Christian political involvement doesn't make any difference anyway. My little vote will hardly make a ripple in the surface."

(e) "Christian activism can become obsessed with the machinery of politics and eventually Caesar (the political process and public policy) will become the new messiah."

29. Does this chapter contain a highly negative message about American consumerism? Americans should feel blessed by God to live in such a land of material wealth and prosperity, but should they feel guilty that others are not so fortunate? And what if Americans have far more cars per capita than any other nation? The operation of millions and millions of cars in this country is costly, to be sure, but the cost in terms of oil, manufacturing, highway construction, deaths on the highway, and so forth is only one side of the coin. How about the advantages of speed and comfort in private transportation? What about all the jobs that the manufacture, sales, and maintenance of these automobiles provide for millions of fellow Americans? What about all the pleasures and hobbies associated with automobiles?

30. Don't the advantages of our lifestyle far outweigh the disadvantages? Isn't it important to keep the American economy healthy and its people employed by economic growth and the increase of the Gross National Product? Is there any moral purpose or advantage in living through another depression?

31. Jesus, standing in the succession of the prophets who emphasized the danger of wealthy people exploiting the poor,

offered clear indictment of greed, acquisitiveness, and putting one's trust in material rather than spiritual goods (cf. Matt. 6:24; Luke 12:15-21). Jesus was forthright on the perils of riches. Yet this does not mean he thought lightly of the material foundations of life, evidenced by a model prayer which included the petition to the Father "Give us this day our daily bread."

Is it morally wrong for Christians to accumulate much wealth and material holdings? At what point does one draw a line between reasonable lifestyle or comfort and security on the one hand and morally unjustifiable affluence and luxury on the other? How much may a person exploit tax loopholes, class advantage, and good connections (e.g., insider information) to accumulate wealth and property?

32. Isn't advertising criticized a little unfairly in this chapter? After all, are there not ads which appeal to the best character traits in people? Besides, advertisements provide consumer education to people who need to know what products and services are available. The worst abuses of advertising can be controlled by watchdog agencies, publications such as *Consumer Reports*, and, as a last resort, our civil courts. Advertising enables business people and manufacturers to present their products and services to the public. Is there any valid reason to believe that advertising contributes to the loss of community or to a moral decline in this nation?

33. As long as a person does not violate a major moral commandment, is how he/she spends a vast amount of leisure time a moral issue?

EPILOGUE

(This concluding statement was written primarily for closure to our thinking about community, but it appropriately states an epilogue for this entire volume.)

Is there a final statement for Christian citizens as the passage of time moves us inexorably toward the twenty-first century?

First and foremost, the church bestows on "community" its deepest and richest meaning. Ideally, no community is any more closely-knit or more involved in providing insight and direction for life's greatest issues than the community of faith in our Lord Jesus Christ. The church is thus a *super-community*, for its members share not only the common core values of their political environment, but share also the transcendent goals and values of a loving heavenly Father who created all the world and its inhabitants.

Second, this super-community, the church, can meet all our deepest needs and longings for association and interrelatedness. The experience of first century Christians is evidence that the community of faith can survive in an environment that legally, politically, and socially is hostile to its purposes. Not coincidentally, the black churches in south-central Los Angeles played an important role in stabilizing the 1992 riot situation and proved once again to be the most stable and positive forces in the black community. The church has always considered itself "the body of Christ" and, as such, it continues the ministry of reconciliation and healing he began during his earthly career.

Third, this super-community must ever be vigilant like any other community, so that insidious evils do not destroy its esprit de corps. Jealousy, envy, pride, gossip, slander, power struggles, pettiness, and other "works of the flesh" can rob the church of its spiritual dimension and render it as worldly and limited in nature as any other human institution or affiliation. Stiff and mean-spirited competition is unwelcome in community. There are no sides. Conflict can be resolved in the spirit of grace by listening, understanding, caring, and healing. Indeed, the church must be the *answer* to rather than the *cause* of individual alienation and disillusionment about the meaning of life.

Finally, Christians should derive their strength from walking in the light and from fellowship with committed brothers and sisters and yet seek to impact in a positive, healing way the larger community (nation) of which they are members. For some this will mean their voting behavior reflects a commitment to spiritual life and transcendent values; for others, thankfully, it will mean also signing petitions, running for office, boldly confronting evildoers, demonstrating publicly, and/or seeking public forums to address vital issues.

Throughout it all, responsible Christians acknowledge the essential freedoms and rights bestowed by the larger national community and realistically resist imposing some minority version of morals or ethics on the larger majority. In the final analysis, good behavior cannot be legislated. Civic virtue, so vital in a democracy, requires what one philosopher has called "obedience to the unenforceable."

The American dream still shines brightly for most people. Our diversity, which often keeps us embroiled in petty, contentious politics, can continue to be a source of our greatness if we attempt to resolve our differences and solve our great moral problems peacefully. We may learn much by listening to the voices of others.

Finally, the great gospel metaphors of *yeast*, *salt*, and *light* underscore the unique quality of the Christian man or woman's involvement in the larger community. The Christian is not simply an armchair critic seated close to a remote-controlled TV. Nor is he or she a spectator in some giant arena while the world's events unfold safely below. Enlightening as the reading and discussing of current events may be, Christians are not citizens who are simply *informed* of the truth about a political community and major world issues and who can discuss these issues with dispassionate objectivity. Committed Christians are people who are not simply custodians of the special revelation from God but who, in the apostle John's language, *do the truth.*

As *yeast* is different from the dough in which it works, as *light* permeates darkness so as to change its essential character, and as *salt* penetrates the meat which it preserves, so then that supercommunity of redeemed believers in Christ provides the moral insight, motivation, and support for a disciplined lifestyle which might, just might, be the salvation of that larger community among nations. After all, the church is the one special community which exists primarily for the sake of those who do not belong to it.

APPENDIX

A. HOW PHILOSOPHERS AND ETHICISTS COMMUNICATE WITH EACH OTHER—

A GLOSSARY OF COMMON TERMS WITH BRIEF DEFINITIONS AND EXPLANATIONS FOR THE JARGON-IMPAIRED STUDENT IN CHRISTIAN ETHICS.

Absolute moral principle: A moral principle that cannot be justifiably violated; a moral principle for which there are no exceptions.

Act Utilitarianism: The positive version of the theory claims that an individual action is right if and only if it would produce more total happiness than any other action available to the agent. The negative version of the theory claims that an action is right as long as it does not reduce total happiness.

Altruistic behavior: Behavior motivated by concern for the well-being of others and intended to benefit others; altruism says we should be self-forgetful and seek the good of others and not of self.

Anthropology: The study of humans. Physical anthropology is the study of human biology; cultural anthropology is the study of human cultures.

Antinomianism: The "rule" of nondirectives; no law; no rules; no principles; every situation is unique, therefore we cannot generalize.

Beneficence: Altruistic behavior directed toward benefiting others or protecting them from harm.

Categorical Imperative: According to Kant's moral theory, there is a basic principle of morality that all people should follow. According to the Universal Law formulation, it is: "Act only on a maxim that you can consistently will to be a universal law." According to the Respect for Persons formulation, it is: "Never treat people merely as a means to your ends."

Christian Freedom: The right and power to fulfill what one ought to be. Generally, freedom may be viewed both negatively and positively, the difference residing in the two prepositions "from" and "for." Freedom in a negative sense means freedom "from" some authority or some alien determination; freedom in a positive sense means freedom "for" action in obedience to high standards. Political freedom connotes the right to "do as one pleases" and Christian freedom connotes the right to "do as God wills."

Consequentialist moral theories: Theories that claim that only the consequences of actions determine their rightness and wrongness. Consequentialist and teleological theories may be considered as the same theory. These ethicists insist that if the consequences are good, the action is right; if bad, the act is wrong.

Consequentialists consider the ratio of good to evil that an action produces. The right action is the one that produces or is intended to produce at least as much good as evil and the wrong action does not.

Deontological moral theories: Theories that claim that some actions are inherently right or wrong, independent of their consequences. Kantian moral theory is usually classified as a Deontological moral theory. Duty-theory is an ethical theory that disregards the importance of consequences and focuses only on the rightness and wrongness of the act itself. Nonconsequentialist theories are deontological. The "divine command theory" is a single-rule nonconsequentialist normative theory that says we should always do the will of God. Whatever the situation, if God says to do it, then do it. (Thus did Abraham move confidently to obey God's commandment to offer his son Isaac as a human sacrifice without any regard for the consequences of his radical obedience.)

Divine Command theory of morality: As defined by philosophical ethicists (that is, non-Christian ethicists), the theory that God's commands make moral laws that are true and authoritative for all human beings. According to this theory, an action is wrong if and only if it is forbidden by God. Christian ethicists respect divine commands and would not speak of such commands as "theory."

Egoism: Doctrine that contends we should always act in a way that promotes our own best long-term interests. This does not mean that we should do anything we want because our immediate desires/interests may not serve our long-term interests. (For example, the Watergate conspirators served an immediate interest but paid for it long-term.) Psychological egoism is a theory that all human behavior is exclusively self-interested. Psychologists who teach "self-actualization" and self-realization would be expressing egoism.

Empiricism: The belief that all knowledge about the world comes from or is based on the senses. The human mind contains nothing except what the experience has placed there. John Locke was an empiricist, claiming that human mind was *tabula rasa,* a blank slate, on which experience makes and leaves its mark.

Epicureanism: The theory that pleasure and the absence of pain are the keys to human happiness. Pleasure is derived from friendship, contentment, peace, morality, and aesthetic pursuits. Emphasizes virtue for its own sake: virtue is its own reward. The ancient Greek philosopher Epicurus (342-270 BC) argued that people should live so as to bring about as much pleasure for themselves as possible.

Epistemology: Theory of knowledge; the method of seeking truth; the nature, basis, and extent of knowledge; one of the main branches of traditional philosophy; how we know; from the Greek, *episteme,* meaning "knowledge."

Epistemological questions are basic to all other philosophical inquiries. Every fact or statement we make must be backed up with evidence or justification. Epistemology presents us with the task of explaining how we know what we claim to know, how we can find out and what we wish to know and how we can judge someone else's claim to knowledge.

Eschatology: The direction and anticipated end of human history. *Eschaton* means "the end" and eschatology has to do with what happens at the end of human history and beyond it.

Eudaemonism: Derived from the Greek *eudaemonia,* eudaemonism signifies a philosophy of happiness—not mere pleasure, but well-being, a happy spirit, a pleasant state of mind. "Happiness then is the best and noblest and pleasantest thing in the world," according to Aristotle (384-322 BC) in his classic *Nicomachean Ethics* (1.10). Aristotle maintained that an individual's state of happiness resulted from a life governed by reason, moderation, and the actualization of one's potentialities.

Existentialism: Radical individualism; a twentieth century philosophy (main proponents: Nietzsche, Sartre) that declares each person is a free individual in a purposeless universe and hostile environment; denies essential human nature and declares that each creates one's own essence through free action.

Existentialism is suspicious of science and scientific method; is concerned with subjective flow of experience; self-definition is found in a passionate commitment to act and deed; nothing is real but what the individual experiences in desires and passions.

Hedonism: Pleasure is intrinsically good and worthwhile; pain is bad; only pleasure is worth seeking for its own sake. Hugh Hefner's Playboy philosophy may be considered a hedonistic philosophy.

Humanism: A doctrine that emphasizes distinctively human interests and ideals. The humanism of the Renaissance was based on the Greek classics; modern humanism emphasizes humans exclusively.

Legalism: The doctrine that moral rules are absolute laws that must always be obeyed; virtually every situation is covered; no flexibility or creativity is needed; fully systematic, highly prescriptive.

Libertarianism: The theory that (negative) liberty or freedom is the most important social value.

Maxim: According to Kant's moral theory, an agent is following a maxim when he/she acts. A maxim is a personal rule specifying how and why one will behave in certain circumstances; for example, "In circumstances C, I will do action X for purpose P."

Metaphysics: The branch of philosophy that studies the nature of reality; literally, after or beyond physics. Metaphysics looks beyond what can be seen and observed in the sphere of natural science. It asks questions such as "What is ultimate reality?" and "Is there a God?"

Moral Absolute: The doctrine that there is only one morally acceptable and correct action in a given situation.

Moral Nihilism: The theory that nothing is morally right or wrong, morally forbidden or required.

Moral Objectivism: The theory that there is only one correct moral code. Some people define it as the theory that some moral judgments and principles are (objectively) true and others (objectively) false, contrasting Moral Objectivism with Moral Subjectivism.

Moral Relativism or Ethical Relativism: A doctrine that denies there is only one correct moral code that binds all people at all times in all places. Moral truth is thus not absolute but relative to certain factors. *Individual relativism* is about individual tastes. *Cultural relativism* relates to the age in which one lives. Slavery would be adjudged harshly in our age, but not so judged in previous centuries among powerful citizens in slave-holding cultures.

Moral Subjectivism: The theory that whatever an individual believes to be right and wrong is right and wrong for that individual. Sometimes moral subjectivists maintain that an individual's moral code is based merely on feelings and is for that reason subjective.

Natural Law: A body of laws considered to be derived from nature or reason that are ethically binding on society; a pattern of necessary and universal regularity holding in physical ratio. Natural laws are established by God; they constitute moral imperatives for the entire created order—human, non-human life, and physical universe.

The Christian philosopher and theologian Saint Augustine presented a well organized scheme of law in his *City of God.* Augustine influenced Thomas Aquinas, who defined natural law as divine law applied to human situations. The moral law, then, is based on natural inclinations (e.g., preservation of life, propagation of the species, etc.) and the ability to reason to discern the right course of conduct. The rules of conduct corresponding to these inherent human features are called natural law.

Negative Duty: A duty to refrain from doing something (or to *not* do something). (Compare with Positive duty.)

Nihilism: The view that nothing exists, that nothing has value; the social view that conditions are so bad that they should be destroyed and replaced by something better.

Normative Ethics: Prescriptive ethics; "oughtness."

Ontology: Doctrine or study of the nature of being; nature of Ultimate Reality; a subdivision of metaphysics. (Metaphysics is concerned with the nature of reality.)

Anselm developed an argument for the existence of God. His point: If God is greater that that which humans can conceive and no human can conceive of anything greater, then God must exist. He also said, "I believe in order that I may understand."

Positive Duty: A duty to *do* something. (Compare with Negative duty.)

Prima Facie Duty: Duties that on the surface dictate what we should do when other moral factors aren't considered; these prima facie duties are duties that generally obligate us; they impose a moral obligation. W.D. Ross contended that circumstances can entail the reality that one has conflicting duties. A prima facie duty, which Ross distinguishes from one's actual (all things considered) duty, is a duty one has that is not absolute and that justifiably may be violated in order to satisfy another, conflicting duty. Ross categorizes certain duties as prima facie: fidelity, justice, gratitude, self-improvement; non-malfeasance (avoiding hurting others).

Rationalism: The belief that knowledge is based on reason alone, not on sense perception, that is we do not rely on sense experience for knowledge. According to rationalists, we know truth by the use of our mental processes. True knowledge does not depend on an experience.

Rule Utilitarianism: The theory that an action is right if and only if it is permitted or required by a correct moral rule. According to the theory, a moral rule is correct if there would be more total happiness produced by following it than would be produced by not following it.

Sin: Radical rebellion against God and his sovereignty; egocentricity; an attitude or act in which one rebels against or fails to be responsive to the will of God and the love commandment of Jesus; self-centeredness and self-love with regard to both God and other persons. This theological definition is at variance with the usage of sin in popular culture which equates sin with vice and bodily self-indulgence ("wine, women, and song") or its dismissal as a vestige of the American Puritan past.

Situation Ethics: According to Joseph Fletcher, the doctrine that contends that the moral action produces the greatest amount of Christian love of all the possible actions. Rules and principles are valid only if they serve love in a specific situation. One must be acquainted with all the facts before taking action. Fletcher therefore is a consequentialist and utilitarian, asking that we choose the course that best serves love.

Soul: That part of humans given by the Creator which is eternal; the immaterial entity that is identified with consciousness, eternal spiritual mind, and personality.

Stoicism: Absolute mental freedom from the vicissitudes of life; inner peace of soul is maintained regardless of circumstances. The Stoics were members of a school of thought founded by Zeno around 300 BC and believed that the world does not operate by blind chance but involves divine providence. The universe is rational, operating by laws the human mind can discover. This order the Stoics called Zeus, nature, or logos. Since people are happy when they act in accordance with nature, their job is to enact laws that coincide with or in accordance with the laws of nature. Hence, natural law is rooted in nature or is a moral imperative, a description of what ought to happen in human relationships.

Augustine thought out the implications of this philosophy in *City of God*. Later, Thomas Aquinas was influenced by Augustine and in the Middle Ages wrote about different kinds of law.

Summum Bonum: Highest good. The major schools of Western world philosophy originated with Socrates who taught that a person's most prized possession is knowledge and that knowledge of the highest good (*summum bonum*) should be one's primary goal.

Teleological Ethics: What is the great goal or end (*telos*) of human striving? What behavior moves one in that direction? Teleology maintains the reality of purpose and affirms that the universe and everything that happens are consciously designed for that purpose.

Utilitarianism: The theory that insists that the promotion of everyone's best interests is the standard for morality; moral actions are the ones which produce the greatest happiness for the most people.

Virtue ethics: To become a good person by developing good virtues (moral excellencies).

B. HOW "CHRISTIAN ETHICS" IS DEFINED OR EXPLAINED BY SOME OTHER WRITERS:

William Barclay: "If you want to put it in one sentence, ethics is the science of behaviour. Ethics is the bit of religion that tells us how we ought to behave. . . . The basis of the Christian ethic is clear — the basis of the Christian ethic is concern." *Ethics In A Permissive Society*, pp. 13, 31.

Henlee H. Barnette: "Christian ethics is a systematic explanation of the moral example and teaching of Jesus applied to the total life of the individual in society and actualized by the power of the spirit." *Introducing Christian Ethics*, p. 3.

J. Philip Wogaman: "Morality . . . includes everything we do to live our lives and organize our world in accordance with our deepest values. For Christians, those values are drawn from the heart of their faith as Christians. Those values represent what seems, in light of that faith, to be good. Evil, on the other hand, is what obstructs the good. So, for Christians, morality is living one's whole life as a Christian; it is acting in the world so as to exert a Christian influence in behalf of good and in opposition to evil." *Making Moral Decisions*, p. 11.

Georgia Harkness: "Christian ethics is the systematic study of the way of life set forth by Jesus Christ, applied to the daily demands and decisions of our personal and social existence." *Christian Ethics,* pp. 30-31.

L. Harold DeWolf: "Ethics is the discipline concerned with the evaluation of human conduct, that is, with determining the goodness or evil properly ascribed to human choices. . . . Christian ethics is this discipline pursued in the perspective of Christian faith." *Responsible Freedom: Guidelines to Christian Action,* p. 3.

George F. Thomas: "Christian ethics is based upon the authority not of the Church but of the Bible. Since the Bible is the record of a divine revelation in history, this means that Christian ethics is ultimately based upon the authority of that revelation. . . . It is a revelation of God and His redemptive activity, not of dogmas about God; of new life in love, not rules of conduct. . . . Christian ethics is inseparable from the Christian faith that God has revealed His will in Christ. A philosopher who does not share this faith cannot accept Christian ethics as a whole, although he may incorporate into his own thinking certain ideas derived from it. Consequently, he cannot give the moral experience recorded in the Bible a 'privileged position' in his examination of the facts of the moral consciousness." *Christian Ethics and Moral Philosophy,* pp. 373-375.

Waldo Beach: "Christian ethics is a discipline of reflection and analysis that lies between Christian theology on one side and social sciences on the other or, to put it in shorthand, between the faith and the facts. From Christian theology, it derives the faith-premises that validate its moral norms. From the sciences that study human behavior, it derives the understanding of the complex factors in the psychology of human nature and the cultural circumstances surrounding the problems of choice and decision." *Christian Ethics in the Protestant Tradition,* pp. 8-9.

John S. Feinberg and Paul D. Feinberg: "To act ethically or morally means to act in accord with accepted rules of conduct which cover moral (as opposed to non-moral) matters. To have ethics or a morality is to hold a set of beliefs about that which is good and evil, commanded and forbidden. . . . Ethics intends to set forth what ought to be, not what is. But it should help us evaluate the rightness or wrongness of what is and tell us how to act in light of it. Unfortunately, changes in what 'is' in modern life have far outdistanced reflection upon how we ought to live in such a time. This seems to be especially true among Christian ethicists, though even secular ethicists disagree about how we should live in this changing world. . . . In our pluralistic societies, Christians can no longer assume that others, our children included, will be exposed to and adopt Judeo-Christian morals or will know how to apply them to concrete situations. Hence, as Christians we must speak to these topics lest we find out too late, as in the case of abortion, that a morality foreign to Scripture has not only won the day, but has even been enacted as the law of the land." *Ethics For A Brave New World,* p. 17. and pp. xiii-xiv.

C. TEN COMMANDMENTS FOR AMERICAN VOTERS

If Jesus Christ had been endorsing a candidate in 1992, would he have selected Bush, Clinton, or Perot? If Jesus were to endorse a candidate for 1996, would the candidate be Republican, Democratic, or Independent?

The whole idea is preposterous, of course, since Jesus lived in a totalitarian society which did not grant ordinary citizens a strong voice in government decisions. Jesus acknowledged civil government's role in a fallen world, urged support for its legitimate activities, but warned that the state must not take the place of God.

No two topics are any more controversial than politics and religion and any discussion of the combination of the two topics is likely to be doubly explosive. Yet, because Christianity provides a perspective for all dimensions of life, we do well to consider carefully the ancient biblical foundation for making contemporary political decisions.

Borrowing the linguistic style of the King James Version (with tongue not totally in cheek), I hereby present Ten Commandments for the modern American voter:

1. Thou shalt remember that the Lord thy God is the Lord of all nations and that all political leaders rule by his permissive will.

2. Remember now that the kingdom of God is not concerned with national boundaries but with lost humanity, spiritual needs, and eternal values. As such, political goals must be sought with honesty, fairness, and respect for opponents.

3. Thou shalt not automatically equate any party platform or partisan policy with the will of God.

4. Thou shalt not pass eternal judgment on those who hold different convictions or cast votes for another candidate, for verily they have their reasons and preferences the same as thee.

5. Thou shalt not complain and nag about the failures of the government when thou hast taken no time to vote thyself.

6. Thou shalt not select, among all the moral issues in an election campaign, only one issue and make it thy litmus test by which the morality and patriotism of all other candidates and voters are measured.

7. Thou shalt not allow simplistic slogans and mottoes to sufficeth for answers to complex issues and problems; nor shalt thou listen to the siren voices of demagogues and fanatics without critically analyzing their appeals.

8. Remember now that compromise is not always evil in a world of conflicting needs and competing values and that politics requires cooperation, negotiation, give and take, goodwill, and courtesy.

9. Thou shalt advocate freedom for all citizens as thou rememberest that America is not a theocracy or a covenant nation with God, but a diverse, pluralistic nation with many nationalities, races, and creeds.

10. Remembering that spirituality is not synonymous with state craft, thou shalt not equate the personal piety and church membership of political candidates and officials with either the deeper issues of commitment to justice, equality, and liberty or with legislative and administrative competence.

(Originally written by the author for the *Fourth Avenue Family Focus*, November 1992, and slightly revised for this work.)

D. ARGUMENTS AND FALLACIES (A few traps to avoid)

Here is a bit of final personal advice for you, the reader. Remember:

Not all viewpoints are created equal. The same is true for opinions. Holding opinions merits no special credit, for all people have opinions. Thoughtful, considered, and well-grounded opinions are indeed better than others, of course.

God has given you a brain. Not only does it store memories of your experiences, but it creates your personal wisdom and intelligence through the process of blending study, logic, and reasoning.

A well-considered, highly-supported opinion is reached at the end of a reliable pattern of logical reasoning. Such reasons are the essence of persuasive arguments.

On the other hand, there are various traps that even thoughtful Christians can fall into while engaged in moral reasoning. Some of these traps are the ordinary fallacies which are common in all forms of moral and public policy reasoning and debate.

For students of Christian ethics, however, there are additional traps and pitfalls to avoid when using the Bible in the reasoning process. When Christians reason with opponents on moral issues, they are more vulnerable to fallacious arguments. Why? Because moral issues strike at the core of human life and spiritual values and commitments — values and commitments on which we have staked our very lives. We can become highly emotional about the values and convictions for which we feel the strongest.

Some of the typical traps or pitfalls to avoid when you are engaged in moral argument and discussion with others:

Ad Hominem: From the Latin phrase for "to the man," a logical fallacy that assumes that because a person is who he or she is, his or her viewpoint must be wrong. Consider that some of the harshest critics of Jesus' teaching attempted to discredit him by asking, "Can any good thing come out of Nazareth?"

Granted, untrustworthy and even unethical people often do present unsound arguments; but as long as they do present valid arguments, we should evaluate those arguments, not the arguers.

Ambiguity: Quality exhibited in an expression or statement that can be interpreted in different ways.

Sometimes we simply talk past one another, not understanding what our alleged opponent is talking about. Sometimes the issues are vaguely defined. Other times, we simply use different words to say the same thing without being aware of a major consensus.

"Begging the Question": Assuming what you are trying to prove. A question-begging argument (also called "circular reasoning") is one that contains the conclusion as one of its premises. For example, "I believe Tom Riley on this matter, because he is an honest man. He is honest because he told me so."

Equivocation: Allowing the argument to turn on different meanings of the same word. The word "natural" could mean "out of the ordinary" or "perverse;" the term "human life" is capable of several meanings. Usually in moral dialogue, key terms must be defined if there is to be effective communication.

"Glittering generality": Casual and vague over-generalizations, such as "Everybody is doing . . ." or "Everybody knows that. . . ." For sure, there are plenty of things that everyone does or facts that everybody knows and they form strong premises for your arguments. But please be careful to avoid careless generalizations about what "everybody" is doing, thinking, or saying. In making a general claim, ask whether *anybody*, let alone everybody, really knows, does, or acts in the way you claim.

Non-Sequitur: Literally, "it does not follow." A fallacy in which an unjustified link is drawn between cause and effect, thus leading others to a conclusion without sufficient grounds. The fact that two phenomena coexist does not mean that one caused the other. There may be no link or other causal factors may be operative. The person who argues, "There is such a high rate of promiscuity among our high school and college youth and that's all because the Supreme Court took prayer and Bible reading out of public schools" may find that statement based on the fallacy of *non-sequitur* — surely there are many other factors which contributed toward youthful promiscuity.

"Paralysis of Analysis": Continuing to discuss questions and issues long after most members in a moral community have arrived at firm conclusions. The danger is that continued analysis and vast information accumulated may become a substitute for committed action. The college or university may properly be viewed as a center of questioning and learning; and, while the church may be a center for dialogue on moral issues, such dialogue must be vitally linked with actual mission. A highly informed but highly inactive church is a lamentable contradiction of all the Lord intended for his church to become.

"Poisoning the wells": A typical fallacy which is intended to stigmatize the one who presents an idea so that others don't have to deal with the idea itself. If the well is poisoned, all the water that comes out of the well will be contaminated.

It's tempting to dismiss everything that an opponent says because that person has been labeled as a conservative or a reactionary or a liberal or a radical. Other labels come to mind: liberal Democrat, socialist, secular humanist, bureaucrat, charismatic, false teacher, fanatic, "so-called intellectual," "self-styled something or other," and on and on we could go. If the in-group has already decided that any member of another group cannot possibly be right ("birds of a feather" fallacy), then all one must do is attach that label to those whose ideas one wants others to reject. If an idea can be branded before it is considered, it need not be taken seriously.

Premature Consensus: Reaching for agreement before all the viewpoints and differences have been aired and examined sufficiently. Some move toward premature consensus because they erroneously feel that open disagreement is unloving, destructive, and non-Christian behavior. What is truly unloving and destructive is a phony, dishonest concurrence.

Proof-texting: The misuse of sacred Scriptural text which involves extracting a single verse or group of verses from its larger context in order to "prove" a point. This "use" of Scripture is highly subjective and is tantamount to Bible abuse. The fallacy is, unfortunately, widespread, even among preachers and Bible teachers.

A **"scissors and paste"** approach to Scripture involves stating a moral or theological point to be proven and *afterward* approaching the Bible in search of proof-texts to be cut out and pasted as an undergirding for the assertion under consideration.

The fact that Christianity is a "religion of the book" has made it a temptation to search the Bible for the final, specific word on every moral issue that contemporary society confronts. Additionally, combine this respect for sacred writings with typical Protestant rejection of the authority of ecclesiastical tradition (at least as compared with Roman Catholic doctrine). The result: many fundamentalists and evangelicals feel compelled to find at least one verse of Scripture to substantiate a moral argument or prove a point. As we have seen in this volume, Christians reading the same biblical material can disagree as to its moral doctrine or specific applications.

"Red herrings": Irrelevancies which are intended to distract your attention away from the real issues. Red herrings often involve appeals to emotion. Be extremely wary of emotional appeals, lest they lead you where logic would not go.

Reductio ad absurdum: A form of argument in which you reduce your opponent's argument or viewpoint to its absurd consequences.

"Slippery slope": A version of the *reductio ad absurdum* argument; you reduce your opponent's view to unacceptable or ridiculous consequences, which your opponent will presumably have to accept or else abandon his/her theory. Your opponent's argument must "slide down the slope" of logic.

The idea here is that what looks like one small step is just the beginning of a series of additional small steps that will be difficult or impossible to stop once the first step is taken. For example, one might oppose active euthanasia by arguing that its legalization will lead to euthanizing the severely mentally retarded, then Alzheimer's patients, then the physically handicapped, and so on.

The way to defeat the slippery slope argument is to "dig in on the slope" and defend your viewpoint on the basis that there is a difference between the "top of the slope" and the "bottom of the slope."

"Straw man": A logical fallacy that consists of attacking and disproving a theory invented for the occasion. Your opponent may attack your arguments. If your opponent fairly represents your arguments, all is well; if your arguments are unfairly rendered, your opponent is attacking a straw man.

Sometimes it is easier to build and then attack a straw man than it is to logically criticize the real issues in moral debate. Watch out when someone attempts to restate your viewpoint. Also watch out when you attempt to restate someone else's viewpoint.

A final word: Techniques you have developed for analyzing and evaluating moral arguments are not intended simply for other people's arguments. Apply these same standards to your own arguments and conclusions. Scripture summons all disciples of Christ both to integrity and to continual self-examination. It is crucially important, then, that you confront vital issues directly and biblically, and that along the way you confront yourself as well as others.

A BIBLIOGRAPHIC COMMENT

Recapturing and citing all the influences and resources which were consulted and drawn from for this volume would be a task of formidable magnitude if not near impossibility. For the years that I have been teaching ethics I have maintained large folders of material on each of the topics discussed in this book. Into these folders were filed magazine articles, newspaper clippings, cartoons, pamphlets, and any other materials relevant to each topic. Drawn from these materials were many of the quotes used in chapters three through eleven of this book, although, regrettably, I failed to record the date for a few of the newsclippings.

Since ethics covers the whole of life, the amount of published material in books, periodicals, journals, and newspapers is prodigious, as one might expect. It is my pleasure here to cite the sources from which I have drawn most of my concepts, arguments, and lines of analysis and which have stimulated my own thinking. First, because such attribution is both fair and ethically appropriate. But, also, it is a privilege to invite serious students to a further exploration of Christian ethics; therefore, I will offer some annotation for some of these sources that I hope will be helpful to interested readers.

At the outset I can recommend virtually anything (I'm protecting myself here, as you can tell) that the following have written or edited as stimulating, thoughtful, and worthy of consideration: William Barclay, Waldo Beach, Harold DeWolf, Carl Henry, Stanley Hauerwas, Paul Ramsey, Lewis Smedes, John Stott, and Philip Wogaman. There are other excellent authors, of course, and not all of those cited here have built their reputation as ethicists, but you will find their writings intelligent and insightful.

With gratitude I now cite, with occasional comment, some of the published books in general Christian ethics to which I turned for background study: Waldo Beach, *Christian Ethics in the Protestant Tradition* (Atlanta: John Knox Press, 1988) draws from the author's

forty years of experience in teaching ethics to write this brief introduction which balances perspectives and issues from the Reformed
tradition; Beach's *The Christian Life* (Richmond, VA: CLC Press,
1966) is an older but more comprehensive work. William Barclay,
Ethics in a Permissive Society (New York: Harper and Row, 1972) is
an older but very sound and readable discussion of perspectives
and problems. Denise Lardner Carmody and John Tully Carmody,
Christian Ethics: An Introduction Through History and Current Issues
(Englewood Cliffs, NJ: Prentice Hall, 1993) and Robert Bruce
McLaren, *Christian Ethics: Foundations and Practice* (Englewood
Cliffs, NJ: Prentice Hall, 1993) offer scholarly, more liberal
approaches to Christian ethics. An older volume that I highly
recommend for serious depth study is L. Harold DeWolf's *Respon-
sible Freedom: Guidelines to Christian Action* (New York: Harper and
Row, 1971). Stanley Hauerwas, *A Community of Character: Toward a
Constructive Christian Social Ethics* (Notre Dame: University of Notre
Dame Press, 1981) is a thoughtful, well-documented work which
emphasizes public ethics and building community.

I also consulted the following: Wayne A. Meeks, *The Origins of
Christian Morality: The First Two Centuries* (New Haven: Yale
University Press, 1993), an excellent scholarly work; Georgia
Harkness, *Christian Ethics* (Nashville: Abingdon, 1957); and Henlee
H. Barnette, *Introducing Christian Ethics* (Nashville: Broadman
Press, 1961). Readers interested in a more comprehensive consideration of situation ethics might elect to read Joseph Fletcher's
original work, *Situation Ethics: The New Morality* (Philadelphia: Westminster Press, 1966), as well as a compilation of the many
responses that this work evoked from professionals, preachers, and
pundits in Harvey Cox, ed., *The Situation Ethics Debate* (Philadelphia: Westminster Press, 1968).

For easier reading that still challenges, please consider: Peter
Kreeft, *Making Choices: Finding Black and White in a World of Grays*
(Ann Arbor, MI: Servant Books, 1990); J. Philip Wogaman, *Making
Moral Decisions* (Nashville: Abingdon Press, 1990), a little volume
which is much lighter reading than most of Wogaman's writings. I
have always maintained the utmost respect and appreciation for the
work of Lewis B. Smedes and the books he has authored which I
recommend here are *Mere Morality: What God Expects From Ordinary
People* (Grand Rapids: Eerdmans, 1983), *Choices: Making Right
Decisions in a Complex World* (San Francisco: Harper, 1986), *A Pretty
Good Person* (San Francisco: Harper and Row, 1990), and *Forgive*

and Forget: Healing the Hurts We Don't Deserve (San Francisco: Harper and Row, 1984). I made a conscious decision to postpone reading a new book by my friend and colleague in ministry Rubel Shelley; his *Written in Stone: Ethics For the Heart* (West Monroe, LA: Howard, 1995) was being released at the time I was writing the final chapters for this book, but I am confident Rubel's book will measure up to or surpass the standards of his prolific number of published materials.

Several writers have produced volumes on the issues, the best of which may be the diverse collection of essays edited by Paul T. Jersild and Dale A. Johnson, *Moral Issues and Christian Response* (4th ed. rev.; Fort Worth and other cities: Holt, Rinehart and Winston, 1988). John S. Feinberg and Paul D. Feinberg have co-authored a substantive issues text which discusses most of the issues treated in this book, but they also include chapters on marriage and divorce, genetic engineering, and the Christian and war. Their 479-page work is entitled *Ethics for a Brave New World* (Wheaton, IL: Crossway Books, 1993). David J. Gyertson, ed., *Salt and Light: A Christian Response to Current Issues* (Dallas: Word, 1993) contains brief essays by sixteen evangelical writers. A provocative little volume from which several quotes were taken is John B. Cobb, *Matters of Life and Death* (Louisville, KY: Westminster/John Knox Press, 1991). John Stott, *Decisive Issues Facing Christians Today* (Grand Rapids: Revell, 1990) ably discusses a wide range of issues.

Two works must be cited as near classics. The first is Carl F. Henry, *Christian Personal Ethics* (Grand Rapids: Eerdmans, 1957) is a masterful exposition by a distinguished evangelical theologian-philosopher. The other is George F. Thomas, *Christian Ethics and Moral Philosophy* (New York: Charles Scribner's Sons, 1955); both Henry and Thomas affirm a clear biblical and Christian ethic over against both ancient and modern alternatives and each work is broad in scope. Speaking of classics, one might add Helmut Thielicke, *Theological Ethics*, edited by William H. Lazareth (Philadelphia: Fortress Press, 1966), a Lutheran approach to ethics by a great German theologian-preacher, and historic essays included with a strong introduction in Waldo Beach and H. Richard Niebuhr's *Christian Ethics: Sources of the Living Tradition* (New York: Ronald Press, 1955). As for classic essays, one might also opt for Harmon L. Smith and Louis W. Hodges, *The Christian and His Decisions: An Introduction to Christian Ethics* (Nashville: Abingdon Press, 1969) which includes writings of Barth, the two

Niebuhrs, Brunner, Bernard Anderson, and others.

There are several general volumes and texts I consulted along the way: Jeffrey Olen and Vincent Barry, *Applying Ethics* (4th ed.; Belmont, CA: Wadsworth, 1992) and James P. Sterba, *Morality in Practice* (4th ed.; Belmont, CA: Wadsworth, 1994) provide excellent collections of essays by a diverse group of authors on various subjects, as does K. Finsterbusch and G. McKenna, *Taking Sides: Clashing Views on Controversial Social Issues* in its treatment of fourteen issues (Duskin Publishing Group, 1984). Mike W. Martin, *Everyday Morality: An Introduction to Applied Ethics* (2d ed.; Belmont, CA: Wadsworth, 1995) is an excellently balanced standard textbook, as is the older text, Harold H. Titus and Morris Keeton, *Ethics for Today* (4th ed.; New York: Van Nostrand and Reinhold, 1966). For a challenging analysis, see Jeffrey Stout, *Ethics After Babel* (Boston: Beacon Press, 1988).

In examining the specific issues discussed in this book, some more specialized sources were consulted, although the above volumes were also searched for ideas and insights on specific moral issues.

Abortion: See Robert Baird and Stuart Rosenbaum, eds., *The Ethics of Abortion* (Buffalo, NY: Prometheus, 1989); Edward Batchelor, Jr., ed., *Abortion: The Moral Issues* (New York: Pilgrim Press, 1982); James T. Burtchaell, *Rachel Weeping: The Case Against Abortion* (New York: Harper and Row, 1984); Daniel Callahan and Sidney Callahan, eds., *Abortion: Understanding Differences* (New York: Plenum Press, 1984); John T. Noonan, ed., *Morality of Abortion: Legal and Historical Perspectives* (Cambridge: Harvard University Press, 1970), especially John T. Noonan's essay, "An Almost Absolute Value in History." R.C. Sproul, *Abortion: A Rational Look at an Emotional Issue* (Colorado Springs, CO: Navpress, 1990); C. Everett Koop and Francis A. Schaeffer, *Whatever Happened to the Human Race?* (Westchester, IL: Crossway Books, Good News, 1983).

As for material on abortion published in periodical literature which was consulted for this volume or which contained quotes used herein: Beverly Coney Heirich, "Abortion Compromise," *Tennessean*, May 1, 1994; Gilbert Meilaender, "Abortion: The Right to an Argument," *Hastings Center Report*, Nov./Dec. 1989, pp. 13-16; John Scott, "The Morality of Abortion," *Mission* Journal, July, 1973, pp. 3-7, which makes a strong case for the neutrality of the Bible on the abortion issue, as does Roy Bowen Ward in "Is the Fetus a

Person — According to the Bible?" *Mission* Journal, Vol. 19, No. 7 (Jan., 1986), 6-9; see also an interview with Professor Ward in, of all places, *The [Wittenburg] Door,* March/April, 1995, pp. 17-18, 35; David Vanderpool, "Abortion: A Look at Questions and Controversies Surrounding a Major Societal Issue," *Christian Chronicle,* Nov., 1993, pp. 14-15; the special issue of *Image,* Vol. 8, No. 1 (Jan/Feb., 1992); Michael J. Gorman, "Why Is the New Testament Silent About Abortion?" *Christianity Today,* Jan. 11, 1993, pp. 27-29.

Sex Morality: See C.S. Lewis, *The Four Loves* (New York: Harcourt, Brace, 1960) for an analysis of the different meanings of Christian love; Stanley Grenz, *Sexual Ethics: A Biblical Perspective* (Dallas: Word, 1990); Richard Hettlinger, *Sex Isn't That Simple* (New York: Seabury Press, 1974); Vance Packard, *The Sexual Wilderness* (New York: David McKay Company, 1968); Letha Scanzoni, *Sexuality* (Philadelphia: Westminster Press, 1984); Dwight H. Small, *Christian: Celebrate Your Sexuality* (Old Tappan, NJ: Revell, 1974); Lewis Smedes, *Sex for Christians* (Grand Rapids: Eerdmans, 1976) and *Caring and Commitment* (San Francisco: Harper and Row, 1988); and Thielicke's vol. 3 of *Theological Ethics.*

In periodical literature, see: Eleanor Clift, "The Murphy Brown Policy," *Newsweek,* June 1, 1992, p. 46; Tim Stafford's articles, "Intimacy: Our Latest Sexual Fantasy," *Christianity Today,* Jan. 16, 1987, pp. 21-22 and "Love, Sex, and the Whole Person," *Campus Life,* 35 (May, 1977): 74-78, and "The Next Sexual Revolution," *Christianity Today,* March 9, 1992, pp. 28-29.

Criminal Justice and Capital Punishment: See William Baker, *On Capital Punishment* (Chicago: Moody Press, 1985); Hugo A. Bedau, *The Courts, the Constitution and Capital Punishment* (Lexington, MA: Lexington Books, 1977) and his edition, *The Death Penalty in America* (3rd ed.; New York: Oxford University Press, 1982); L. Harold DeWolf, *Crime and Justice in America* (New York: Harper and Row, 1975); Bonnie Szumski, Lynn Hall, and Susan Burrell, eds., *The Death Penalty: Opposing Viewpoints* (St. Paul: Greenhaven Press, 1986); Van den Haag, *The Death Penalty: A Debate* (New York: Plenum Press, 1983); James Q. Wilson, *Thinking About Crime* (2nd ed.; New York: Basic Books, 1983).

In periodical literature, see L. Harold DeWolf, "The Death Penalty: Cruel, Unusual, Unethical, and Futile," *Religion in Life,* 42 (1975): 37-38; the Greenhaven Press "Opposing Viewpoints" series contains three interesting essays from which quotes were drawn: John Dear, "Seventy Times Seven," *Sojourners*, Aug/Sept., 1989; Michael Pakaluk, "Till Death Do Us Part," *Crisis*, September, 1989; and Lloyd Steffen, "Casting the First Stone," *Christianity and Crisis*, Feb. 5, 1990; the quote from Rubel Shelley was published in the Nashville *Tennessean*, November 15, 1993.

Obscenity, Pornography, and Censorship: Harry Clor, *Obscenity and Public Morality: Censorship in a Liberal Society* (Chicago: University of Chicago Press, 1969); Perry C. Cotham, *Obscenity, Pornography, and Censorship: A Christian Perspective* (Grand Rapids: Baker Book House, 1973); also, many of the books on human sexuality already cited deal with the issue of pornography.

In periodical literature see: Perry C. Cotham, "Rights and Responsibilities: A Christian Perspective," *Integrity*, Vol. 22, No. 6 (Nov/Dec., 1991), 4-7; "Fine Art or Foul," cover story in *Newsweek*, July 2, 1990, pp. 46-52; Ann Garry, "Pornography and Respect for Women," *Social Theory and Practice*, Vol. 4 (Summer, 1978), 395-421; "The Selling of Sex," cover story in *Newsweek*, Nov. 2, 1992, pp. 95-103; Stephen Monsma, "Yelling Fire in a Crowded Art Gallery," *Christianity Today*, Oct. 22, 1990, pp. 40-41; Judge Jerome Frank's dissenting opinion in *United States v. Roth* (353 U. S. 476, 1957).

Work: Most of the quotations and lines of analysis on this topic were drawn from works already cited, to which may be added Paul de Vries and Barry Gardner, *The Taming of the Shrewd: A Marketplace Handbook for Smart Ethics, Scrupulous Strategy, and Sound Decision-Making* (Nashville: Thomas Nelson Publishers, 1992); Kevin R. Murphy, *Honesty in the Workplace* (Pacific Grove, CA: Brooks/Cole, 1993) and essays by Edmund Optiz, Tibor Machan, Mary Scott, Howard Rothman, Kenneth Labich, Robert J. Samuelson, and David Moberg in *Ethics*, edited by Carol Wekesser for the Greenhaven Press Current Controversies Series, 1995.

Euthanasia: See Norman Anderson, *Issues of Life and Death* (Downers Grove, IL: InterVarsity Press, 1976); Ray S. Anderson, *Theology, Death and Dying* (New York: Basil Blackwell, 1986); James Childress, *Priorities in Biomedical Ethics* (Philadelphia: Westminster Press, 1981; Richard M. Gula, *What Are They Saying About Euthanasia?* (New York: Paulist Press, 1986); Gerald A. Larue, *Euthanasia and Religion* (Los Angeles: Hemlock Society, 1985);

James B. Nelson and Jo Anne Smith Rohricht, *Human Medicine: Ethical Perpectives on Today's Medical Issues* (Minneapolis: Augsburg Press, 1984); Leonard J. Nelson, ed., *The Death Decision* (Ann Arbor, MI: Servant, 1984); Paul Ramsey, *The Patient as Person: Explorations in Medical Ethics* (New Haven: Yale University Press, 1970); Paul Simmons, *Birth and Death: Bioethical Decision-making* (Philadelphia: Westminster Press, 1983); Harmon Smith, *Ethics and the New Medicine* (Nashville: Abingdon Press, 1970).

In periodical literature, see "Choosing Death," a cover story in *Newsweek*, Aug. 26, 1991, pp. 40-46; Victor L. Hunter, "A Time to Live, A Time to Die," *Mission* Journal, Jan., 1976, pp. 7-9; "Mercy's Friend or Foe," *Time*, Dec. 28, 1992, pp. 36-37; "The Mystery of Suicide," *Newsweek* cover story, April 18, 1994, pp. 44-53; Douglas K. Stuart, "'Mercy Killing' — Is It Biblical?" *Christianity Today*, Feb. 27, 1976, p. 9.

Homosexuality: See Derrick S. Bailey, *Homosexuality and the Western Christian Tradition* (London: Longman, Green, and Co., 1955); Edward Batchelor, *Homosexuality and Ethics* (New York: Pilgrim Press, 1980); Ruth Tiffany Barnhouse, *Homosexuality: A Symbolic Confusion* (New York: Seabury Press, 1977); John Boswell, *Same-Sex Unions in Premodern Europe* (New York: Villard Books, 1994), which presents a startling thesis, and the work is reviewed in *Time*, June 20, 1994, pp. 76-77; James P. Hanigan, *Homosexuality: The Test Case for Christian Sexual Ethics* (Mahweh, NJ: Paulist Press, 1988); Jerry Kirk, *The Homosexual Crisis in the Mainline Church* (New York: Thomas Nelson, 1978); John J. McNeill, *The Church and the Homosexual* (Kansas City: Sheed, Andrews, and McMeel, 1976); Letha Scanzoni and Virginia Ramey Mollenkott, *Is the Homosexual My Neighbor?* (New York: Harper and Row, 1978); and John Shelby Spong, *Living in Sin?* (San Francisco: Harper and Row, 1988), which presents an ultra-liberal position.

In periodical literature, see "Born or Bred?" a cover story in *Newsweek*, Feb. 24, 1992, pp. 46-53; Joe Dallas, "Born Gay? How Politics Have Skewed the Debate Over the Biological Causes of Homosexuality," *Christianity Today*, June 22, 1992, pp. 20-23; "Gays Under Fire," cover story in *Newsweek*, Sept. 14, 1992, pp. 35-41, and the quote from Eric Marcus comes from this issue; Christine Gorman, "Are Gay Men Born That Way?" *Time*, Sept. 9, 1991; Mark Hartwig, "Public Backs Scouts, Stands Up to Gays," *Focus on the Family Citizen*, Oct. 19, 1992; Bennett J. Sims, "Sex and

Homosexuality," *Christianity Today*, Feb. 24, 1978, pp. 23-30; John R. W. Stott, "Homosexual Marriage: Why Same-Sex Partnerships are Not a Christian Option," *Christianity Today*, Nov. 22, 1985, pp. 21-28; and "What Causes People to be Homosexual?" *Newsweek*, Sept. 9, 1991. The quote from Leroy Garrett came from his *Restoration Review* series, "Visiting Other Churches," New Series, No. 7, 131-34.

Animal Rights and Environment: Robin Attfield, *The Ethics of Environmental Concern* (New York: Columbia University Press, 1983); William Baxter, *People or Penguins: The Case for Optimal Pollution* (New York: Columbia University Press, 1974); J. Baird Callicott, "An Ecocentric Environmental Ethic," in *Matters of Life and Death*, ed. by Tom Regan (New York: Random House, 1986); Tony Campolo, *Rescuing the Earth Without Worshiping Nature* (Nashville: Thomas Nelson, 1992); Center for Science in the Public Interest, *99 Ways to a Simple Lifestyle* (Garden City, NY: Anchor Press, 1977; Paul R. Ehrlich and Anne H. Ehrlich, *Healing the Planet: Strategies for Resolving the Environmental Crisis* (Reading, MA: Addison-Wesley, 1991; Paul R. Ehrlich and others have excellent essays in *Environment in Peril*, ed. by Anthony B. Wolbarst (Washington, DC: Smithsonian Institute Press, 1991); C. Dean Freudenberger and Paul Minus, *Christian Responsibility in a Hungry World* (Nashville: Abingdon Press, 1976); Al Gore, *Earth in the Balance* (New York: Houghton Mifflin, 1992); Hessel, Dieter T., ed., *Energy Ethics: A Christian Response* (New York: Friendship Press, 1979); Tom Regan, *All That Dwell Therein: Essays on Animal Rights and Environmental Ethics* (Berkeley and LA, CA: University of California Press, 1982) and *Earthbound: New Essays in Environmental Ethics* (New York: Random House, 1984); Bernard Rollin, *Animal Rights and Human Morality* (Buffalo, NY: Prometheus, 1981); Roger Shinn, *Forced Options: Social Decisions for the 21st Century* (San Francisco: Harper and Row, 1982); Paul Taylor, *Respect for Nature: A Theory for Environmental Ethics* (Princeton, NJ: Princeton University Press, 1986).

In periodical literature, see William A. Dyrness, "Are We Our Planet's Keeper?" *Christianity Today*, April 8, 1991, pp. 40-42; Christina Hoff, "Immoral and Moral Uses of Animals," *New England Journal of Medicine*, Vol. 302, No. 2, Jan. 10, 1980; Sallie McFague, "Should a Christian Love Nature?" *The Spire* (bulletin of Vanderbilt University Divinity School), Vol. 15, No. 3 (Spring/

Summer, 1993), 1, 11-12; Adrian R. Morrison, "What's Wrong with 'Animal Rights'" *American School Board Journal*, Jan., 1992, pp. 20-26; "Of Pain and Progress," *Newsweek*, Dec. 26, 1988; and Paul Taylor, "The Ethics of Respect for Nature," from *Environmental Ethics*, Vol. 3 (Fall, 1981), 197-218.

Community: The best work I have read on community is M. Scott Peck's *The Different Drum: Community Making and Peace* (New York: Simon and Schuster, 1987). "eck describes community life through its different stages: pseudocommunity, chaos, emptiness, and genuine community. Almost equally insightful are two works by Robert Bellah: *Habits of the Heart: Individualism and Commitment in American Life* (Berkeley, CA: University of California Press, 1985) and *Individualism and Commitment in American Life* (New York: Harper and Row, 1987), each written with the collaboration of other contributers. I have also drawn from my own *Politics, Americanism, and Christianity* (Grand Rapids: Baker Book House, 1976) as well as my article "The Disunited States of America: A Call for Christian Realism and Action," *Wineskins* (Vol. 1, No. 6), October, 1992, 8-11. On volunteerism and American heroes, see "What Works," the cover story in *Newsweek*, May 29, 1995, pp. 18-39. As for lifestyle, see E.F. Schumacher, *Small is Beautiful* (New York: Harper and Row, 1973) and Ron Sider, *Rich Christians in an Age of Hunger* (Downers Grove, IL: InterVarsity Press, 1977); the quote from Leroy Garrett was taken from his "occasional newsletter" *Last Time Around*, no. 12 (June, 1995), p. 1 and the one from Douglas Davis from his *Achieving the Self-Directed Life,* privately published.

About the Author

Perry C. Cotham is Involvement Minister and Administrator of the Fourth Avenue Church, a Church of Christ in Franklin, Tennessee, serving the Williamson County/Nashville area, a church he has served previously as pulpit minister. He is also adjunct professor in Bible and Political Science at David Lipscomb University and in Philosophy (Ethics) at Nashville Tech. He has also taught for several years as an adjunct professor at Belmont University.

Dr. Cotham earned graduate degrees from Wayne State University in Detroit and has done extensive graduate work at Harding Graduate School of Religion, Middle Tennessee State University and the Divinity School at Vanderbilt University. He is certified to teach in colleges and universities in the fields of religion, communications, psychology, history and political science.

Dr. Cotham has enjoyed a wide range of business and professional positions, though most of his years he has been connected with a church or Christian college. He has served in full-time church ministry, taught full-time in communications and political science at Lipscomb for seven years, served as consultant in labor-management relations and continuing education at Tennessee State University, taught in the Staff Development Unit with Tennessee' Department of Human Services, and worked as a copywriter and editor in advertising and public relations.

American history and politics is one of Cotham's major fields, as he wrote a doctoral dissertation on Harry Hopkins and Franklin Roosevelt. In the autumn of 1995, Cotham's definitive study of Tennessee labor was published in conjunction with the state's bicentennial and is honored in Hillsboro Press' Tennessee Heritage Library collection. His work is entitled *Toil, Turmoil, and Triumph: A Portrait of Tennessee Labor.* An earlier work, *Handbook of Labor History: The Tennessee Edition* (1989) enjoyed wide circulation in the state and a copy is given to each new worker at the Saturn plant. Cotham has spoken or read papers on subjects related to Christianity and politics at several national conferences. His writing on a wide range of subjects — including John Kennedy, Myles Horton, current issues — has often appeared in the "Nashville Eye" column of the *Tennessean* newspaper.

Articles in religion by Dr. Cotham have appeared in a wide range of journals and periodicals. *Mission Journal* has granted him two awards for published articles demonstrating "outstanding literary achievement." He has published several books including: *Christian Social Ethics: Perspectives and Problems* (1979); *Politics, Americanism and Christianity* (published 1976 and awarded one of the year's best religious books by *Christianity Today*); *Obscenity, Pornography, and Censorship* (all published by Baker Book House); *Marriage in the Fast Lane; Trust at Work* (with Douglas Davis); *The Church of Christ in Warren County*. He collaborated in the authorship of a major volume, *The Bible in Modern Culture* (Fortress Press, 1985) and in 1994 administered a project in church history, published as Anderson, *Landmarks* (Gospel Advocate).

Cotham has written articles or reviews for the following: *Christianity Today, Mission Journal, Wineskins, Image, Integrity, Firm Foundation* (under Ruel Lemmons' editorship), *Gospel Advocate,* for *Upper Room* and *Disciplines,* two publications of the Methodist Publishing House, and for *A Closer Look,* which reviews new religious books for national circulation.

Cotham is married and is the father of three children. He enjoys nearly all collegiate and professional sports, as well as walking, jogging, and tennis, and following the American political scene.